PRICED OUT

Building Homes at Fair Prices

- Future Generations Included

By Troy Deckert and Lydia Deckert

Public Policy Press

Copyright 2024© by Public Policy Press, LLC

All rights reserved. Reproduction, scanning, or distributing any substantial portion of this book without written permission is prohibited by law. Using short excerpts or quotations from the book is encouraged by the publisher and is allowed by copyright law.

Style is guided by the Associated Press Stylebook, 56th Ed., 2022, Basic Books, New York and The Chicago Manual of Style, 15th Ed., University of Chicago Press, Chicago, Ill.

ISBN 978-19524990-0-5 paperback edition
Printed in the United States of America

Public Policy Press LLC
332 South Michigan Avenue
Chicago, Illinois 60604

www.PublicPolicyPress.com

One-Page Summary: Good News! This Could Work.

For an average household, how about a home price or rent payment based on what you can pay? Like at 30% of your current monthly income? For singles, or for large families. With a reasonable commute, in a safe environment. Or, in time, how about a paid-for home? No mortgage, no rent, and fair property taxes.

If you rent, what if the rent stayed low with a lifetime lease? Increases would be modest, just enough for upkeep. How much could you save? For a decent lifestyle, and a stable retirement.

These deals are ongoing. Now. As you read this. They're in some U.S. locations and are widely available in Austria in Europe. See p. 75 and p. 100. It is possible, anywhere. This can be in your area. It should be in your area. Don't believe it? That's understandable. Because it's not widespread yet, most people haven't heard that this is even possible. We implore you to check this out. Not that we have all the answers, but we are trying to ask the right questions.

This isn't the same-old housing projects idea. It's about owning a home, paid-in-full. Or a rental that leaves you plenty of money. On your current income. To save. For upward mobility. For stability. For peace of mind. Future generations included. For 100 million people in the U.S. and billions of people worldwide, livelihoods and living conditions are at stake. Let's get this going.

Three methods for fair prices are *here on this _one_ page, outlined below.*

(Method 1) Cap property tax increases at 2% for average-income homeowners and rental residences in every town, county, city, and state: Then, people can remain in their homes into retirement, even if prices skyrocket around them. From our suggestion, Zarek Drozda and Benjamin Guzman of the Paul Douglas Institute have initial research.[1]

(Method 2) Add enough starter homes and apartments with commitments at regional or state levels, or a national standard, based on population. Have homes and rentals at fair prices for the middle class, the workforce, and retirees:
- enough homes and rentals for the middle class, priced at 35% or less of household income; and for
- enough starter homes and rentals for entry-level employees, priced at 30% or less of household income.

This has no limit on upscale development. (See the legislation on p. 7.)

(Method 3) Offer future generations fair prices with affordability agreements, which are binding contracts. An average-income buyer gets a lower price, and sells at a similar lower price to an average-income buyer later, which includes a fair profit. For a good deal now, the buyers agree to give a good deal later to others. Rents follow the same pattern. Property taxes for such units should match the lower prices. Prices can only go up gradually. People can switch to the regular market any time. It's free choice. There should be a choice, other than sky high prices.

Table of Contents

      One-Page Summary: Good News! This Could Work 1

      Summary in 13 pages: Making a Commitment and Details to Work Out 5

Reasons to Act 21

Chapter 1   Building Economic Stability 23

Chapter 2   Homes as a Human and Social Necessity. 25

Steps to Take 41

Method 1: Cap Property Taxes

Chapter 3   Cap Property Taxes: Do Cities Have to Kick Out the Working Families? Then the Middle Class Too? 43

Method 2: Add Starter Homes and Apartments

Chapter 4   Add Starter Homes and Apartments: Otherwise, It's Like Buying a Car and Only Rolls Royces are Offered 49

Chapter 5   Add Starter Homes and Apartments: So a Doctor, a Teacher, a Lawyer, and a Janitor Can Live in the Same Area 57

Chapter 6   Austria has Homes at Manageable Prices: Let's Do What They Do 71

Chapter 7   Use Available Financing: The Math Works 83

Method 3: Add Agreements for Future Generations

Chapter 8   Add Affordability Agreements: Keeping Prices Fair for Future Generations 95

Chapter 9   A Young Couple Gets Out of a Bleak Situation 107

End of Main Part of the Book

Additional Information 115

Chapter 10 Related Political Factors, Social Factors, and Economic Factors 117
Topics include: • Examples of change in political & economic power • The U.S. housing balance sheet. • Raise the wages? • The U.S. & Austria spend the same on homes. • Ineffective use of U.S. tax funds. • Most U.S. housing welfare goes to homes worth $350,000 to $750,000. • Free market failure. • Reversing landlordism is worth trillions. • Labor is capital's only customer.

Bibliography 135
Notes 141
Index 163
Appendix 173

Summary

In 13 pages

A Summary: Making a Commitment and Details to Work Out

Let's offer a lower price to buy or rent homes, townhomes or condos. For all sizes of living spaces, for singles to large families, in adequate space and privacy. Where the jobs are. In cities, suburbs, or further out. Take your pick. At lower prices, would people sign up?

Let's find out. Developments that are already set to make a profit can add extra homes and units to the available airspace to allow lower prices on some of the homes and apartments. Buildings can add floors. Single-family home developments can mix in some smaller lots or townhomes, or a mid rise, sectioned off. Homeowners and renters can pay the costs, not taxpayers.

Under affordability agreement contracts, future generations keep low prices. Anyone at any time can switch to the regular real estate market. There are methods for this. It's a decision to work out the details. With no strain, people have stable living. When construction and land costs are paid off, the renters, homeowners, and condo owners only have to cover upkeep costs, so monthly payments can drop, a lot. The property tax can be kept reasonable. People build assets, into future generations. Retirement is secure. Such methods have worked for 100 years, around the world.

Or put starter homes on the fast track for approval, as Los Angeles has done recently, with a significant effect.

Here's an example of a national standard, with local adjustments.[2] It covers (1) property taxes, (2) housing inventory, and (3) lower prices for the future.

Sample Legislation: A Commitment: Add Enough Homes at Fair Prices

> All states shall commit to an inventory of homes, condos, and rentals for employees, residents, and retirees of the middle class (the 2nd & 3rd lower quintiles by income level) and of entry level employees, (the lowest quintile by income level) equal to their employment and population ratios of the regions of a state within generally accepted commuting times. Sufficient housing inventory shall be available at costs not to exceed 35% of gross income for the middle class and 30% for the entry level employees as defined above. Government shall act deliberately to provide such inventory with all due speed using all methods as needed, including financing, with bonds, purchase of land, and construction. Net property taxes for such inventory, new or converted, shall adjust to meet the pricing ratios.
>
> This shall include future generations with affordability agreement contracts for defined prices via purchase or lease with no expiration year as part of the inventory commitment above. This shall include ownership options equal to market demand. Sales and rent price increases shall match average regional inflation rates and wage rates, not to exceed 5% increases annually, whichever is lower.[3]
>
> If for long periods of time (excluding prolonged emergency circumstances such as natural disasters, severe downturns, civil unrest, and war) no buyers or renters sign up under affordability agreements, then vacant units in the inventory can be sold or rented at market prices, or converted to other use, and action under this statute can cease until such time as needed. Financing is to be paid by owners and renters to the highest extent possible, with longer payback terms if needed. After costs for rentals are paid under such agreements, rents will be lowered so renters pay only upkeep and management costs.[4] For all primary residences and for all rentals for primary residences, net property taxes will not increase more than 2% each year.

Should we put it to a vote?

About This Book

For a short read of a few minutes, the summary runs to only page 19, so readers can understand all the main points. Also, to shorten the time to read just the main material, the book splits off the extra information at page 109.

We intentionally write in a conversational style to reach all levels of readers, including students. For readers with specialized expertise, serious economic, political, and sociological factors are examined in some detail. When concepts are explained for general readers, those readers with expertise can skim forward. Questions for students are in the appendix, on p. 176.

The supplementary, second part of the book adds more details. We review many books relevant to housing in the bibliography.

The Income Scale Includes You

Because housing inventory matches up to household income, all of us must consider people's wages and income group, whether higher, middle, or lower. Since income is considered a personal matter, we hope no one takes it as an affront when they see their income level discussed, along with everyone else's income level. It's not disrespectful to recognize the plain facts that there are different wages and income on any national income scale and that people are in different income groups.

Definitions

As of publication editing in Sept., 2024, the U.S. Census Bureau's latest released figure for real U.S. median household income was $80,610 for year 2023.[93] Median household income is defined as the middle point on the national household income scale.

The book refers mainly to three income groups:
- working families
- the middle class
- upper income earners, or the wealthier

We generally mean that the middle class is the group of households around the median income, including those moderately above and moderately below median income. The terms working families and working class[94] are meant to include households that earn less than the middle class. We use the term entry-level employees for the 20% quintile of households that earn the lower wages. Many of those jobs, still, are lifetime full-time jobs for those employees. The wealthier are households that earn more than the middle class.

A Development Plan With Fair Prices, With Luxury Units Too

On this page and the next, a sample development plan is provided with specifics for inventory, acreage, pricing, and building types within a major city.

It's exciting to see when a development has lower prices for entry level employees and the middle class. This isn't new. This is being done, after astute people took action, in the nation of Austria in Europe, 100 years ago. What's new to most nations is committing to middle-class and entry-level units. That's the majority of the people, after all. The people, the majority, shouldn't be an afterthought, never gotten to. In any nation, this can be done. This isn't a giveaway. Household income pays the way, to profit all involved. Renters profit, by saving so much. This is a payback system.

Los Angeles has put starter units on fast track approval. It is in effect a commitment, since it moves starter units ahead of luxury units, not relying on optional incentives alone at equal start times. That method could meet the demand.

When demand exists for fair prices and that demand is not being met, if local housing boards must put out bids, so be it. It is in the pressing public interest, which is the basic definition of when government is required to act.

The inventory commitments are proportional to the population of employees and retirees, and minor children living with them. It's fair. It only meets a market need, nothing more. Remember that the 30% and 35% ratios in the commitment on page 7 refer only to the monthly prices of units (at 30% to 35% of a monthly paycheck), not the percentage of units built. The percentage of units adjusts with the area's need for employees. If a region needs 25% of the workforce to be entry level employees, then 25% of housing should be priced for those employees, including in retirement.

If none of this happens, people will make do, as they always have. When they are priced out, they move. But what if they didn't have to? Consider one high-rise development, for example, City Point, in downtown Brooklyn in New York City. It included 200 lower-priced units. There were 87,000 applications for the 200 units.[5] Any building can add floors. In a busy region, add more floors at lower prices. In suburban subdivisions, add some smaller lots for starter homes. Add some cottages, with clusters of studios around courtyards.

A Sample Regional Plan

For a sample plan, Seattle is a typical big city, one which has worked to address home prices. Recently, the Seattle City Council vote came in, after a decade of work.[6] It was exciting to see something enacted. There were congratulations all around. Some 6,000 new homes at practical prices in 10 years. Then we wondered, how does 6,000 homes compare to Seattle's total households?[7] We looked it up. The 6,000 homes will be 2% of Seattle's 300,000 households. Only 2%? After being hopeful, that's deflating. It's not enough. The math is the math. It's only 2%.

So 98% of new housing will be at higher prices. And 100% of existing units will go higher, excepting the few public housing units and other units under low-price agreements, until the agreements expire. Landlords even get to jack up the rents for Section 8. And most suburbs are not trying for new units at lower prices, even just 2%. Median-income households may have gainfully-employed breadwinners, but they will have to squeeze into a small apartment or some type of house sharing, still flat broke, or just above broke.

Instead, let's consider 20% of inventory at lower prices. That's adding 70,000 new units at lower prices to Seattle's 300,000 households. Then, a noticeable change in prices can occur for employees and retirees living on lower incomes.

Once the 20% level is reached for the whole city, upscale developments can continue at 80% of new residential units with 20% of new units included at lower prices, adjusted up or down to business payrolls for workforce needs. (The suburbs should also add needed units at lower prices, but that's a larger discussion.)

The mix of types of units can adjust, like with more floors added to mid rises or high rises, if acreage for townhomes is limited. Here is a sample plan to get to 20% of total units at sensible prices within the city limits of Seattle.[8]

Sample City of Seattle Housing Development Plan

With 300,000 households in the City of Seattle, as of the 2020 census[9]

70,000 new homes will be close to 20% (after being added in)

    60,000 new homes in mid rises and high rises in underutilized airspace

        20 developments of 3,000 units

            (20 x 3,000 units = 60,000 homes)

            One 3,000 unit development has (at 20 units per floor)

                2 mid rises of 25 floors (2 x 500 units = 1,000 units) and

                2 high rises of 50 floors (2 x 1000 units = 2,000 units)

    10,000 new homes in townhomes, 30 units per 2 acres, such as

        • reuse of scattered acres
        • teardown of old residential use
        • commercial/industrial conversion

        2 acres = 30 units

            20 regular two-story townhomes
                with extra

            10 one-bedroom garden apartment units or

            10 one-bedroom units in a multi-story building
              (with underground garages and elevators as needed)

10,000 units ÷ 30 units per 2 acres = about 667 acres needed. Seattle has 53,000 total acres; 667 acres is 1.3% of the land for conversion to new townhomes; or more use could be in mid rises.

Where Do We Find the Space?

◊ In busy regions, since many buyers and renters are already priced out of central cores, or are in cramped housing, or have long commutes, they will accept a smaller yard for a townhome, for example, than will an upscale buyer. Average households can still have adequate space with good amenities, but the location doesn't have to cater to upscale sensibilities, like having huge yards. Average households will buy on a smaller lot, or a townhome, or three-bedroom condo. It still beats a high-priced, cramped apartment they'll never own. Or sharing a place. Thus airspace now underutilized (awaiting upscale use, or empty per upscale sensibilities) can provide viable locations for average-income buyers and renters. Parking can be underground or in parking structures.

◊ When a building is already going up, just add some floors for moderate income units and middle class units. Larger units and penthouse units sold at higher prices help on costs, profits, and property tax revenue.

◊ The wealthiest of the wealthy raise their families in high rises on the Upper East Side of Manhattan in New York City and on Lake Shore Drive in Chicago. They choose high rise living. There's no social harm to well-off families living in high rises. So too, then, for average households in well-managed buildings.

> Complexes can include exercise rooms, gyms, sports courts, common areas, and meeting rooms. Extra floors can include outdoor areas, decks, and plazas with picnic tables, benches, jogging paths, and play lots for children. This meets individual and family needs, and provides community interaction.

> When space, bedrooms, and amenities match family size, then normal and positive family life can occur in high rises or mid rises.

◊ Place mid-rise buildings on busier commercial streets or above transit lines to reduce "not in my backyard" (nimby) concerns.[10]

◊ Units can rise above malls, parking lots, grocery stores, offices, warehouses, and light industrial uses, with parking floors included. Use soundproofing as needed. Business use can remain. New residential complexes can be near such areas with proper sound-blocking buffers, with tree lines and greenery. Businesses benefit from new customers and employees in the new homes. The new tax revenue supports schools.

◊ Add more mid rises and high rises along highway corridors.[11] Such buildings are already adjacent to highways running through cities in the U.S. One nice high rise with a Whole Foods at 798 W. Madison St. in Chicago is right next to Interstate 90/94, with no complaints.

The Overall Situation: With Some Effort, Success Looms

This will take effort. But it's eminently doable. Yet, we offer analysis as realists, not idealists. If none of this is addressed, average people will make do, as they always have. But why just make do, when much better options await? Any corrective movement is welcome, pointing the way to further success.

The customers are ready and waiting: If enough people and businesses conclude that more homes at fair prices are needed, governments can respond. Or people can use referendums. A commitment for enough homes at prices for average households is beneficial. It's within fair free enterprise, rather than a monopoly of upscale real estate. Builders and landlords will still profit with new development, with some lower-priced units included.

The National Interest

So let's get the job done for America's middle-income households and America's working families. This majority is the heart of the people in the U.S.A. Our people deserve this effort. Yes, there will be difficulties. Yes, it will take time. It will be time well spent. This is vitally important.

This is in the national interest. Such as in the 1930s when the U.S. decided to keep the elderly from destitution with Social Security. Or in the 1940s when the U.S. built the world's mightiest military from scratch to help win WWII. Or in the 1960s when 75% of seniors had no health insurance so Medicare was added for all seniors. Or in the 2010s when health plans finally covered preexisting conditions.

Those complicated tasks were completed, after it was decided to be in the national interest. The investment and effort made the nation stronger. Would you say it wasn't worth it? Because, well, it sure took a lot of effort. Yes, it did take a lot of effort, rather than leave the elderly destitute, or rather than lose WWII to dictators, or rather than leave seniors with no health insurance, or rather than leave people with preexisting conditions unable to get health coverage.

There are rebuttals to housing at modest prices. Let's examine them:

"It's too complicated,"   indicates a need for more rigorous thinking.

"It's too much to do,"   indicates either unconcern, or mental laziness.

"We're busy with other things,"   indicates a lack of logic in prioritizing.

"It's too hard to pass any changes,"   indicates an unwillingness to make anyone any bit inconvenienced, which is not the same as harming them in a significant way. Profits from upscale real estate will remain.

These rebuttals to housing at sensible prices don't hold up, considering the huge scope of the serious intergenerational effects.

A Monopoly Effect in Real Estate by Upscale Use

In the U.S., a market effect skews prices to the upscale. Even when price fluctuations lower U.S. housing costs, the entry level inventory is so limited to begin with, waiting for housing downturns is not a lasting solution for U.S. working families.[12]

The key 30% level of housing cost to income is of little consideration in rental pricing in the U.S. as prices are driven by demand from the top income levels. Landlords will keep raising the rents as long as enough people are showing up to pay what the market will bear.

If someone who earns a higher income will shell out a high price per month for a one-bedroom place, then that's the going rate. That's even if that price is double the 30% level for what an entry-level employee earns per month, working in the same area. High prices are less of a deterrent for the more substantial incomes of the upper-middle-class households and on up, so this won't slow down much. The middle class on up might gripe about high prices too, but they pay those prices, because they can, and landlords squeeze the prices upward, because they can.

Households cram in more people to cover the price. In many regions more of the workforce is sharing housing. Homes designed for 4 people have 8 people. Apartments designed for 2 people have 3 or 4 people. A lot of U.S. developers don't even bother planning for the lower-middle class or for entry-level employees in busy areas, or in the suburbs, or, increasingly, in rural areas.

With homes for purchase on a mortgage, sure, some cushion is required since mortgages are only approved when the payments start at around 30% to 35% of income. But homes or condos for sale at that level for the entry level workforce are about nonexistent in busy areas where the jobs are. Going up the pay scale, even the middle class is having a harder time qualifying for mortgages for the homes that are available for sale.

Even after approval for a mortgage payment at 35% of income, in some time, or quickly, the property taxes may be 50% higher or 100% higher. So the monthly payment rises above the 35% of income it was originally set at, to 45% of income, 50% of income, and up.

Including Homes at Fair Prices

We in the U.S. strain and struggle as serious problems mount. But when one knows a little bit more about the situation, the excuse of "That's just the way things are" does not hold up. It does not have to be this way. The U.S. can commit to a self-sustaining inventory of homes at manageable prices. Americans can pay the financing for their homes by themselves for themselves when prices are manageable.

It is in the national interest to fit in homes and rentals that are reasonable for the majority of society. Some things are worth an effort. This is one of them.

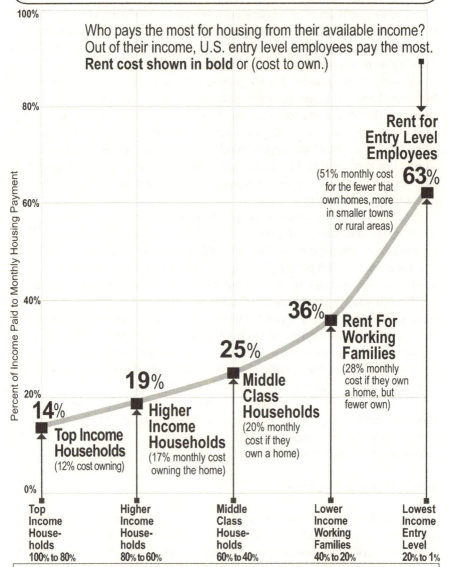

Summary

Effects of the Gentrification Curve
Cash Left Over Per $1,000 of Household Income After the Monthly Housing Payment

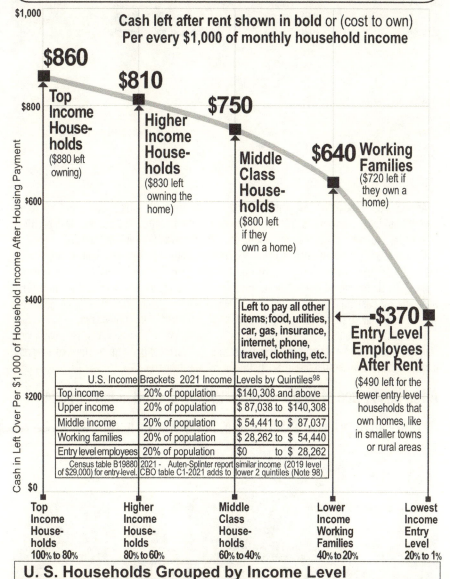

As the gentrification curve increases more steeply upward (page 14) it inversely drives net income down for employees. Overactive gentrification is a linchpin of unfair economic inequality, perhaps exceeding other factors.

Where New Homes are Going in at Regular Prices Add Some Starter Homes Too. There is Space.

Any U.S. area can adjust by its regional prices and by adding more units. These were actual new homes built at all of these actual prices. Infrastructure costs, permit costs, and labor are included. These were among the lowest priced standard new homes in the Phoenix region in 2023 and 2024.

On lots above (A) homes such as below (B) from a standard builder were built for regular full profit at $275,990, base price, for 1,168 sq. ft. in suburban Phoenix, in Coolidge, Ariz. From (A), Phoenix Sky Harbor Airport is a 45-minute drive. The Intel factory in Chandler is a 35-minute drive. Shopping, the post office, city hall, and a public library are a 5-minute drive. There is municipal bus service, and senior transit pick-up and drop-off service. It's a safe, low-crime area.

Base prices are from Oct., 2024 price sheets, as distributed by builders and online. Homes were built and offered for sale at each base price per square foot shown, at that date, by standard, for-profit, corporate builders, in the area shown. See p. 154 for documentation.[99]

A top base price of $236 per sq. ft., $275,990, 1,168 sq. ft., Oct. 2024

At mid-range price of $196 per sq. ft., build starter homes ➡

Sept., 2024, example of homes at $275,990 base price, 1,168 sq. ft. in suburban Phoenix.

Summary

Own or Rent a Cottage Home for $1,119 a month.
$142,500 base price, 750 sq. ft., Oct. 2024 prices, 6% mortgage

(C) $1119.66 per month
$142,500
3% down FHA 6% APR
0.5% PMI
Included in payment:
$ 57.59 PMI
$125.00 property tax AZ
$108.33 insurance in AZ

Using the same pricing per sq. ft. of the homes actually sold in (A) & (B), the same development could have fit in cottage homes, as shown above (C) and some studio condos as shown below (D). The studios below are fully rented about 10 blocks from the homes at (A) & (B).

The home (B) was sold at $236 per sq. ft. base price, and larger homes were sold at $162 per sq. ft. for a 1,980 sq. ft. home. So, on smaller lots, starter homes can be built and sold at a profit at a mid-range of $196 per sq. ft., $1,1119.66 a month (C) and $715.25 a month (D), for FHA loans including tax, PMI, and insurance; which are shown so to not understate prices unrealistically.

OR LESS: Also, a site nearby had move-in-ready new homes at $155 per sq.ft. ($328,990 for 2,127 sq. ft. to $173 per sq. ft. ($284,990 for 1,650 sq. ft). The avg. of $165 per. sq. ft. would be:

$165 per sq. ft
- (C) Cottage $969 a month $123,750
- (D) Studio $645 a month $ 74,250

The municipality & builders sold bigger homes at each price shown, per sq. ft. of $142 to $236

They skipped starter homes. As usual. But starter homes are possible.

Own or Rent a Small Studio Condo for $715.25 a month.
$88,200 base price, 450 sq. ft., Sept. 2024 prices, 6% mortgage

(D) $715.25 per month
$88,200
3% down FHA 6% APR
0.5% PMI
Included in payment:
$ 35.65 PMI
$ 83.33 property tax AZ
$ 83.33 insurance in AZ

Small? Yes, but these studios (D) are just 10 blocks from the location of (A) & (B), fully rented out, so there is demand. Some studios can be larger, for a bit more in price. Photos pp. 16-17 by Lydia Deckert © 2024

Current U.S. Housing Policy: Nobody Has to Do Anything

For housing, nobody has to do anything. So developers hold veto power. Sure, profit is required for any business. Business isn't charity. But, it's a matter of ratios. Right now the U.S. requires zero consideration for average people's salaries in overall housing inventory.

Developers can get by, saying that no significant amount of new development at lower prices is reasonable, since they say so. That is not a proven business certainty, as shown on pages 16-17.

That's because not one government in the whole of the United States has taken the responsibility to stand up for the average households with starter homes in more than a pittance of market share. The only exception is Vermont, which has made some more serious efforts.

Most areas or states won't pass even a measly 10% to 20% commitment to starter units amidst new construction. That would leave 80% to 90% at full prices. Can our businesses add extra units to manage that? Sure they can. Let's embrace U.S. business dynamism and a can-do attitude. Let's use that good ol' American know-how that we're supposed to proudly display in these here United States of America.

Under the guise of a free market, an upscale monopoly of real estate is taking over, whether it's necessary or not and whether it's right or not. Legal expert Robert C. Ellickson used the term the cartelization of housing supply. Ellickson used the term in the context of "proponents of growth controls" such as homeowners who want to "protect their major financial asset" which is their home value.[13] It is an apt and reasonable description of gentrification effects. This market isn't like luxury cars where, fine, refuse to sell for less. Or only make so many of them, as no one requires a luxury car. This goes further than just specializing in luxury units, when it in effect eliminates or bans starter homes and starter apartment prices.

Everyone requires a home. People work. People have income.

People need homes.

If the usual investors and developers think that it's not worth their time and money to meet any commitment for homes that people need, then fine. Yes, then, that's fine. They may invest elsewhere.

If Most Developers Won't Include Any Lower Prices, Then Get Someone Else

Then let's use someone else's time and money to include a few homes and rentals at fair prices. Other investors will likely step in and take the 5%, 10%, 20%, or 30% deal, as it still leaves, for example, 70% to 95% at full prices. That is what happened with such commitments in place in Europe. That is also what has happened in the U.S. In one example, the builders proposed only a few lower-priced units. That's all they can afford, they said. At first. Then when the city council required more at lower prices, the builders signed the deal.[14]

This doesn't mean that rich areas, like Beverly Hills or the Hamptons, won't remain rich areas. The housing of regional workforces need not occur in high rises directly in Beverly Hills nor in apartments directly on the ocean front of the Hamptons. That's not really under discussion. For a regional workforce, somewhere in the general area, starter units could be added, so employees do more in life than barely break even, to end up barely making it on Social Security in retirement. There is usable, compatible airspace in a region.

The one market of starter homes is just one subset of the economy. The inventory commitments under discussion wouldn't be an attempt at broad price controls, like President Nixon tried in the '70s. Nor should the U.S. have rent control takeovers which obliterate investor capital. This is for investors who agree to join in.

People can own their own homes, independent of government, independent of private exploitation. Or people can rent at very low prices in nice buildings over a lifetime. They can save so much that their private funds can be adequate in retirement, reducing reliance on government.[15] The apartment buildings can be paid in full, independent of government, independent of big-business greed.

Fees should match relevant government costs. Exorbitant fees which are designed to cover other government expenses should be contested and should end.

A property tax bill should match the income level of the home owners and renters, so costs are reasonable to builders and customers. The surrounding higher prices with higher property taxes will provide money for government services. So will overall sales taxes and income taxes, which are relative to income, thus fair.

As needed, governments can temporarily play the role of investors with full repayment by rents and home sales. Cities, counties, and states, in conjunction with federal agencies, can use bond proceeds from private investors to put out bids. Developments could be 70% full price and 30% lower price. Some general contractors, construction crews, and management companies will take the contracts.

Would starter homes sell? Would lower-priced rentals fill up?

What do you think? Perhaps? Maybe? Yes?

If so, then, there is a proper pricing equilibrium in residential real estate.

Fair prices, for everyone.

Success looms, with enough concerted effort.

Reasons to Act

Chapter 1
Building Economic Stability

A U.S. economy that is better able to handle downturns and shocks is in everyone's interest. For the wealthy as well as the workers, it is best to have a profitable economy that is well positioned to compete globally. What's a great way to do that? Provide housing security for those who don't have it. Here's a two-page summary to appeal to the self interest of U.S. investors, business owners, government officials, social leaders, union leaders, and employees for U.S. economic stability and growth.[16] For readers in other nations, these conditions apply in their nations as well.

U.S. Economic Stability

• Many people cannot make their home payments for very long after an extended layoff, of one or both spouses, or after events like divorce, a serious injury, or a protracted illness. These situations could often be overcome, but for the high home payment which leaves little margin for error.

• High residential prices prevent entry level employees and the middle class from having capital, the building block of upward mobility. With homes with reasonable prices, and thus with more capital, people can build wealth, succeed in businesses, and expand careers, not just scuffle along.

• High residential prices are a main cause of U.S. working-class financial instability, which causes personal problems, which cause society huge spillover spending, such as emergency rooms, welfare, child services, addiction rehab, police, courts, jails, prisons, and on and on. Western Europe and Japan, for example, don't spend such huge amounts on working-class dysfunction, but, rather, have relatively stable entry-level employees, financially and personally.

The current course of U.S. residential real estate is not viable for the social compact or for economic stability.[17]

When will business owners look up from the last quarterly returns and when will government leaders carve out some time to look at this seriously? This is a vast, long-term, encroaching, enveloping problem. For business leaders, this is in their business interests. For unions and advocates for the working families, solving this goes a long way to adding significant take-home pay for the U.S. workforce. For government officials, the stability of society is their responsibility. If it comes to it, entry-level workers may join with middle-class voters to pass binding referendums for a commitment for homes at fair prices.

People can collaborate and compromise to find an on-the-ground solution that's fair, as closely as is possible, to all parties. Glitches and unintended consequences will occur. We should expect that. Adjustments can be made. Psychologists find that people tend to settle for what they have already, rather than try for a better result. At some point, however, a situation gets serious enough to warrant effort for change. Then it's time to proceed with the best, well-researched methods for change, in order to see what the results will be, in order to make further adjustments.[18]

While seeking growth, let's not disdain a steadier base. Let's retain a rock-solid American middle class and workforce, from which to propel U.S. comparative advantage further, and profits further. By utilizing fair housing costs, let's recapitalize our working families and average-income seniors. U.S. employees from the lowest levels on up can prosper, moving into higher wealth of their own.

The U.S. workforce can rest assured on a staid normalcy. The broad reliability can establish a springboard to bring forth fresh ideas and innovations for future generations to achieve even more. From positions of strength, all levels of society can calmly, patiently overcome bad conditions when they occur. That's better than having to live nervously, on edge, reacting to bad conditions with impatience, intemperance, and panicky overreactions.

From all the varied members of society, from all corners of the United States, a calm, deep-set, sober confidence can take hold. In confidence, those who want to begin new pursuits can better do so, like starting businesses, or getting degrees, or starting research, things that had been out of reach for them in the past. Others can go further, launching unusual, bold, and brave pursuits, and see what happens. All under dependable governance and dependable business management that comes from steadiness.

Building homes at fair prices sounds peripheral at first, easily enough put off, left for a future date down the road. We'll see, maybe later, who knows; that has been the story about housing at fair prices. But how the broad majority of people manage their biggest expense of housing has huge consequences, effects, and reverberations. Building homes at fair prices will build a better economy and will build a better society.[19]

Chapter 2

Homes as a Human and Social Necessity

A nicer, bigger house is fine, in and of itself.

Spending is relative. To a family with only beans to eat, a pizza delivery is an out-of-reach luxury. To a family that can afford only a pizza delivery, a dinner in Paris is an out-of-reach luxury. The scales of spending apply to any product and to any household. It's the definition of private property. Spending *is* private property, like your spending, for example.

Just as the law can't limit pizza deliveries, or trips to Europe, the law can't limit what people choose to spend on a house. In a democracy, the law can't tell people how to spend their money. It's without limits. That's freedom. In a democracy, the law can't tell people who start a business, or make an investment, how much money they can make, or can't make. It's not set by limits. That's freedom. Do you want anyone telling you that you can't order a pizza, or move to a nicer place? If you take a more demanding job to earn more, or start a business, do you want anyone telling you how much money you can make, or can't make?

We bring up this old concept, of the freedom to spend one's own money however one wants, because a lot of people fervently defend this freedom of private property rights when it's for their own spending choices on themselves, but leave it out of their thinking for everyone else.

When people know their situation is not great, they may resent the freedom to spend that other people have, people like the 1% to 5% to 40% of the wealthiest, or someone down the block. Some people have less than is comfortable. It is valid and important for them to be included in a nation's prosperity, so things are good for them as well. Analyst David Brooks pointed out that you can't argue people out of the distrust they feel from being insecure financially.[20]

Better housing gives security to people, and hope for their futures. When they are secure, people don't have to give much thought to people who are ahead of them financially. The economy can roll along with everyone included. Those who started a business in their garage and made a billion can make a billion more; and a person can just put in a 40 hour week and have peace of mind too.

There is a Large Pool of Wealthier Buyers That Keeps Getting Bigger

In housing worldwide, a key factor is that many families have moved into the middle to upper income levels. Like a janitor who starts a cleaning business and retires well off, with two children, who finish college, become professionals and start families. One lower-income household (a janitor with two kids) morphs into three upper-income households (a retired business owner and two professional households). The next generations have more money as adults and pass more along. That's inclusion and transformation to empowerment within free enterprise. It's success that anyone would want to see for their own family.

Next add the households that were already well off, whose children follow, some with more children. Assets grow. That's normal, lawful, and to be expected. It's mathematical:
- From 1950 to 2020, U.S. population more than doubled. In the U.S. since 1950, 180 million more people live within the same land mass.
- Thus millions more households can afford nicer homes, and even more are on the way, both from natural growth and people who move here. Millions of wealthier households will keep buying whatever they want.
- In addition, 5% to 8% of U.S. sales are to well-off families from around the world who buy second homes, or buy homes to rent out.[21]

Thus real estate is skewed by more and more people who have more and more in resources.

A New Type of Monopoly

Residential real estate is in effect becoming more and more an upscale monopoly, but it is different than a standard-style monopoly. Gentrification pricing monopoly can't be pinned on one company, one investor, or a group of companies or investors. It involves every real estate transaction in a region. It's from each single-family home sale and each apartment rented, including from mom-and-pop landlords and handy-man rehabbers.

Pricing has effects from all over. Boise, Idaho and St. George, Utah are affected by what goes on in Portland, Ore. and Seattle. The ever-growing number of wealthier households buy more and more of the land and airspace, even in rural areas. There are lulls, price drops during slowdowns, and crashes, but waiting for a crash is not a lasting solution for entry level employees to have a place to live. In price crashes, the wealthy buy more. After a crash, prices edge up steadily again. Over time, wealthier households keep their real estate and buy more. Adjustments and unanticipated trends occur.

Who Should Determine the Housing Inventory? A Big Glitch

U.S. housing is provided by developers as they work their way down from the highest bidders. They stop when they want to. Building nothing at all is always an option.

That's a glitch. It's a big glitch.

Housing companies do not have to provide *any housing at all,* not if they don't want to. Sure, when demand slackens, developers and landlords drop prices, which can then include some buyers and renters at lower incomes, but if developers don't get the profit levels they want, they can limit production.

We won't build, is what they have said, for example, when cities have floated ideas for a certain percentage of new housing units to be priced lower. Left to investors' profit motives alone, no more homes or apartments are built until prices reach what investors seek.[22]

A market equivalent would be to raise prices of electricity, water, and basic insurance to what only the wealthier half of the nation has money to pay; and claim it's fairly what the market can bear. Even if the other half of the nation is left to fend with only limited electricity, water, and insurance, or none, when prices exceed income levels. The equivalent effect is happening in housing.

The utility companies could today remain profitable for investors with only the wealthier half of the nation paying higher prices for their products, thus it would be wholly accurate to say that's what the market will bear.

As long as the wealthier have enough to pay the higher costs, tough luck for everyone else? No matter how bad the conditions are for the majority of people? Yes, that's the U.S. method, the official policy, in housing, and for housing in much of the rest of the world.

Housing developers are in the same category as any other company, to sell any product to willing buyers who can pay the price. So anyone can understand how a developer of houses or apartments follows the market. So would anyone who starts a business, for take-out hot dogs or for designer handbags. Developers will raise the prices to the highest that buyers will pay, and when they don't get the prices they want, they will build less. That's free enterprise.

The problem is that a place to live is a basic need, unlike a nicer handbag. So when housing developers go for the highest prices they can get, it leaves out a lot of society on a basic need. It's also leaving out a valid use of the commons, so to speak.

Housing Status

Housing supply for all employees should have the status as a product that's essential, not discretionary.[23] Upscale buying is discretionary, and will provide the profits that it normally would. The need is for homes for average households that match the paychecks of the average users, just like water supply, electricity supply, and basic insurance. That's done by passing a commitment.

This is a change in one specific market sector, residential real estate that is non-luxury. Thus it would have some effect on residential real estate developers, just as the changes in pricing ranges had some effect on the water companies, electric companies, and insurance companies, which remain profitable

Electricity was originally sold only to the rich, because at first the product could only be afforded by the rich. Electricity was at first only for lighting, as electric appliances and electric heating units hadn't even been invented and air conditioning didn't exist until later. Electricity wasn't even considered a necessity at first, since everyone, including the rich, had always used lamps with oil, kerosene, or gas for light in homes, businesses, and for street lights. To have electric lights was a high luxury, a discretionary purchase, only for mansions and the richest corporate headquarters.

Gradually, electricity became the social necessity it is today. Thus, when society made a commitment that everyone should have electricity service at a price within their income level, the electric companies had to lose some profit potential. They still do lose some profit opportunity. A wholly unadulterated free market would allow the electric company to jack up the price to what only the well-off can easily pay, squeeze the middle class for more, and cut off entry-level employees, who would do without. That's a complete free market option, like for designer handbags, for example. The free market producers won't lower the price for a designer handbag, if they don't want to. Can't afford a designer handbag? You do without one. That's what the market will bear.

For housing, the U.S. system is to permit whatever the market will bear.

A U.S. Housing Inventory Minimum? There Isn't One. Just a Small Safety Net

The housing task remains to add pricing options at the bottom, by defining regular, sustainable housing as
   a. essential
         instead of
   b. discretionary, as
   c. the determinant factor in housing inventory. A commitment to pricing options for modest-income employees would alter the inventory. This then places some basic housing beyond how discretionary items are produced in the market, which is at someone's discretion.

There is specifically not a significant minimum commitment of inventory to match workforce income.

There is only a safety net of minimum housing inventory that reaches only a few percent of the poorest of the poor citizens through some scattered public housing apartments and some Section 8 payments to some landlords. Section 8 is limited to the poorest 2% of the whole nation, about half are seniors. The perception that a huge percentage of the U.S. workforce has it on easy street on

Section 8 is not accurate, but that's in some of the public's mindset. Again, it is a mere 2% of the nation, the poorest of the poor, mostly seniors who would be in homeless shelters or tents otherwise.

Adding in other housing safety nets of charity shelters, government shelters, and other governmental supplements, it's maybe up to 4% or 5%.

The effects of high prices on the broad workforce and retired population reach into the households of perhaps 40% or more of the total U.S. population.

This isn't a 5% problem. It's a 40% to 50% problem.

Inventory changes of only 5% won't be the answer.

Minimums and Maximums

Human effort and spending is either on
  (a) essential minimums or
  (b) discretionary items and activities.

Human life has the basic needs of water, nutrients, calories, protein, transportation to work, shelter from freezing in winter, and shelter from heat stroke in summer. Those are objective, factual human essentials. All human spending and activity beyond meeting these essentials is discretionary effort.

In proper civilization, there are minimums to each citizen, such as not letting people die of malnutrition. Nations have had malnutrition to the point of death, including large numbers in large nations in the 1970s.

Minimums and maximums in economics need recognition, in order to develop systems to meet the minimums. Along with required minimum standards, in free democratic republics, extra initiative has no limits.[24] One person is free to work more than others. People can start businesses, learn new trades, study for professions, and then spend their higher earnings however they like. It's freedom to gain more, including for nicer housing.

In housing, there will be someone who outbids others for the highest-priced property. Someone will build a new mansion somewhere. It's their money. To stop that would necessitate limits on personal spending or private business spending, which won't work. That's because:

(1) There are no spending caps or income caps in democracy. That's because there aren't limits on how many customers you can have, or on how much customers can spend. In democracy, rather, the limitation is that you can't force anyone to be your customer. (That's done in a dictatorship or a cartel.)

(2) Limiting discretionary spending by households that have the extra income would not directly provide inventory of products at lower prices for households with average income, for any product, including housing.

Which is why, the answer for starter homes is not to complain about nicer homes of the upper-middle class, or the most expensive mansions and condos of the wealthiest people. The solution is to not even bother thinking about those maximums that some people will spend, because that's their free choice, to spend to their maximum, after they paid their taxes, like you do.

Do you condemn the rich person who donates all his or her money to charity, and then moves into a modest apartment? That's happened. Well, that doesn't get you a cheaper home, does it? Nor would it get you a cheaper home, if a rich person donated nothing to charity, and bought another mansion.

The solution is for the system to build starter homes and lower-priced rentals. That is what is not being done, while fretting about other people's money. If you have some extra money, should we all fret about how you spend it? How much money should you chip in towards someone else's housing selection?

Why Do Some Have So Much, While Others Have So Little?

"Why do some have so much, while others have so little?" people ask. Now, that's a topic of immense depth, the topic of unfair economic inequality. About 3,000 years ago, a sociological analysis in the book *Ecclesiastes*, for example, noted "...all the oppressions that are done under the sun: and behold, the tears of such as were oppressed, and they had no comforter; and on the side of their oppressors there was power; but they had no comforter."[25] That book is still in print, and available. After thousands of years, humanity is still working on it.

Other, more recent commentators seem to have just discovered the topic as they emphatically proclaim, "This is clearly about unfair economic inequality, pure and simple, no doubt about that." Well, ... that's what the author of *Ecclesiastes* pointed out already, some time ago.

Regarding unfair economic inequality within societies and nations:

> The "what" is the wide gap in income between those at the top and those at the middle and bottom of the income scale. The "what" is well documented (see p. 124).
>
> The "why" is a lack of will by society to change the status quo, fed by uncertainty as how to do so.
>
> The "how" is a method to correct unfair economic inequality, if society decides that people from the lowest wages to the middle class deserve stability, along with the wealthy.

Statements about the need for empowerment for workers are valid. Statements about making things better for average households are valid. These statements are valid observations about the strain in average people's lives.

In this, however, we've grown utterly fatigued of reading from beginning to end, page after page, yet another book or article about poverty or about unfair economic inequality. Such works repeat the unfair conditions, with some slight or new variation of data, with more statements about the lack of progress. Or they claim that the fix is in.

Then, nothing much practical, or specific, in detail, is offered about how to bring about change. Pointing out a problem that is pretty self-evident and apparent to us all, is not much of an analysis for citizens to work with, when few details are provided, specifically, about what to do next.

This short book isn't going into too much depth on this broad topic, but this book aims to make a few meaningful points. Solving unfair economic inequality involves the vital matter of committing to minimums by society. To requirements. To binding commitments. Not, perhaps. Not, let's hope. Not, we'll see if something might be done, later, maybe, sort of, kind of, possibly. Minimums are at the core a decision of distribution. Proper income distributed at first eliminates any need for redistribution.

And it could be important to notice the sum in total of trillions of dollars worldwide that the workforces and future generations will spend on housing to benefit landlords and lenders. That immense sum of capital, which is being sucked out of the payrolls of the world's businesses and out of the paychecks of the world's employees could, rather, be under the control of billions of working families.

Those trillions of dollars could benefit the households of the workforces themselves by supporting rentals at fair prices, or paid-for homes. Then the capital saved provides the working families further compounding investment capital for centuries. See Reversing Landlordism is a Revolution Worth Trillions on pp. 127-129.

That could be a change for those who have so little.

Why don't we find out? By trying it.

In a discussion about why some have so much, while others have so little, remember to remember about the minimums.

Again, minimums are at the core a decision of distribution.

Again, proper income distributed at first eliminates any need for redistribution. This would also strengthen all other business sectors (other than landlordism and lenders) when the workforce can buy from the businesses.

It's a sign of human progress to move past bare existence to be able to spend time and money on efforts such as recreation, music, art, entertainment, fashion, sports, literature, history, inventions, exploration, and travel. This is freedom, from simple fun to the most serious matters, like social betterment, or scientific research. Yet, with our freedom, let's have some minimums set in place, for all of us.

Opportunity Costs

A commitment to starter homes and to starter rental prices will have some opportunity costs. An *opportunity cost* is an investment term. It means a cost when someone passes up one opportunity, to do something else. When you hold a property now, to sell later, you incur an opportunity cost; the cost of not selling now for what you will get now, in hopes of making more money later.

For a home builder, there may an opportunity cost to include a few starter homes. A developer of starter homes, for example, may have to deal with more buyers in total than they do now they do now for regular homes.

For example:

2 buyers - each buyer gets 1 home of 1,500 square feet (sq. ft.) on 1 standard lot
= 2 standard lots used by the builder

Home 1 = 1,500 sq. ft.
Home 2 = 1,500 sq. ft.

= 3,000 sq. ft. of construction on 2 standard lots
at the same price per square foot

3 buyers of 3 cottage homes - each buyer gets 1 cottage home, 3 of which
= 2 standard lots used by the builder

Cottage Home 1 = 1,000 sq. ft.
Cottage Home 2 = 1,000 sq. ft.
Cottage Home 3 = 1,000 sq. ft.

= 3,000 sq. ft. of construction on 2 standard lots
at the same price per sq. ft. (or more, see below)

(Equal prices per sq. ft are one example. Home builders' standard practice is to charge less per sq. ft. for larger amounts of square footage. See actual prices on pp. 16-17.)

It's the same lots (2) with the same square footage of construction (3,000) but with 3 buyers to deal with; instead of 2 buyers to deal with.

Selling to fewer buyers makes it so much easier to sell out a subdivision or a building, which is why all the developers love selling standard sizes, or larger sizes, to fewer buyers. It's fully understandable, what's happening.

There is the can-do aspect of free enterprise and there is the why-bother aspect of free enterprise. It's understandable that a lot investors will balk at any adjustments. Yet, people need homes. And understand that current practices, which are freely accepted by builders and buyers, have lower per-square-foot prices for putting more square footage of new construction per lot.

A fair ratio can apply to starter homes, so the profit margins could work out fine. So, yes, dealing with 2 families who get starter homes, instead of 1 family on a regular home is a different product. This is putting a different investment scenario in place, but a worthy one, and it's still profitable.

Once a new scenario is in place and understood, investors who do not want to participate do not have to. For development with extra units for more families, there is no coercion that they must invest. They are free to select other investments with their money. Then different investors can sell to more families or the local housing boards can do so. A housing board can buy some real estate at full and fair market value, including business relocation or buyout costs, just as any other investor would negotiate. Construction can proceed, backed by different investors, or by society through local housing boards.

Conditions of home building have changed over time, like for minimum electrical safety, fire safety, and plumbing sanitation, and builders have adjusted. So can expectations change? Sure. Expecting some starter homes shouldn't be considered unreasonable. Including starter units is not taxation without representation, because commitments to starter homes and starter apartments will be set by officials who are selected by voters. Referendums passed by voters are another option. This is for the public good, as determined by the public, the voters, and their duly elected government. This relates to ideas about use of the commons.

That's capitalism under republican democracy, which is still at the core free-market capitalism. Some opponents of starter units will paint this idea as meddling with the market and as government overreach. They will cry "confiscation!" at the loss of any level of profits otherwise to be had selling at full maximum prices, to only those who can pay the full maximum prices.

When you include some starter homes, that is the case indeed, that for all the effort and investment, you might make less in profit ratio, than if you sell only what wealthier people can pay for. Which all businesses and housing analysts who understand the math agree upon. As do buyers who understand the math.

Which is exactly the point, remember, that some prices should be lower, so the workforce has some money left over, i.e. capital. So conversely, then yes, some ratio of capital won't go to developers or landlords. So, yes, there is some opportunity cost to developers and landlords. That ratio of capital remains within the workforce's use. Yet, that is not blatant unfair confiscation of property, not with full market value paid for all development land and airspace, and with all other luxury market opportunities still available in the surrounding region. Nor, one might conclude, with 70% full prices, and 30% lower prices, for example. Nor only where needed by all of the businesses for their workforces, as part of an interactive, well-functioning economy. This is good old-fashioned, Chamber-of-Commerce business common sense, not dictatorial Bolshevism.

Investors are free to invest elsewhere. As with today's electric companies, water companies, and insurance companies, investors are free to invest their money elsewhere, but democratically elected officials of the republic have a say in base-level pricing for the public good now in utilities and insurance, so say the voters.

When electricity was originally sold only to luxury mansions and corporate headquarters, electric company owners probably liked the practice of charging whatever they could, and shutting off those who couldn't pay higher prices.

Now, however, does anyone think that any group of voters anywhere in a republic is going to let the electric company provide service only to the wealthier households, and deny electricity for the middle class and working families since they can't pay the highest possible prices? Of course not. It is ridiculous to even suggest that, isn't it? Well, that's the deal for housing. And the housing payment is a whole lot more than the electric bill. That this is going on for homes should be considered ridiculous, or worse. It's reckless. It's feckless. Thus, it seems, there might have to be one more market segment, residential real estate for average households, in which society says that a minimum level needs to be provided.

That's unless the real estate providers will build starter homes and rentals, even just at a price close per square foot they are charging for larger homes, as is possible as shown in the actual market pricing per sq. ft. on pp. 16-17, with infrastructure, and *no* government welfare. It remains to be seen in most nations.

The Broad, Lifetime, Social Effects of a Modest Home

How important is a home? Let's look at people's whole life spans. Many people freely choose to be single. Many people freely choose not to have children. But we also read and hear about people around the world who don't get married, or don't start families, because they can't afford adequate apartments or homes. That reflects on how adequate housing space, or the lack of it, has a deep effect on how we live as humans.

Because they don't have a proper place to live, some people agonizingly give up basic human choices of companionship through marriage, raising a child, and of growing old with a companion. As people enter old age, the lack of a proper place to live denies them a proper quality of life and dignity. These things are deep in the human core, and should be available so that full, vibrant, and joyous lives are possible, including on modest wages.

With adequate space to live, young people can start well rather than flounder. As people settle in to a home, it contributes to community as people develop lasting links. For children, basic stability in a home is vital to ground them with relatives, friends, teachers, activities, and a house of worship, as they so choose.

With such security, the children grow into stable habits and stable frames of mind into adulthood.

These options are vital for people, especially those of average incomes, who have fewer resources to start with. They need all the resources that they can muster to build a better life. These personal and social things are fundamental in life, liberty, and the pursuit of happiness.

This all involves so much more than how much profit new condos for the wealthy will bring to investors.

This involves the human condition.

It shouldn't have to be a major political battle to have fair home prices. It looks as if it will be, however.

What does that reveal, that in this century, with all of the progress and profits of society, that this idea even might have to be a major political battle?

How important is a home? Even the most modest one? Much more so, than at first glance. It is not just a percentage point.

The 60-Year High-Payment Plan

Here's a symptom of the problem: The 60-Year High-Payment Plan.

We will refer to this specific, distinct plan again a few times in the book, using a capitalized title for it, The 60-Year High-Payment Plan.

That's because it describes the specific set of circumstances used by actual people, as defined next, like the terms in a specific contract.

If you read it elsewhere in the book, please remember how it indicates this specific set of circumstances:

The 60-Year High-Payment Plan

You Might Be Already Signed Up

Starting at **age 25**, most average employees make payments for 60 years on

(a) high rent or

(b) a high mortgage followed by

(c) much higher property taxes in old age, followed by

(d) death at **age 85**. If you live longer, continue longer than 60 years.

It's always a strain. A large number of people in the U.S. and people around the world are signed up, like it or not, whether they've realized it yet or not. Pause to consider your expected housing payments, including property taxes, until age 85. You might be on this plan. Should you have to settle for that? It depends on what type of housing methods your nation and your state uses.

Remember that even a paid-off house doesn't get you off The 60-Year High-Payment Plan in busy regions in many states and nations, those with no meaningful property tax cap. Gentrified property taxes can rise to $1,000 a month, then more. Don't forget to look forward to enjoying those payments in your old age, in most U.S. states.

The American Dream? Half the nation wearily faces The American Reality: always being either barely ahead in life's monthly expenses, or a little behind, on The 60-Year-High-Payment Plan, unto death at age 85.

Is This Our Future? Cots, Campers, and Renting Out Your Bedrooms

In any nation, when people are so broke after paying the rent or mortgage payment, many of them skip medical coverage, skip medicine, avoid trips to the doctor, get inadequate nutrition, or live with some unhealthy or unsafe conditions. Worldwide, lack of reasonable housing leads to lower lifespans as people's health falters prematurely, or from preventable or treatable illnesses, which they don't take care of for lack of money and time, since they're working all the time, but have no money left.

Housing options affect safety. A leading cause of death of U.S. citizens under age 18 is from shots fired, which relates to where children and young people have to live, which is all that some households can afford.

In London, researchers found that high home costs have pushed one million people into poverty conditions, not that they don't have jobs, pensions, or health coverage.[26]

In Hong Kong some full-time employees live in closet-sized units with bunk beds, hot plates, and mini-fridges.

In Seoul, Korea, as of 2023, housing prices in five years went up 80% higher than pay raises and a three-bedroom unit costs around $1 million. "I thought I would live well by working at a good company after college, but the reality is that we are the poorest in our neighborhood. Living as a salaried worker, there are so many limitations," a college graduate who had a good job at a corporation told a reporter.[27]

In Miami, some employees rent entryways of homes to sleep in, using cots.[28]

In Silicon Valley, Calif., and Sedona, Ariz., some employees live out of cars, vans, and campers. And these aren't derelicts, but dependable people in full-time jobs, who grew up in these areas. Is that the future for these employees, whom society needs? Work full-time for a bunk bed, couch, or cot.

In Orange County, California, homeowners rent out bedrooms to make their payments. Is that the future for the middle class? Rent half your house.

In the U.S., 85% of all Americans, of all political parties, say the situation of financially struggling households ranks as a top concern.[29] Of all Americans, 92% say they prefer financial stability, over potential upward mobility, if forced to choose between those two options.[30] An economy should offer basic stability in living standards, and upward mobility for responsible effort. Too bad the U.S. housing system could care less, it seems, about those possibilities.

For housing expenses, the mortgage approval amount is recommended to be not more than 30% of income, although some mortgages allow a little less income. That's to have $700 left per every $1,000 you make. Housing costs above that cut into an ability to pay all other expenses without strain. That doesn't mean a U.S. employee in the lower income brackets is flush with savings at that 30% level, mind you, as that's the cut-off for loan approval. So it's right on the line of being too risky for a home loan, not a ticket to ride the gravy train. With sensible spending, people earning in the lower 20% to 40% of wages and salaries can save, certainly, but only so much, even at the housing cost level of 30%. And it's more like 40% to 50% or more for the 20% of Americans who work full time at jobs that pay the lower amounts at U.S. workplaces, the bottom income bracket.

The wealthier and upper middle class may choose to pay more of their income to homes, and still pay minimum living expenses comfortably. Still, census data shows their average spending is only at 16% of income, even paying for upscale units. For employees who hold down full-time jobs the economy needs, but are at the lower 20% of wages, it's not comfortable. This was shown in the gentrification curve on p. 14, but it bears repeating for this section. U.S. Census data show that:[31]

For the wealthier 40% income brackets, after housing at 16% of income
    per every $1,000 you make: $840 is left.
For full-time workers in the low 20% of wages, after housing at 60% of income
    per every $1,000 you make: $400 is left.

That's U.S. life, and U.S. economic inequality, in a nutshell.

Workers up to the middle class rely more so on their wages from jobs for income, not investment income. It is harder for households to get ahead when housing leaves someone only $400 to $500 per every $1,000 they earn.

With a change in housing, workers could get ahead, and faster, and in higher levels. Tax policy won't reliably create housing inventory. Wage increases for average workers won't outbid the wealthier in real estate. Only commitments specific to housing inventory will reliably create housing inventory.

Without changes, people may see a Manhattanization of prices in more areas, meaning harder times for the non-wealthy, the majority of people.

Altering A Curve.

A complex equation might win some recognition, which is valid. An equation examines economic factors. It can take considerable effort to document economic statistics in meaningful ways. Those statistics can be shown in charts. Often a curve on a chart is a good way to show the statistics.

Yet, much more so than identifying a curve, altering a curve might be the hardest task. To alter a curve, economists, political operatives, and social leaders must materially alter the factors that led to the statistics in the curve. That is the task at hand where high levels of unfair economic disparity create problems. That is the task at hand in housing. Given the obstacles and risks, it gives anyone pause to even try. Let's itemize:

- Some positive signs may beckon, yet odds of success could be scant. It could take a long, long time.
- Does acclaim await? Or ridicule, heartache, and heartburn?
- Will an elected official or appointed official be heralded? Or ignored? Or shown the door?
- Having good motives? Who cares. Good motives get steamrolled all the time.
- Is something is the right thing to do? Yeah, so what. That doesn't mean it'll pass the legislature or parliament, or override a veto.
- Economists and lobbyists for the working class don't get the more lucrative contracts, if any recompense at all.

With all that going for us, shall we get started then?

Maybe economists could give some recognition to recognizing what's before everyone's very eyes, the real estate market, which is average people's biggest expense. It's a huge factor in economic inequality between the haves and the have-nots. Considering that a lot can be done, more of the general public should express concern specifically about starter homes, rather than go along with the incorrect conclusion that nothing much can be done.

The next steps are that society's leaders, political officials, and economists to decide to start work on specific, detailed solutions to this abundantly apparent economic dilemma of society.

The task is to implement economic methods to alter the situation for billions of people worldwide, soon enough, one can hope, and also well into the future.

Fixing the Ratios

Let's look at ways to lower unfair economic disparity by going to where a whole lot of the money is: the highest single non-discretionary expense usually for most households, the monthly housing bill.

For housing, it's a matter of ratios of the market, as with other economic ratios of input and output between business owners (capital) and employees (labor). We will show in detail how and why a certain inventory of homes can cost less, should cost less, and can remain profitable.

From our experience on political campaigns and in government, we're analyzing the following things: What can we propose? Now. What does it cost? Will tax money be saved? Will it work? Soon? Or later? Or ever?

Conclusion: What's Needed? A Decision

Is this easy to do? Well, it's no small undertaking.

Yet, since the resources and methods are available, it only requires the mental fortitude to make the decisions. That's the most difficult part. A decision. Then the next decision. It's a series of decisions. Who's up for it? Then, the details will work out as demand is met. People can collaborate on solutions.

To conclude, the problem is that it's getting to where half the nation strains to find a sensibly priced, adequate place to live. People need enough left from their paychecks to build a better life. A societal necessity is being neglected by society.

Let's examine the possibility of combining the three methods we've highlighted:

Method 1: keeping property tax bills reasonable for average households
Method 2: committing to an inventory of sensibly priced homes for average-income earners
Method 3: keeping prices reasonable for future generations with binding affordability contracts

The three methods can include these additional concepts:
- In all areas and regions, society can have space for upscale homes, and space for homes for workers and the middle class.
- The financing will work, as people will pay for what they get, without handouts.
- These methods require binding commitments. Model commitments are available (see Chapter 5).
- Then enforcement.

That's it.

If you've got the gist of Method 1 (fair property taxes), Method 2 (inventory), and Method 3 (agreements for the future), then you understand more about housing. You also understand how housing inventory might change.

If you can explain this to others, we hope, then the word can spread that there are possibilities for solutions. Housing in any nation doesn't have to be like it is. We provide more details in the rest of the book.

Any person can suggest new ideas in articles, in blogs, or in social media. Any city council member, county board member, state legislator, or member of Congress can request research, hold hearings, and put legislation on the agenda.

People, like you, can email officials, or call, or send a letter, or speak at a meeting. Ask basic questions. Make suggestions. These are sensible things to bring up. It's then the duty of the officials and their staff to look into the details and then do something. Or explain why they won't do anything. It's their job. It's what they signed up to do. When these officials won't pass anything, binding referendums are available in some areas.

For average Americans to improve their lives and for more permanence and durability in society, it isn't enough just to see to the real estate market's rate of return on investment. That's where the effort on housing has gone for the last 30 years; to see to percentage rates of return for landlords, builders, and lenders, not to see to the stability and prosperity of the majority of America's citizens.

Could we citizens, as a nation, in a democracy, in a free republic, our commonwealth, our people, together, to our combined and mutual benefit, decide to take action? For the stability and prosperity of the majority of America's citizens? Yes. We could do that. And so could citizens of any nation.

Steps to Take

Chapter 3

Cap Property Taxes:
Do Cities Have to Kick Out the Working Families?
Then the Middle Class Too?

Should local governments decide to kick out the working families and the middle class? Is that proper? In order to bring in the well-to-do families who can pay higher tax bills, in order to balance the city budget, or the county budget?

This is what's effectively happening, as mayors and city council members usher in the wealthier folks. That's to shore up local government budgets. So what if it also pushes out the working families, is what the mayors are thinking. Soon enough middle class families are priced out too.

What's mostly unspoken, but well understood, is that for mayors this also pushes out some of the social problems to who knows where. Which is fine by most mayors. Let someone else deal with the social problems of the U.S.'s dysfunctional households. Covering the whole topic of social problems and remediation is not possible for this book. It is still highly relevant to this book, because the issue of neighborhood safety affects housing inventory decisions, which are the topic of this book. Thus we have some analysis in Chapter 5, starting with the section Avoiding Mistakes on p. 59.

Property taxes are forcing households to move,[32] so let's get to that.

Each municipality and county wants ease of governance, while letting municipalities and counties elsewhere deal with complications. It is an age-old pattern. To be responsible to the majority of society, we must find workarounds which will meet housing needs and have fair home taxation. Fair taxation means, for what people earn. And what people earn, is what local businesses can afford to pay employees and remain profitable.

Using appraised value for setting property taxes is using the going sales prices in an area. That seems to make sense, at first. But there's a built-in catch that needs to be fixed. Over time, as wealthier folks move in, home and apartment building sales prices may quadruple, and thus appraised value quadruples, thus the property tax bill quadruples. But for a homeowner or renter who was there all along, his or her income may not go up much at all, and likely won't quadruple.

For average-income homeowners and renters, property taxes should not exceed their wage and pension levels. A property tax cap of 2% a year for households at median income and below is a starting point for this debate.

What about the local government budgets? What's the fiscal impact? Is a property tax cap for average households fair to local governments? Yes.

Local governments welcome gentrification for the higher property tax revenue. Yes, wealthy households can pay more in property taxes. If you buy a $1 million condo, then you have the available income to pay the high property tax bill.

The question remains, must working families and middle income homeowners also pay the higher and higher property tax bills on homes and condos?[33] As they work over the decades, it reduces their their ability to pay down debt, save, and get ahead. They struggle after finishing their working lives and proceed into retirement, in the home they've bought, or even paid off.

Homeowners with modest pension income struggle with a high property tax bill. They do so for years, trying to hang on to their property, the one it took 30 years to pay off, the one they raised their children in, the home they thought they could keep in retirement. As the tax bill exceeds their income, they must sell. Then, they leave that town, never to return. Off to somewhere further out if possible, and if not, to shared housing.

Seniors and working families who rent face rising prices from two factors: (a) upscale renters who will pay more, and (b) higher property tax bills as apartment building values rise. Even a building owner who wants to keep rent lower for seniors or working families cannot do so when the property taxes rise from surrounding gentrification. So renters struggle as they work, and in retirement.

As all of this happens, the new upscale home and apartment values bring in new tax money. So the cities and counties ought to be able to leave the property tax bills for school teachers, fire fighters, clerks, janitors, and seniors at similar levels to when those folks first bought or first rented. That's with property taxes prorated by unit, by household income. The social benefit is worth the hassle of prorating the tax bill.

Rich folks moving into cities are generally not creating undue costs for government agencies. A lot of them pay for private schools, saving the public school districts a lot of money at the same time that they pay high property taxes into public school districts.

Upscale residential, retail, and office use (with supporting warehousing and industrial use) provide proper funds for the city, county, and state budgets. Let's keep that going. But let's mix in the entry level employees and the middle class employees as well.

When the average income households can live with affordable rents and home prices for the first time in a long while, these households will cost less to city budgets, as the households become more stable and self-sufficient. Stable households create fewer costs to local governments in social services, police, courts, and the like.

Should Increases on Upscale Property Taxes Follow Gentrification's Prices?

What about a cap on property tax rate increases for more upscale buyers? Is that fair?

At first, one would think, well, no one's forcing anyone to pay a high price for a luxury house or condo, with the expected tax bill. That's correct. If they can buy at that level, let them pay at that level. But what about later? If the prices double and triple over time, for example, then those people who bought are then paying double, then triple, the property tax bill, just as if they bought it for double or triple the price, which they did not. That could be a serious strain for them, especially in retirement when income can drop.

People at any income level may end up staying at about their same income level over time.

Two Spouses, Each Makes $500,000

Let's consider two spouses or partners who each make good salaries as corporate managers, say $500,000 each. They are a $1 million couple. Let's say they buy a $1 million home. They may not be able to increase their income with higher promotions, as competition is even more stiff for those jobs higher up the ladder. Maybe they just don't want to move further up the corporate ladder. Why should they have to? They've worked hard. They are doing well enough.

Why can't they just use their existing income to pay off their house and retire? So they can see each other through old age. When one spouse passes away, the other can remain in the home, until passing away. But maybe not, if the property tax bill has quadrupled, and may quadruple again. Retirement income usually drops from regular income.

Home values rise over 20 to 30 years of working life, and then rise further 10 or 20 more years into retirement. A couple can be priced out in retirement, or earlier, by property taxes, if the taxes soar along with the soaring prices.

Yes, people with higher income have options when prices rise, and thus when the property tax bill rises as well, and can plan accordingly, but still, must everyone always have to move, because of prices going up, often rapidly?

The manager couple might want to keep the jobs they worked so hard to get. They might need to remain at that location to keep those jobs, but what if they have to sell and move much further out? In some time, even further out, the prices go up and will keep going up, along with taxes, so they have to move again. Then they end up too far away to even commute to their great jobs. Those great jobs were the whole point of being professionally successful. This is another example of how gentrification unduly subverts standard economic patterns. Perhaps there should be options for people to keep their jobs and stay where they are, on into retirement, all along the income scale.*

The Next Generation

What about the idea of a middle-class retiree, at their death, passing along a paid-for home to a middle-class daughter, son, granddaughter, or grandson? It's a free country. That should be possible, right? A person should be able to inherit a house with no mortgage, so the person has a better life and better retirement, to be passed along to another family member, and so on. That should be possible. But, again, not if the property tax bill has quadrupled, or more, and will keep going up more for the next generations beyond their income.

This comes back to a major point, that the U.S. should use methods that

---

*Homeowners in poor towns sometimes pay double the property tax *rate* that homeowners pay in rich towns.

Local tax rates on residential real estate in the U.S. vary widely, from 00.5% to 5% of market value. A town with only low-value homes and few shopping malls, few offices, and few upscale homes, for example, paradoxically, can have a much higher percentage rate of property tax paid per the price of the home, than a town with high-priced homes and lots of shopping malls and offices. That's a *rate* paid, not the total amount paid. Each town has to pay for schools, police, and the like. Lower-priced homes might be taxed at 5% of value to pay for local services, since there are few shopping malls and upscale homes paying in. Meanwhile a mansion in another town with a lot of shopping malls, offices, and lots of other luxury homes. In this town, the total of taxpaying square footage is much greater at higher value, to cover a similar number of schools, police and the like. Thus, the mansion might be taxed at 00.5% of the market value. The $5 million mansion pays a higher overall bill of $25,000 each year, paying at 00.5% of value. A low-income town charges 5%, which is $1,750 each year on a $35,000 house. The homeowner in the poor town pays a much higher rate. This is even after significant federal education money is added to pay for local schools in poor areas. Federal education money never goes to schools in wealthy areas, since they don't need it. Adding new development can bring in new taxes, lowering the tax rates, thus lowering the bills, if the home values stay even. But new development in a town may raise residential values, so at the same rate, or even at lower rates, the total tax bill may still rise for homeowners and rental buildings, unless a property tax cap is in place. That's a catch, for the lowest-income residents especially, as values rise.

stabilize working families and middle class families, not destabilize such families. Therefore, should people be able to pass along a home to family members, or other people that they want to help, and the new owners get the property tax cap? That might be best.

That case brings up the income level of the next generations. While the parents may have been middle class, what if the daughter or son is making more money? Should she or he still get the tax cap? Maybe the tax cap and thus the rate can be indexed to the heir's income. Wealthier heirs would not pay middle class rates, but a new rate set within their income. This involves having some enforcement against fraud, but so does all taxation. So that's no reason to ignore these options to help future generations to succeed.

Decades ago, California voters approved Prop. 13 for a 2% increase cap per year, starting at the value at the date of sale. In California, for example, after you purchase, the tax bill on your primary residence goes up just a bit each year, not more than 2%. In California, that's for the less expensive homes and for the more expensive homes.

Along with the helping the working family, the California system does help an upper-income couple. And when and if anyone sells decades later for a high price they can do so. Then the new owners, who can afford that higher price since they're buying at that higher price, will settle in at that higher level. Those at the higher level get the 2% protection too, and so on.

That's fair and that's the intended result.

Unintended Results

Here's one of the unintended results, but one for which there is a solution:
One thing that's happened in California is that local governments aimed for tax revenue by approving plenty of higher-priced new development, like shopping malls, office towers, upscale homes, and industrial use. The towns and counties most often skipped over any new entry-level housing.

Working class people and middle class people aren't leaving or avoiding California because they can't get a decent job there. It's because even with a decent job and even with the property tax cap, homes with tolerable prices aren't available because of inventory. Thus, going back to page 1, a property tax cap is logically best combined with an inventory commitment for sensibly priced homes, where such inventory is lacking.

A tax cap could be for everyone up to a middle class level. It could be lower, or in expensive regions, it could be higher. Or the tax cap could cover all income levels. Like with any tax bracket, people do the math for their situations and adjust. Each household would like the property tax bill to stay within their income level and not be forced to sell, until they want to sell. That seems fair.

These are the choices that city council members, county board members, and state legislators have to make.

So elected officials could decide whether to give the tax cap of 2%, for some examples, to:

    a.   households up to $ 200,000 of income
    b.   households up to $ 500,000 of income
    c.   households up to $1,000,000 of income
    d.   or to all households

Then at the same time, there should be a housing inventory commitment for workers and the middle class, or they won't get enough housing built for them, as is happening in California, even with the property tax cap in place.

It is a dereliction of duty by society and government to fail to accommodate the entry level employees or the middle class households in the areas in which they are employed. In the best that society could offer its members, people should be able to remain in an area in their retirement as well, if that's the best choice for them. People should not be forced to move away from their roots of family and social support, just because of the real estate market.

Chapter 4

Add Starter Homes and Apartments: Otherwise, It's Like Buying a Car and Only Rolls Royces are Offered

All regions, in all nations, should provide enough starter homes and starter rentals. Yet, in many places that's not the case.

It's as if you go to buy a car, and only Rolls Royces are offered. That's what the housing market is like. Real estate markets aren't offering all price points. Not in safe areas, in the busy regions, where the jobs are. So much for the free market for homes.

The equity/affordability paradox in housing inventory is when the average-income worker or retiree gains home equity, a great thing for him or her, but then the home is too expensive for a future average-income worker or retiree. Some average-income households gain equity. The rest are priced out.[34] Where the equity/affordability paradox exists, it is because of a low supply of one product, the product of homes for average-income earners.

Free markets usually meet all price points for a category of a product among sellers and buyers, for example, from a Corolla to a Rolls Royce.

Those who buy an upscale product, a Rolls Royce, don't hinder those who buy a lower-priced product, a Corolla. One product, like a Corolla doesn't morph into another product, like a Rolls Royce. That's except in real estate, when working-class areas morph into upscale areas. This occurs as economy and time move forward to create wealth for more high prices for locations that the wealthy didn't use in the past. But no new working-class homes are built in the vicinity.

In the 1960s the Lincoln Park neighborhood in Chicago was working class, cheap, and considered run-down. A basic two flat was worth about $100,000 in 2023 figures. It has become a $1 million home. Sure, it had fixture upgrades, but those didn't cost $900,000. It's basically the same structure with the same square footage on the same lot, but now worth $1 million to wealthy buyers because Lincoln Park is now an upscale location.

That product, a home in the central core, is never affordable again to its original type of customer, a working family. Nor are any replacement units added nearby, like in condos above a commercial strip. Real estate markets don't meet all price points.

What's a Fair Mix of Homes?

In a fair mix of homes, all employees could afford to own homes and rent within an area. In the U.S. this is ceasing to exist. That's highly unfair to the employees. To make their livings, to survive, they must provide their time at the region's workplaces. There's no other choice for them, like investment income. So for the employee's best interests, it's bad.

Next let's look at the best interests of businesses. For the businesses, these employees are needed or they would not be on the payroll. Business productivity and profits are threatened, and reduced, when access to a stable, productive workforce is hindered, or when payroll costs are prohibitive.

So, for both the survival of employees earning their livings and for the survival of business operations, a fair mix is best.

In any region, to completely exclude homes for average households is outrageous. That is a sensible conclusion. Yet, the exclusion grows. Enforcement against this outrageous exclusion is needed. How? It's simple. Commit to starter units. Then enforce it, just a certain ratio. Ratios can adjust as conditions vary, such as employment levels, population increases, or population decreases. A requirement is the key.

Otherwise, it's just a nice idea.

Like, would the job pay overtime, if it wasn't required?

New Inventory

There are no market limits inherent in a commitment to a fair mix. That's because the inventory growth is not limited by this. Rather, it restores market equilibrium of inventory for all income levels. Like going to buy a car, and a less expensive car is offered at the same time a Rolls Royce is offered. For a time, the U.S. can build more starter homes. Then as needed or desired, inventory for all income levels can increase, including all the luxury the market will bear.

Rich areas, like Beverly Hills or the Hamptons, will remain rich areas. Rich areas already attract employees by paying employees higher wages to get them to show up, considering the commute, or even provide worker's quarters.

Average households don't have to live in Beverly Hills or the Hamptons. There is ample airspace close enough in the general area to jobs in the area.

An inventory commitment is not a broad price control. It is not a communist collectivization which outlaws private property or exploits anyone. On the contrary, people can own their own homes and condos in the end, paid for in full, independent of government control,[35] independent of private exploitation. Or people can rent at very low prices in nice buildings over a lifetime, and save so much that their 401(k)s can be bulging in retirement.

This isn't for poorly-run projects to be overrun by bad elements. Are there bad elements in society? Yes, but with the precautions found in any standard leasing agreement, they won't find a place in these buildings. People will need legal income to be approved for the mortgages or leases. They will have to make the payments, follow the rules, be good neighbors, or be kicked out. For people in extreme emergencies and in extreme, unexpected financial problems, such as the death of a spouse or co-owner, extra time can be given to responsible residents who fall behind on payments temporarily.

This is for employed people in regular apartment buildings, condos, townhomes, and houses. These are to be built and run by the same real estate companies that operate any other building or development successfully, just with some extra spots at moderate prices.

This is a limited real estate adjustment.

It's fair.

Along with the majority of residents who are employed, the mix will include some retired people on pensions, a few people on disability, and a few on temporary assistance. That reflects our society.

Real estate has a catch to it. Until you buy (or have a lifetime lease option), the rising prices are your enemy as you watch with trepidation as it gets harder for you to buy at your income level. As soon as you buy, however, the rising prices turn into your new best friend and partner, as a rising price means rising equity. Now you want the highest values possible. After you buy, those rising prices are the other person's problem. This affects owners of the richest homes to the most modest homes.

But what if you can never, ever buy in? What if you cannot find reasonable rentals where the jobs are? That unfairly puts a means to upward mobility out of reach. It's the lack of means to upward mobility that's the problem.

So this is not a jeremiad against rising prices per se. Or a rant against material gain. Except ascetics, like monks or nuns, most people want some material gain. Higher income pays for better living, or increases savings, or pays for acts of benevolence. Take your pick. It's a free country. We are proponents of profit. Having some money is not a vice, but rather *not having enough money* to get by, that's a problem. The problem is a lack of the means to get any wealth for that person, for their own stability; and for national stability. It's a person's lack of even a modest level of wealth that presents problems.

Reviews of All the Proposals

Many housing experts provide guidance. Francesca Mari provided a comprehensive review of housing practices and proposals in a long article in 2023 in the New York Times Magazine. Madeline Carlisle also had a full review of programs and proposals in The Atlantic magazine. Both articles are cited in note 36.[36] Housing expert Jenny Schuetz published an excellent review of the factors in her 2022 book *Fixer-Upper: How to Repair America's Broken Housing Systems*. Other surveys of policy are in the bibliography.

Our book doesn't attempt to explain every proposal, nor have we monitored most journals, articles, or research papers prior to finishing the writing in 2023, and publishing in 2024. Other proposals abound, of which we're not aware, as we haven't agreed to run a legislative or research clearing house. We have endeavored only to complete this book to prompt more discussion.

Austria in Europe has an excellent system that includes the middle class, that's covered in Chapter 6 - A Nation that Already Has Homes at Manageable Prices. Even upper class renters choose it. Rents can be from 30% of income for low-income renters. Net costs can end up lower if income rises.

A couple in Austria, a school teacher and an office professional, for example, cited in Francesca Mari's article mentioned above, pay only about 10% of their combined income on rent for a modest one-bedroom.* Sure, it's not huge or luxurious, but it meets their needs, and they're saving a lot of money.

Would you and your spouse, or partner, or roommate consider a monthly payment of 10% to 20% of your monthly income? If you want to pay more, fine, pay more. But a lot of people will consider that deal.

Austria has been highly successful at this because it takes the high profits out of rentals, by charging renters only for upkeep, once mortgages for the land and construction costs for apartment buildings are repaid.[37]

Landlordism is removed.

And since Austria has been building solid, well-constructed apartment buildings for 100 years, a lot of the inventory is fully paid for. So the only payments are for upkeep. It's very hard to argue against that logic, unless you are a landlord insisting on the highest rents. Even those landlords might agree it makes perfect sense, for everyone else but those landlords.

Most U.S. proposals just jigger things, and are voluntary, without any meaningful commitments where the jobs are. It's all optional. Since it's optional, we all know what that means: It won't get done, mostly.

---

* For that same one-bedroom in Austria, for a single person, for example, who stocks shelves full time, a lower-income job, the rent is 30% of income, since the income is lower. The same ratios adjust anywhere, like when a single person adds a roommate who adds income, or a person to add income gets steadily promoted at work. When household income goes up, but with the same 1-bedroom place at the same price, the percentage cost of rent at 30% of income could drop to 10% of income.

The Size of the Inventory is Too Small in Most Proposals

Yet, even hoping that most optional proposals get done, then the size and pace of the new inventory in the proposals seem to be well behind the need. One of the most ambitious proposals, from a U.S. senator, could add 3.2 million lower-priced units over 10 years.[38] It sounds ambitious, at first. Yet it's only 320,000 lower-priced homes nationwide, for example, built in a year. That doesn't seem to meet the needs of 30 million (30,000,000) to 40 million (40,000,000) households, or more, whose standard of living is held hostage by high prices.

The idea of up to $25,000 in government assistance to some first-time buyers *won't add* inventory. Like other current programs on housing, the money will just funnel into further high prices. Where's any reason to lower the price, with the government kicking in another $25,000?

Then, with population growth and people moving here, the U.S. might add 20 million working-class households to middle-class households in 30 years. Added to the 30 million to 40 million households that struggle now, that's up to 50 million to 60 million households to plan for.

Does 3.2 million homes in 10 years, and at that rate getting to 9.6 million in 30 years do the job? Not for 60 million households, who may be holding their own sometimes, but in effect have few assets going into old age. It's reaches 16%. Reaching only 16%, leaves 84% struggling. That's not success. Let's think bigger. At three times that, 28.8 million units would reach closer to 50% of struggling households. Then effects for overall stability should occur.[39] Current proposals are not adequate.

Or there's no enforcement. New Jersey's Supreme Court ruled specifically for such housing, but no one is enforcing anything, pretty much. How's that for a great example of inertia and the "why bother" attitude of the free market? Here's a state's highest court ruling in no uncertain terms in favor of starter homes, in favor of the workforce, in favor of someone standing up for the average people, and still hardly anything's happening. See note 74.

Or it's voluntary. Will developers voluntarily quit building highly-profitable, higher-priced homes and condos to build modestly-profitable, lower-priced homes and condos?

Let's Have Both, Upscale Prices and Modest Prices

Let's have both, gentrification by choice, and modest prices, at our choice. With lots of new starter units, would prices drop on the existing inventory for the entry level employees and the middle class?

Perhaps.

That's the goal. To return to a sane economic pattern of life for average-income people, our national majority, our society's core.

Otherwise, What Are the Options?

Let's run through the options for median income households in the U.S.

Group #1 Median Income Buyers

First, to even buy, they must have high enough income to qualify for a mortgage for homes within commuting distance. Then it's no cakewalk for them because their cushion disappears into the higher property tax bill later. They're still broke. They might have to sell even before they get the mortgage paid off. Where do they move then to live by their jobs? Not nearby, since prices went up. They can't even get to retirement in the house they bought. Much less stay there in retirement.

Group #2 Median Income Renters

Staying in the same place, renters have no hope of lowering their rent payment. Over time, it's going up. Perhaps by a lot.

So, neither of these two groups of the workforce have a particularly easy time of it throughout their working lifetimes.

Let's look further at retirement:

After covering other standard expenses, at age 62 a homeowner's pension and 401(k) might not cover property taxes, even with the mortgage paid off.

For renters, their payments have been going up and up and will keep going up. That's one reason why so many seniors are taking jobs while on Social Security or other pensions.

After they sell or when the rents are too high, then where do they move? When prices and taxes in their region have risen beyond their 401(k)s or pensions? Out to the sticks.

But what will the prices be in the sticks in coming years?

- When millions of retiree homeowners who cash out will also have been moving to the sticks.
- Joined by millions more senior renters who will have been moving to the sticks to try to live on pensions or 401(k)s, since their 401(k)s won't have much in them, since rents were too high their whole lives to leave extra cash for their 401(k)s.
- Joined by millions of younger people whose earnings after high school or college won't cover the rent or purchase in busy regions.

This has been steadily occurring nationwide. Outlying areas in the U.S. aren't necessarily inexpensive areas for homes and land anymore, not on a retiree's lowered income, or a younger person's starting income, or on the income of a lower-level employee. (And in outlying areas, will a similar job at similar pay be available?) To get a lower housing payment requires that you move to an even more remote area, or to the dicey part of a town or city.

As high prices move into more territory each decade, even with cash from a home sale, many people will run low on money, or run out of money.

In nations with population decline, like China and Japan, prices in outlying areas are showing declines. That may lower prices in busier areas. But that depends on a lot of factors, like if immigration occurs after birth rates drop.

In the U.S., with so many millions clamoring to enter, population will rise. Without changes, the housing equity/affordability paradox continues.

A Statewide Standard or a National Standard

Perhaps statewide standards can do the job. Perhaps a national, federal standard for housing inventory is warranted to provide for the fair housing mix. Then local and state governments don't have overcome the local nimby obstructionists.[40] Such standards are accepted in all sorts of things.

Those who object to meeting such standards are those who don't want to meet such standards. It's not that the standard is unreasonable. Instead of meeting a standard, opponents usually switch the topic to something else, rather than admit why they don't want to meet the standard.

So many national standards have become the norm that they're overlooked, taken as a given. It's a good exercise to remember that these standards weren't always in place. And it's good to remember that standards were only adopted because certain segments of society kept violating proper and best practices, as long as these were not written into the law, and then enforced by local law-enforcement officers. Local control is fine, except when it's illegal conduct.

Which of the following national standards do you think we ought to let some of the people decide they can ignore, when it's getting a bit too much in their way, according to them?

- there's the 40-hour work week, which includes overtime pay
- laws against unfair discrimination in mortgages, for renting, or in selling residential real estate to willing customers who can buy
- laws against unfair discrimination in hiring practices
- there's a national standard that consenting adults can marry, with the corresponding property rights and spousal rights, or do you want your local government deciding whom you can marry?
- no state, county, or city can restrict movement around the nation to work, own a business, visit, or reside, a national protection of freedom of movement
- there is a national standard against unfair discrimination in providing open accredited public schools or allowing accredited home schooling to any and every child, which cities, counties, and states must follow
- the freedom of interstate commerce, for willing sellers and willing buyers to conduct business across the whole nation without local interference, is a national standard, enshrined in the constitution

A national housing inventory standard could be fair like any other national standard.

Businesses and individuals have to meet many different national standards all the time, and they do so, and the economy doesn't collapse and the sky doesn't fall. In all other business sectors other than residential real estate, no one set of customers, like only the wealthier ones, nor one set of business owners gets to exclude the rest of the nation from having a full choice of products or producers. Except for housing, we have choice, from a rowboat to a yacht, from an inexpensive used car to a Lamborghini, from Goodwill to Gucci.

With accepted national standards, citizens can go to court to hold government and private parties accountable for blocking or failing to meet the national standard. A national standard would end the lack of accountability we see now in providing a sensible housing inventory. This is true for any state as well. If the state passes a state housing standard, then regions and towns can be held accountable.

Chapter 5

Add Starter Homes and Apartments: A Doctor, a Teacher, a Lawyer, and a Janitor Living in the Same Area

The case of entry-level households, middle-income households, and upper-income households being in the same vicinity can work out. All types of households can have their needs met. The United States has enough land and airspace to house its people properly.

In the U.S. and many other societies, the wealthy, the upper middle class, and much of the middle class will be in higher-income areas anyhow. That's expected. It is the exclusion of enough starter homes, and the exclusion of enough middle class homes, that must end. All employees and retirees must be accounted for, none excluded.

In the not so distant past, regions with entry-level jobs and middle-class jobs had homes for all income groups. Businesses and the wealthy understand the concept. Businesses and the wealthy have regularly embraced the concept of homes for employees nearby, when they provide apartments for their staff.[41]

Nowadays, however, an employee from the large pool of entry level employees, like a full-time cashier at a grocery store, might have no homes that are available that he or she can afford to buy. And this isn't just in New York City or Los Angeles. It's also in a medium or small town in the lower Hudson Valley of New York, or in or around Austin, Texas, Nashville, Tenn., or Seattle. The modern economy requires some adjustments to obtain fair home prices.

People have worked for what they have. Middle class and wealthier people are protective of their neighborhoods. Working families are also protective of their neighborhoods. Good intentioned people of all walks of life do what they can.

It's fine that a nice middle-class area remains a nice middle-class area. But working families also ought to have some units in a region where the jobs are. That's reasonable. New developments can have sections for less expensive homes. The basic concept of homes for employees blended in can be readily accepted by all citizens, the wealthier, the middle class and working families.

A Janitor, A Lawyer, A Teacher, and A Doctor Living on the Same Block

Regions, neighborhoods, and developments can have homes for a doctor, a teacher, and a janitor. Different-sized homes with different prices can even be on the same block or in the same building. This now occurs in Austria in Europe in as shown in the photo on this page, and in Singapore. This is in neighborhoods, in individual buildings, even in downtown-style areas in those nations.

Lower-wage employees and high-wage employees already co-exist in the workplace, using the same streets to arrive at the same buildings for work. People can also co-exist in residential use.

This type of social mix in the same area can work with mixed-income developments and mixed-income buildings. Already in the U.S., there are downtown residential buildings that have some lower-income residents mixed in. It's just that such agreements are few, and then they expire. Modest single-family homes for modest incomes can be in one part of a development, with the larger homes in another part. Modestly priced units can be in within mid-rises and high-rises.

Photo by Harald Schilly, 2014 Creative Commons license.[100]

Doctors, teachers, lawyers, and janitors live in this well-kept apartment building. It is located in Austria in Europe, with fair prices, full of willing customers.

Effects on Schools Can Be Managed

Regarding the effects on schools, solutions are possible. Schools have flourished with both wealthier students and working-class students attending. Often wealthier families select private schools.

In any school, gifted programs, extra credit options, and advanced classes can be offered for the college-bound students. U.S. high schools can add advanced placement classes as needed with federal funds and state funds, which are available for this. Extra free tutoring is readily offered to those students who show up for it at U.S. schools, online, on laptops and on phone apps.

Western Europe has proven that a properly educated workforce saves society tax money in the long run, since there are fewer social problems to fix with tax money spent on social programs and criminal justice programs.

Japan as well, to give a second example, has a fraction of the crime and social remediation problems and the related costs per capita than the U.S. does. If any school district needs more state and federal funds, it's probably simplest to just increase allocations to these funds, which are from the pool of federal and state taxes. Regional property tax pooling formulas are possible.[42]

Avoiding Mistakes

Mistakes in some U.S. public residential buildings are well explained by scholars such as Howard Husock of the Manhattan Institute. In a 2018 article, Husock lists some of the main errors:

- Ownership wasn't an option.
- Commercial use wasn't mixed in to improve livability and help cover costs.
- Rents didn't cover expenses, so maintenance lagged, to become abysmal in some places. Tenants who could afford to leave, did so. Then, only the poorest remained, concentrating poverty into these apartment buildings.[43]

Housing scholar Francesca Mari also points out that:

- Meager construction budgets alloted in the 1940s and 1950s left some buildings cheaply built, so utility and maintenance costs became more and more expensive. That was on purpose, based on lobbying (and campaign donations, likely) at that time by landlords. Later, maintenance was skipped, so in some buildings conditions decayed.[44] (Austria does the opposite and builds sturdy structures to last into the next centuries. Some, indeed, have done so.)

Those are dismal failures in implementation, which can be avoided in future developments. Such conditions are not present in Singapore and Austria.

Also realize that many U.S. public residential buildings avoided those mistakes and are very well run and safe. They present no such problems.[45] Many are in conservative Republican areas. Yes, there are public housing buildings in conservative, Republican areas which are successful and ongoing, right now. These have the ongoing support of the conservative voters in those areas and their conservative elected officials (see p. 72).

The problems that occurred in public residential buildings have left an image deeply embedded into the minds of Americans, that of the failed "housing project," often better known in cities as "the projects."

The word "affordable" may refer to most products, like affordable groceries, affordable cars, or affordable electricity with no negative connotation.

But for the product of housing, the vivid images of the projects and pockets of poverty mix together with the words "affordable" and "housing," whenever those two words are used together.

Think about this: When someone says, "affordable housing" what is one thing that comes to mind? Decrepit housing projects. That's what comes to our minds too. It's ingrained in the public perception. And decrepit housing brings to every American's mind the picture of dysfunctional households that perpetuate social problems. Thus, just the generic term affordable housing, which is technically a term that is supposed to refer only to price, like affordable groceries, has morphed into a pejorative, a social term with a negative connotation.

To discuss housing inventory responsibly, it is vital to recognize that this negative perception is present and is in large part based on the facts of serious past problems. This perception is serious and heartfelt. People of all income levels, including working families, do not want to live in problem neighborhoods or problem buildings, or on blocks with problems. No one wants problems nearby, not for their families.[46] This negative perception blocks new efforts for homes at fair prices.

There is a conclusion, by some, that the upscale real estate market alone should have supremacy in determining where housing inventory is added. People with that conclusion then use the image of pockets of poverty to block any new homes at all for working families to be mixed into any new development anywhere nearby.

Normal Working-Class Living Compared to Social Remediation for Dysfunctional Households

Thus in housing, two topics mix together in the public mindset. We must force our brains to consider them separately in planning, while recognizing the intertwining factors and overlap. The two different topics are:

Topic #1 - average working families living in standard working-class neighborhoods, or in starter units in developments with varied prices.

Topic #2 - dysfunction in some households which need social and educational remediation for some dysfunctional people.

The image of nice new modest homes on cul-del-sacs and nice condo buildings with some starter units could be primarily linked to Topic #1, average working families. Yet, the term affordable housing creates an image of social problems, Topic #2.

With Topic #2, we're talking about people and their problems. It gets touchy. It's complicated, controversial, and beyond the scope of this book. It involves society's way of doing things, neighborhood expectations, and individual choices. The debate often boils down to determining the extent of responsibility between society and the individual. This book is not designed to make conclusions in these matters, but these matters come up in people's thoughts every time housing is mentioned for working families, so we must acknowledge these factors.

All of the many factors of a residential area are recognized in the pricing of housing, *by buyers and renters, most to the point*. What neighborhood will you select for yourself and your household? Who will buy or rent a house or apartment, at what price, is what primarily and foremost determines price. If there are many people who want to buy or rent that unit on that block, bidding goes up. If few people want to live on that block, because of safety for example, bidding goes down. If there are no offers, zero applicants, what does that tell you?

Quicken Loans, to use the example of a standard U.S. mortgage lender, does not determine the price on a block. The bidding of people who choose to live on that block determine the price on that block. It is by what they are willing to pay. After the price is already set, by the willing seller and the willing buyer, Quicken Loans is only involved if the buyer needs a mortgage. If, on a block, anyone is willing to bid higher, the price goes up, and by nothing more.

Anyone can move into any working class area if they want to. The question is, do they want to? Would you? Owners in dicey areas who want higher prices for their homes or rentals, can't take issue with buyers or renters who will not pay more to live on a dicey block, but will pay more for a safer area.

So, after a price is agreed to, Quicken doesn't just hand out the money with no questions asked, as Quicken needs some collateral for mortgage loan, which is the value of the house or condo.

Neighborhood Safety Affects Housing Decision Making

Lack of safety stems from dysfunction, which occurs in all types of households, including the wealthy, middle class, and working class. Yet, conditions are clear that working-class areas have the highest ratios per population of violent assaults and shootings. That is what the victims of violence themselves report, shown in the reports from victims themselves, like by those reporting the murder of a household member.

The deaths of people are evidence of local conditions, as most bodies from murder are found, by someone, so there's a murder report. Factoring in unreported violence might not change those ratios by much. A lot of shots fired, assaults, strong-arm robberies, and thefts in working-class areas may not be reported because of fear of retaliation, or because of an expectation that filing a report won't help a victim much. A theft in a wealthy area may be reported more often, although an assault in a wealthy or middle-class area over a dispute between residents may be not reported, by wealthy or middle-class households who want to avoid police involvement. But overall, shots are not fired as much in most middle-class or wealthy areas, compared to working-class areas.

Safety affects how people choose neighborhoods and housing. Safety affects development. Safety affects what gets built and where it gets built.

Quicken sends out an appraiser to verify what a home is worth based on what people have been paying who choose to live on that block or in the immediate area. The same supply-and-demand economics apply to rental prices.

At that point, then, yes, sometimes along comes an appraiser, or a leasing agent, or a loan officer who wants to hinder a certain buyer or seller with unfair discrimination.

How is that proven? By the actual prices from who has indeed paid to live on a block and in an area, that's how. Enforcement of legitimate appraisals, leases, and loans protects all buyers and sellers from unfair discrimination.

Appraisers and agents who practice unfair discrimination need to be caught and sanctioned. There is no dispute that prices will match up, since willing buyers know the going prices for an area. And the willing sellers know the going prices for an area. We all know what the real estate market is like. Prices aren't any secret, and bidders are informed of competing bids, so bid prices aren't secret to those bidding. If a valid high bid is ignored, because of unfair discrimination, the paperwork is available to prove it in civil court, or for other sanctions. About pricing, nothing's secret, really.

After any unfair discrimination is proven and removed, then prices still come down to the actual amounts paid by willing customers. Do you really want to buy or rent on that block? No? Then do you expect others to? So, who is going to pay to live there? Those who can't afford anywhere else, and will live with that level of risk, that's who. Whoever that is. That's who buys or rents on a dicey block, in a dicey area.

How bad is an area? Who will tell you that? The person already living there, that's who will tell you; and frankly and honestly, usually, not sugarcoating what's going on. That's what we found and you will too, if you will go and talk to people in their neighborhoods, as we have. That includes the areas with the most shootings in the United States, where we have gone to check conditions across the U.S., over many years, from South Central Los Angeles, to Salinas, Calif., to Memphis, to Chicago's west side, to Detroit, to the South Bronx and

---

Books About Neighborhood Safety in the United States of America - in order by year

- *Do or Die: For the first time, members of L.A.'s most notorious teenage gangs - the Crips and Bloods, speak for themselves*, by Léon Bing, 1991
- *Winning the Race: Beyond the Crisis in Black America*, by John H. McWhorter, 2005
- *Gang Leader for A Day: A Rogue Sociologist Takes to the Streets*, by Sudhir Venkatesh, 2009
- *Don't Shoot: One Man, A Street Fellowship, and the End of Violence in Inner-City America*, by David M. Kennedy, 2011
- *Ghettoside: A True Story of Murder in America*, by Jill Leovy, 2015
- *Locked In: The True Causes of Mass Incarceration and How to Achieve Real Reform*, by John F. Pfaff, 2017
- *Locking Up Our Own: Crime and Punishment in Black America*, by James Forman, Jr., 2018
- *Bleeding Out: The Devastating Consequences of Urban Violence - And A Bold New Plan for Peace in the Streets*, by Thomas Abt, 2019
- *Walk the Walk: How Three Police Chiefs Defied the Odds and Changed Cop Culture*, by Neil Gross, 2023

Bed-Sty in New York City, and to Overtown in Miami.

In 2022 and 2023 we went to the south side neighborhoods in Chicago, to Gary, Ind., and to the Sandtown-Winchester neighborhood in Baltimore. We systematically drove the blocks. We walked many blocks, checking the status of vacant homes, of rehabs, of rentals, and the prices. We viewed properties for sale, going into the homes, including board-ups for auction. We interviewed residents and business owners. We attended church services, to ask local pastors about the situation. When we asked about buying, it was the people living there themselves who warned us not to overpay, and questioned our judgment about a home purchase or rental in an area with safety concerns.

Neighborhood conditions are recognized as pricing fundamentals by economists, Realtors,® and everyday renters and buyers. These conditions may be dressed up in terms of a "desirable" area, of "livability." The most basic factor, perhaps, is safety, or lack of it, which is measured in degrees. Safety factors into decisions, along with what a household can afford, resulting in how high or low the prices will be in an area.[47]

The discussion of Topic #2, of personal problems in dysfunctional households, is at times quiet, glossed over, or even left unspoken. But as soon as living in a specific neighborhood or street is the topic, no one's shy about the topic, telling you right away if they think it's a good idea. The specter of problem households is sure to loom large in some people's minds when housing decisions are being made, such as what housing is going to be built, and where, _or not built_. Linked to new housing, the topic of avoiding dysfunction is phrased in terms of preserving property values, keeping an area's way of life, and having tranquility.

Tranquility ought to be within the reach of all members of U.S. society, and any society, not preserved only for those in gated communities, with a sigh and a shrug of the shoulders for everyone else. Look at what Western Europe and Japan have accomplished. They have, by and large, literate workforces living without undue violence. The children are in activities, sports, and the like, and then join the workforce. In time the U.S. can accomplish this.

So, we have addressed this briefly because this factor of social dysfunction by some households lies underneath objections to housing for the masses of households. The case of

> members from some subset of households who need remediation
>
> does not mean

working households as a whole should not have adequate housing inventory. It's quite the opposite.

Forcing more working-class households into pockets of dysfunction, or taking 60% of their income for cramped housing, only worsens the conditions of the regularly employed households, who are doing nothing wrong otherwise. They're going to work. Their kids are in school, with many kids striving and excelling higher. At the least, the kids can come out of school able to start entry-level jobs. They're not creating 911 calls.

While doing things right, they still strain unnecessarily to get over the hump into stability, because of housing costs.

The strain also enters into the middle class.

Even for middle-class students, extra tutoring services, or extra time from parents isn't a given, not as the parents work and spend extra to meet a huge mortgage or rent payment. Over-worked middle-class parents arrive home after 10 to 12 hours on the job, plus the hour commute, and then are too exhausted to help the kids with algebra or chemistry, if the parents remember how to do the algebra or chemistry. For all households, with more money left over each month, it lowers household strain and improves household conditions. All students can better succeed, creating empowerment and upward mobility;

(a) the regular students at grade level can do even better, and

(b) those who need extra remediation can also be in a better situation.

In summary, steps are available for making progress for households, for neighborhoods, and for students who need extra tutoring.

That there is work to be done, is in no way a valid reproof to having adequate housing inventory. Having fair home prices is a good economic method to improve household results and neighborhood results. More so than letting landlords extract more and more of the income out of a neighborhood's families. More so than cramming more families into doubled up spaces. More so than the only lower prices being in unsafe areas.

Objections and Adjustments

Further objections come from middle-class and upper-class homeowners when their home values aren't quite as high as they'd like, when working families are living nearby. Yes, that happens. This is a few percentage points of adjustment in real estate valuations of what are already valuable properties.

Well, is that the worst thing ever for civilization? That the wealthier adjust a little? Let's consider the adjustment that the current U.S. system expects of average employees. They must adjust as high home prices take half or more of their money, ruining their standard of living.

Why? Well, it's not some mean-spirited conspiracy or master plan to harm people. It's the left-over effects. It's the tide rolling in of economic conditions left to their own.

In this case it is when real estate practices are in place mainly so gentrification provides living space and profits for the more well off. As we've pointed out, gentrification is a valid economic function, even at the highest price levels. The wealthy have always been outbidding each other for whatever they want, and at least in functioning democracies they're not murdering each other to settle disputes, as in dictatorships or cartel economics. It's not the actual existence of the higher prices that's the problem. Those will always be there. Thus, price caps are irrelevant.

It is the absence of entry level inventory that's the problem. Let's go over the situation:

(A) Housing methods are left in place for new residential construction by officials primarily in support of gentrification pricing. By *primarily*, that means 95% to 98% of the market.[48] A 2% to 5% effort for lower prices out of an area's total inventory doesn't change what is *primary*. (When 40% of people live on the edge after the housing payment, even 20% of new units may fall short, since it's still 80% new at high prices and 100% of everything else going up.) Here's the main reasoning for the end result;

(B) so the gentrifiers have all the ample real estate that their hearts desire, with very few exceptions; and other factors in the economy are not allowed to diminish that upscale real estate's market value, except by the most minuscule amounts, if any; and

(C) not for any other important, compelling economic factor or social necessity.

Please review previous items A, B, and C. Is each point accurate?

If you conclude otherwise, please list out where in the United States in busy regions that points A, B, and C are not *primarily* accurate descriptions of the residential real estate market, along with some documentation. Please add it to the public debate in a post, video, blog, article, or book. We can also add it to an updated version of this book or it can be placed on the publisher's website.

If the assessment of A, B, and C is largely accurate, think how that indicates how patently unwise and unfair this is for about a third to half of the U.S. employees and retirees.

In effect, the whims, fancies, and real estate valuations of the well-to-do determine the development patterns which set the living conditions of much of the middle class, the whole of the working families, and of business payrolls in vital economic regions, and increasingly out into the hinterlands.

Fundamental Economics Are At Stake

These development patterns have uprooted and replaced the foundational economic and social results of basic employment in all sectors of the economy, which are supposed to provide adequate living conditions for the entry level employees to the middle class.

This is fundamental. This is serious.

This is risky. This is unnecessary.

Many of the world's highest-ranking capitalist practitioners have publicly stated that unfair economic disparity has reached levels whereby significant segments of society are in detrimental conditions. These are highly credible conclusions, from investors who control business investments in the billions, cited in note 49 on p. 145.[49] But the attention alloted to such logical economic conclusions is a trickle of the broad coverage of business and economic events and trends.

Attention to this basic economic problem solving is a pittance of the torrential flood of the regular media, social media, and entertainment that consumes the public's attention span. The fairly simple, easy to understand solution, to provide starter homes, is not noticed.

Working families have adjusted, to their severe detriment. Must only the workers and the middle class adjust? But never the well-to-do?

Yes, if a middle-class or working-class building were to be next to an upscale building, the prices in the upscale building may not go up as fast. But is that catastrophic harm for the well-to-do or the nation's economic well being? Hardly. An upscale building, with its high prices, will still be exclusive, with spacious units and all the amenities. Enough real estate should be left over for average, employed households at a fair price to them, including some profit, and including use of this asset for their children's children, if they so choose.

Under a better system, there will still be separation by income level. A lawyer need not be housemates with a janitor. Could a janitor have a 1-bedroom condo or rental in the same building as a lawyer, who is paying a lot more for a lot larger place? Yes. Let's end the denial by income level to some people of homes within their salaries or pensions.

Starter Prices of $715 to $1,119 a Month, To Rent or To Own

In a suburban subdivision, small starter studio cottages might come in at a price at $88,200 and larger cottages with one or two small bedrooms at $142,500 in Oct., 2024 figures. The developments can have other units to sell at higher prices. In Oct., 2024 figures, those are payments of $715 to $1,119 a month, using 6% mortgage rates.

These are examples of the basic minimum payments, without any large monthly welfare payment included to help make the payment. This is so there are some minimums available, like for a single senior, for new couple, and for a young person on his or her first job. These are examples of what is possible, as shown with actual Oct., 2024 market prices using 6% mortgage rates, shown on pp. 16-17, with calculations in the notes.

These examples are reasonable ballpark figures that show the wide range of households that can have better prices. These examples are not any type of a promise of prices by any means, but were examples in a busy region, Phoenix, Ariz. as of Oct., 2024 using the lower-priced, standard suburban new home prices at that time. Even in pricier areas, by utilizing ample available airspace in mid-rises or townhomes, similar ratios would ease the strain for many households, and the examples show the possibilities being bypassed.

Yes, some arrangements are tighter fits, while some arrangements are less so. Condo units can have patios. Townhomes can have rooftop decks. Town homes can have third floors and elevators for larger households. Developments can have exercise rooms and common areas, for some breathing room.

Cottage homes can have yard space that is private and access to common-area courtyards for some breathing room. Compared to being destitute, people might settle in and at least they can remain solvent, and can retire in these units. They can also make do for a while to build up savings, to move on later to something larger or with more privacy.

(A) Studios can fit:
- singles
- two roommates
- couples with an infant or toddler
- senior singles
- couples without children

(B) Cottages or units with 2 sleeping quarters and a second bathroom with a shower can fit
- two roommates
- one couple and one roommate
- a senior couple and a caretaker
- two seniors
- couples with a teenager
- two couples
- couples with one child, or with two small children in a bunk bed

(C) Small homes with an extra two small bedrooms and bathrooms with showers fit more combinations of people. An extra kitchenette nook adds extra convenience.

(D) Three-bedroom and four-bedroom homes, townhomes, and condos can fit even more combinations of people.

If the price is higher, those on lower-incomes might receive extra amounts of $100, $200, or so, from a welfare stipend, which housing expert Jenny Schuetz of The Brookings Institution advocated in her 2022 book. Any $100 or $200 of welfare could end when the unit's original land and construction loan is paid in full, in a rental building or in a purchase.

It is only when starter inventory is indeed in place, that government assistance, when appropriate, becomes fiscally more responsible, than just sending government assistance into never-ending high payments. With lower prices in place, then perhaps an option is a one-time grant or secondary loan of some amount towards the sales price, to lower the monthly payment. If it's $10,000, to get someone into a lower mortgage payment, that's still a lot lower than taxpayer costs of about $160,000 with 20 years with Section 8. And even more so, if it avoids even more years of Section 8 payments for a household into old age.

A person on disability using Section 8:

- in 50 years costs taxpayers $400,000, with no equity retained, or

A person on disability can get a $175,000 mortgage to own:

- in 50 years pay off and use the unit, with retained and growing equity capital. Or a housing board could own the unit, reserved for the disabled.

A paid-for unit never requires full payments again, generation after generation, unlike Section 8 for disabled people, which always requires a full-priced payment, for the next disabled person too.

The Gentrification Rent Trap
Housing Policy of the U.S. and Much of the World

The Results of High Rent, After 60 Years

$1,400 a month rent = $1,000,000 for a 60-year total paid (age 25-85)

1st generation (parents):   household paid rent of $1,000,000
2nd generation (daughter):   household paid rent of $1,000,000
3rd generation (grandson):   household paid rent of $1,000,000

3 generations: 3 households: rent total: **Paid $3,000,000**

For 3 generations: total assets: $0

The Results of Owning, After 60 Years

Mortgage & property tax paid for 30 years, then property tax paid for 30 years.

$1,400 a month mortgage & tax payment = $500,000 paid
    for 30 years, plus
$ 275 a month property tax   = $100,000 paid
    for 30 years
                           equals $600,000 total paid in 60 years

1st generation (parents):   paid $600,000 and saved $400,000, versus renting
2nd generation (daughter): paid $600,000 and saved $400,000, versus renting
3rd generation (grandson): paid $600,000 and saved $400,000, versus renting

3 generations: 3 households total mortgages & taxes: **Paid $1,800,000**

    Leaving: savings of $1,200,000
Plus three homes at $275,000 value each = total equity of $ 825,000

For 3 generations: total assets: $2,025,000

In Standard Markets, What's Better? ↑

    This compares gentrification-priced renting vs. affordability agreement owning. A similar result comes from gentrification-priced renting at 40% to 50% of income vs. lower rents at 10% to 30% of income. The figures are in 2023 values and market rental prices. The figures use prices in an affordability agreement, whereby the home value matches general inflation and wage growth, not regular housing market increases as explained further in Chapter 8. In an affordability agreement, a house in 2023 prices would be priced similarly in price relative to income in the future, because the price would be relative to average inflation and wage increases, not gentrification pricing.
    This example does not rely on timing the real estate market or buying in a certain area to realize the most gain, or avoid loss, a common criticism of home ownership, but shows an affordable home staying at a similar price. A home may drop in value. Buyers do take that risk. But in most areas? In most areas of the U.S., would you accept an inheritance of a paid-for home? In most areas, most people would.
    This compares renting vs. owning at the base level with steady property tax payments following a steady value used above. If property taxes rise to necessitate a sale, the owner still profits from a much higher sale price, versus renting which nets $0. When a paid-for home is passed down through generations, only one home value is in the total, but future generations might pay much less in monthly payments, so the net asset total in that case can be higher than the above example.

In summary, the smaller payments, of $100 or $200 a month, or a one-time payment of $10,000, rather, may cost taxpayers less. Payments from taxpayers can end when the unit is paid in full. It's also possible, after the unit is paid in full, that the taxpayers could be paid back some money.

What About Welfare?

About people on welfare; well, Europe has people on welfare, some who are disabled and some temporarily, who mix into society in regular buildings, not in pockets of poverty. The U.S. should do that. The few people on welfare require a whole other set of policies. As we help the employed majority with lower-priced homes, the extra inventory can then reach down to help our lowest-income people with lower-priced housing, which helps reduce welfare dependency.

Households Overcoming Past Discrimination

Many people who have faced unfair discrimination have fewer family and household resources to overcome obstacles. This is the intergenerational legacy of unfair discrimination. Over the generations, the gap has been substantial, and isn't yet close. Middle class and wealthier families have dysfunction, but have more resources to overcome a household member's dysfunction, like the ability to pay for lawyer, when a law is broken, or to pay for substance abuse rehabilitation, for example. Dysfunction is hard to overcome. Providing resources as needed, to whom they are needed, remains a serious task at hand in many nations, and certainly in the United States. A society of full accountability, and transparency takes time to achieve under a functioning democracy. It's hard enough to get to a functioning democracy in the first place, and then maintain the basics. So, much work remains.

As improvements proceed, individuals should use previously blocked opportunities. Society should keep all opportunities fair and open for every citizen. Diligence is the price of freedom, and progress. To make such progress, the impact of being priced out of adequate housing, or not, is profound.

The Real Estate Market Creates Pockets of Poverty

Along with dealing with those things, another reason for U.S. pockets of poverty is the problem of the real estate inventory, perhaps more so than just what people's levels of income are at.

Most employees are law abiding. Most employees do all that society asks of them, working and paying their bills. They have jobs and usually can get another job with some effort. They work up from entry level. Some attend school, training, or college. They have deeply-held hopes and dreams for a good life through honest work. So, what has driven them into areas where local bad elements recruit their kids? It's the only place they can afford. This is all that the real estate market offers them.

This happens to U.S. people on their honest, average-level full-time incomes. This doesn't happen in modern democracies in Asia and Western Europe to nearly the same extent for most workers.

As one German economic development official said in conversation, German workers live in areas where they participate in sports in evenings or and weekends, and attend concerts, or relax in the parks, and not worry about safety, or shots fired. In many U.S. working-class areas, people do worry, a lot, about safety. And shots are fired.[50] Local officials can address problems by ways other than denying homes at fair prices to a huge amount of the workforce.

The difference is not primarily the general income levels of the German janitor and the U.S. janitor. The difference is in the neighborhoods that are available to the janitors, to the working families.

Let's provide striving working-class families places to rent or buy in their price range that are not in rough, crime-ridden areas. That's so families are not exposed to pressure from drugs, crime, gangs, cartels, and predators. Then better social reinforcement can take hold.

In steady, well-moored neighborhoods, they can have economic and social normalcy and upward mobility. In plain terms, instead of being stuck on lousy blocks, with nowhere else to go, regular people can live in a decent house, townhome, or building unit, own it if they choose to, and get ahead in life.

Chapter 6

Austria Has Homes at Manageable Prices: Let's Do What They Do

Picture Vienna, Austria. European charm, with vibrant, safe streets. Austria is similar to the United States, as a first-world democracy, with urban, suburban, and rural areas. Austria is by Germany, France and Switzerland, in the heart of modern Western Europe. It is by no means out of the free-market economic mainstream. It is by no means some autocratic backwater. It has strong business profits. The wealthy want for nothing. There is a solid middle class, and stable entry level employees.

So, in a democratic, modern, thriving, high-tech, first-world economy, they have made the commitment to building homes and apartment buildings at fair prices. Even the lowest-wage working families pay only around 35% of their income. The methods can be adjusted for home ownership as well, for single-family homes in the suburbs of the U.S.A., for example.

People pay only 10%, 20%, or 30% of their income to rent. That's for their whole lives. They can get ahead, even renting, never needing to own. Austria has taken the landlordism out of it by only charging for upkeep, once the land and building is paid off. It's somewhat like having a paid-for home, because of the lifetime lease, but you don't have to own it. You just pay upkeep. For a single school teacher, it could be 20% of income. For a couple, both working at Walmart, it could be 25% of their income. Is anyone in the U.S. interested in those prices?

In the capitol city of Vienna, 6 out of 10 residents choose such homes under affordability agreements, in nice, safe places. Just search the internet for Vienna housing to read about it. Articles are listed in note 51 on p. 146.[51]

The key is that Austria has decided to:
- build an adequate inventory of homes at moderate prices; and
- use affordability agreements, so enough units stay at lower prices.

A modern nation presents a successful supply of homes. This isn't a false utopia, or a fool's errand, but an ongoing reality, in a leading free-market, capitalist economy. Any nation can adopt such methods.

People might prefer privately-owned homes, so see the example of the well-regarded homes in Cooper Square in Manhattan, New York City, which are lower priced. Those are under binding affordability agreements, as explained in Chapter 8.

And as well, the U.S. does have some very well-run residential buildings with public financing and public oversight involved. Vermont does well with this idea, with 3,000 units. Arlington, Virginia has some nice units. Bend, Ore. has added some units. In Texas, Houston has some nice-looking developments.

The Upper Peninsula of Michigan is where local governments have stakes in successful, neat, and safe residential buildings. One example in Michigan is the Iron Mountain Public Housing Commission. Look up Iron Mountain, Michigan on a map. It's rural.

Conservative Republicans Who Want Their Public Housing Commissions

Let's look at what the sensible folks in the Upper Peninsula of Michigan are doing.

Yes, there are housing projects, nestled in the small towns and forests of Upper Michigan.

The Upper Peninsula is the opposite of a hotbed of socialism, voting 80% to 90% Republican. It has strongly conservative, pro-business voters. Although it's a working-class area with people on minimum wage jobs, it's not ramshackle or rough. Homes, streets, and businesses are modest, neat, and clean, with some of the lowest crime rates in the nation.

Yet, some people strain to get by at times, since it's a working-class region, so the Republican officials, backed by the Republican voters, have some Republican publicly-run Housing Commissions. That's because, done right, the economics, aesthetics, and livability work. Thus the Republican residents, the Republican voters, and the Republican officials support it where they live.

This housing helps the community, while avoiding dysfunctional pockets of poverty. Nothing that we can see is misguided about these homes with societal involvement in the financing and oversight, supported by some of the strongest conservative Republican voters and strongest conservative Republican elected officials in the nation.

Go ahead and ask the Upper Peninsula Michigan Republicans to get rid of their public Housing Commission apartment buildings.

They won't do it, most likely.

In Europe in Austria, this started some 100 years ago, which is a long record of success. Austria has this nationwide. No one's overly concerned about home prices in Austria. Elected officials weren't run out of town. The wealthy haven't left in disgust, but have ample luxury. After decades of getting a good deal, people of all walks of life know exactly what's up.

People are paying for their own housing, entry-level on up.

The affordability agreements are open to people from 80% of the income brackets. Some developments include various levels of income. Picture fairly well-to-do residents, middle class people, working families, and entry level employees living near each other; a high-salary sports star living in the same building as a school-bus driver and a dishwasher.[52]

It's happening and ongoing.

Renting there is so reasonable that it has eliminated, in effect, the high rent trap that is still in place in the U.S. and most of the world (see p. 68).

In the U.S., for example, buying a home at the same payment per month as renting at that same payment per month has an advantage. That's because the mortgage payments can be eliminated in 20 to 30 years. Renting at the same price lasts for 60 to 80 years. And the U.S. rental price is usually quite high, so the renter builds up little in savings, ending with few assets, and not much in the 401(k), and more high rent. That's what we mean by the high rent trap.

In Austria, with much lower rents, the comparison between owning and renting evens out, more so. In Austria, over 60 years at lower rent prices of 10% to 20% of income, people build savings and assets. They can take extended time off a job now and then. They have assets to pass on. That's all while renting, without having to finish paying off a mortgage to rely on home equity.

Bank financing can mix with government financing. But the first point is that without the inventory commitment and agreements for the future, then the financing method and any tax spending will not matter in a significant way.

Let's Be Blunt About Who is Being Too Blunt

Let's compare U.S. attitudes, decisions, and results with Austria's attitudes, decisions, and results. In the U.S., it will keep coming up that some developers say that commitments for lower prices will prevent development.

To not sugarcoat the statistics, since businesses need to hire employees, and since housing costs are so high, a 40% to 50% commitment in some areas to starter units in new development for a while could be wholly relevant. That would be in an area where half the workforce and retirees are paying half their income, for example, and middle-class people mostly can't buy a home or condo anymore. Does that sound like anywhere you know?

That's if we're being candid.

And serious.

That is, however, not even on the radar, in most discussions.

In busy areas, if:
- only 20% of units in new development are priced for average households, that leaves
- 80% of new development to become high priced, and
- 100% of existing homes to become high priced, so over time
- average income households and retirees have only perhaps 5%, if that, of the area's total units priced for them. So 95% is higher priced.

And that's with a 20% goal of starter units in new development, which is touted as a good level to shoot for, according to some officials and developers. It sounds so reasonable at first, a 20% ratio for new affordable homes. Sounds pretty good, doesn't it? Yet, how does it sound when after time, that results with 95% of homes being out of reach of average income paychecks?

So, 95% of places to live in a busy area will end up costing too much for average folks, so they have to double up, then triple up, or drive long distances, or have barely any money after rent. That sounds a little different, doesn't it? Follow the logic, please, from 20% sounding so reasonable, to 95% sounding so unreasonable.

The high price levels undermine average households, and impede business hiring and payrolls. Households have to move, leaving good jobs. School children have to transfer, leaving established social support. Businesses can't hire to survive or expand, and must alter their operations, with some locations shutting down. Such disruptions don't have to be.

Let's examine a 30% starter ratio. For a 30% total, a developer could have one building be all full-priced condos or rentals, and the second building could have 60% at modest prices, for a 30% total. Or some other mixture, maybe with more floors.

That's too blunt?

Well, U.S. developers bluntly now tell average workers to shell out half or more of their income to rent a place in many areas.

U.S. developers bluntly price out half or more of the employees in many areas from buying new homes.

Who's being too blunt?

Another effect is to hinder movement around the nation when people can't even think of moving to a busy region since they can't afford to live there.

The U.S. ought to follow Austria's market-supported system. Yes, it takes a societal, government commitment, but Austria's system is essentially paid for by private investment and private repayment. The private investment comes from investment loans, from buyers of housing bonds, or a mix.

The proceeds are used to pay for the purchase of land, buildings, and for construction costs. The private repayment is from the renters in apartment buildings, from their paychecks or pensions. Private repayment of units for purchase is from buyers, from savings, or from their paychecks or pensions through mortgages. The starter inventory still has profit for investors.

Photo by Thomas Ledi, 2016 Creative Commons license.[102]
The Alt-Erlaa complex in Vienna, Austria includes park space, balcony patios, and retail shopping.

Prices at all levels can be included, as with the apartments shown here.

These apartments include:
- retirees on pensions,
- entry-level employees
- the middle class, and
- the wealthier

all in the same development, with transit, safety, community, amenities, and nice views. This is the Alt-Erlaa complex in Vienna, Austria., in Europe.

The same can be done with condos, townhomes, and single-family homes (see pp. 16-17).

Photo by Harald Schilly, 2014 Creative Commons license.[101]
A church in a plaza. Residents add balcony plants.

Photo by Thomas Ledi, 2016 Creative Commons license.[103]
The complex has rooftop swimming pools, community rooms, fitness centers, and sports courts.

If some investors take a pass? Fine. Austria is a free country, so some investors got in and others did not. U.S. investors can also invest elsewhere.

Capital needs to remember its vital roots, those of risk and reward. Since when was a constitution for a democratic republic established to guarantee top profits to anyone who shows up waving some money in the air, or top profits to anyone who gets a deed to a property? A democracy can include just getting by and just doing OK. It's about guaranteed freedoms, not guaranteed riches.

Developers and landlords act like their high profits must be guaranteed. How dare anyone offer starter homes at a lower price with a lower profit margin! They avoid open competition, disguised by the language of "unfair competition" when the general public seeks an open market for starter homes, even if by local housing boards, under open competition, with full market prices paid for the land used.

Investors, banks, and developers can fund and build starter units. It's profitably done, in Austria, and in U.S. land trusts. This can work in any nation.

As well, analysts Saoirse Gowan and Ryan Cooper of The People's Policy Project, among many, describe how public financing can fit in,[53] even with the same companies who've been building luxury units, but for starter units.

If developers refuse to build other than 100% upscale, then city councils can use eminent domain to buy property at full and fair market value, to build for-profit units by another developer, with some starter units, for the general good. Even the developers who first opted out could bid on the new construction.

True Free Markets vs. Elitist Communistic-Style Exclusion

Let's expect rebuttals that starter units are unwarranted intrusions into free markets. That's an exaggeration. The proposals examined here and elsewhere are a modest market adjustment, to meet a market need, housing for needed employees, in a fair manner.

Further, gentrification is far from a truly free market. Gentrifiers use all sorts of government controls, like zoning, parking requirements, and setback requirements to skew the free market. They use market manipulations like homeowner association rules and unnecessary pricing exclusions in new development proposals, to skew the system to benefit their luxury equity values. It's in effect an elitist-controlled system, not a free market.

Such thinking is exemplified in elitist, communistic dictatorial justifications. That shouldn't hold sway.

Let free enterprise and private property flourish for average households. Let's have expansion and protection of private property rights from elitist exclusion. Such exclusion is a violation of free property rights in the same effect as is communistic confiscation; the denial of full, free access to the ability to purchase, own, utilize, and profit from one's own private property. The opportunity loss is massive.

Let's promote private property owned by working families which will be their very own homes, which elites and developers are now denying to working families. Workers of the world, own your own home! Workers of world, get a lifetime low lease! At the very least, these should be free-market options, to buy something, to own something, or to choose reasonable rents.

That would be systemic provision of capital accumulation for workers. With a much lower price of lodging, workers can avoid exploitative confiscation of the only property they have starting out (the capital in their paychecks) by landlordism and lenders. A lower lodging cost avoids their lifetime exclusion to property rights and capital accumulation. They can own their own assets, such as stocks, bonds, 401(k)s, real estate, stakes in a business, or other investments.

When a person, because of the real estate system, can't save enough money to own any of these things, ever, in any substantial amount, it is a denial and exclusion of their fair access to property rights. Free and fair property rights, asset accumulation, financial independence, more freedom with one's time, and the ability to pass those things to future generations can be available to people.

That's *if* housing doesn't take all of their money.

And that's a big if under the current U.S. system, and in a lot of nations.

Nimbyism and Free Markets

Opponents of homes for working families have not in my backyard (nimby) concerns. Nimby means not by us. This is a natural and often reasonable response to when something bad could be near you.

No one wants problems near to them. Such issues can be addressed by ways other than denying homes at fair prices to a huge amount of the workforce. See the section Avoiding Mistakes, on p. 59. Nimbies can be working-class residents just as much as wealthy residents. We are all nimbies, to some extent, are we not?

It is fair to conclude that extreme nimby elitism in housing inventory has become bad for society and bad for the economy. The lack of fair housing prices for a lot of the workforce is bad for the nation. This is trouble. This is a radical result, that a huge number of people can't afford to live properly on their full-time wages, risking society's well being. It should be treated accordingly.

Reasonable concerns should be addressed. But the U.S. has unreasonable ratios of exclusion of homes for average employees who need homes in order to work at jobs that need to be filled. That is what the U.S. has, as compared to Austria. Austrian society has not let nimbyism reach such extremes, whereby any amount of concern or objection (or lower profit) is allowed to become a veto which results in an absolute prohibition of housing at fair prices.

For new development at fair prices, the full current fair-market value of real estate should be paid to current owners of land and buildings. That's what regular developers do; they pay the going price. So can developments initiated by local housing boards, if needed. Businesses should be properly paid, including for relocation. Businesses could remain, with the new housing units above and around the business use.

The Austrians Use Available Methods Wisely. The Americans Do Not.

It is Austria's methods that create great results, not Austria's spending levels.

Here's the proof for that. The U.S. spends federal tax money on homes at about the same rate as Austria. So:

a. The U.S. is pricing people out.

b. Austria in Europe is not pricing people out.

> While spending *at the same rate.*

Yes, that's accurate. Don't believe it? We didn't believe it at first either. We discovered it after going over the U.S. federal budget line by line for every single line item for housing. We checked U.S. figures repeatedly, and confirmed the European figures with a leading European housing researcher, for which we provide full documentation in the appendix and notes.

Both nations have been spending approximately the same 1% of their whole economies, (i.e., the gross domestic product [GDP]) on federal tax spending on housing, in the non-pandemic years. The exact totals were 0.724% for the U.S. and 0.9% for Austria.[54] The difference is 0.176%, which is less than 2/10ths of a percent. Local spending is also similar.

It's fair to explain this by rounding up to 1%, which is easy to remember and relay to others. It's about 1% in both places. The U.S. federal budget housing amounts are in the appendix, line by line. These are compared directly to Austria's budget, as reported by European housing economists.

This is an important point to understand, that the spending levels of tax money in both nations has been similar in non-pandemic years. If the spending amounts of federal tax dollars on housing have been similar in two nations, both at about 1%, then what does that tell you?

Again, they're both at 1%. They're the same. Thus, if there is a difference in housing inventory between the U.S. and Austria, the difference can't be the result of the amount of taxes spent, not when the spending rate is the same.

The amount of tax money spent is not what makes the vast difference in results between the two nations in housing inventory. The difference is that:

- Austria commits to fair prices for all of society, then accomplishes it.
- The U.S. is not committed to providing homes at fair prices for anyone, except the wealthier in effect, since they can afford the higher prices.

In the U.S., nobody has to do anything, pretty much, about housing, other than our safety-net spending for the poorest, from which landlords still receive the ample proceeds going to the landlords' higher prices.

Furthermore, using current U.S. methods even with huge increases in housing tax spending, would just further gentrification and landlordism, which would grab that new money as profit. The point is still that the U.S. results won't change, until the methods change. Which could even lower U.S. tax spending, as explained further on pp. 91-94.

Kicker #1: The U.S. & Austria Spend About the Same in Tax Money on Housing, 1% of GDP

Yes, for housing, this 1% figure is very much against the common perception of a tax-and-spend European nanny state compared to the perception of a fend-for-yourself U. S. of A. We had that same perception as we began the research. But we found that the Austrians *do not* pay for excessive tax spending on housing. How's that for a kicker. We'll call that kicker #1.

This needs to be hammered home. One more time, federal spending is about the same amount in Austria, 1% of GDP, that the United States spends, at just under 1% of GDP. We're being intentionally repetitive, on purpose.

If the numbers change by a lot, the housing stability in Austria's system is a still a better version for a nation's economics. In Austria, the rich can still get richer, which they probably are, and everyone else is fine.

On top of that, in Austria those average households that want to increase their upward mobility faster and further have the means to do so, from the extra savings accruing to them. Average people can get richer too in Austria's system, building wealth, patiently. It is basic, sound economics. But not in the U.S.

Kicker #2: With Lower U.S. Tax Rates, the U.S. Allocates More Tax Money to Housing

Austria has no property tax on homes or apartments. Austria has higher personal income tax rates (see the box on p. 80). The Austrians choose and get every item they pay for, like roads, health care coverage, or unemployment insurance. It's whatever they decide of their own free choice to spend tax money on, which their elected government then does for them.

Austrians have a democracy and those folks vote in higher numbers than Americans do, so the Europeans get the spending levels they want, by simply voting for whatever they want.

No one's marching in the street in Austria about government spending. They don't have to march, since they already voted for the exact federal spending they want, or don't want. The Austrians are grown-up, mature adults who vote regularly. Americans, on average, don't vote regularly. (In mid-term elections, to select Congress, which decides tax rates and tax spending, well over half of American adults don't vote. Of those who don't vote, most never have voted, and most have no plans to do so.)

So, the point that we Americans need to understand is that in Austria they *are not* unduly spending *extra* taxes *on housing, directly compared to the U.S.*

When one looks at it in even more detail beyond the 1% figure as pointed out, there is even more proof to conclude that Austria has the correct logic, which is to add methods to create and maintain a housing inventory which is fiscally sound for the whole nation. The U.S.'s methods are not creating a housing inventory that is fiscally sound for the whole nation. The U.S. system is logical only for those who are profiting, and highly illogical for everyone else.

There is an additional, finer nuance to comprehend. It turns out that it is the American government that allocates *more in tax spending* on housing per each citizen's taxes chipped in; than does the European Austrian government in this second category of comparison. That's because the American citizens pay less of their income for that same 1% tax spending level.

If you want to stress that comparison, go ahead: The American government allocates more to housing, than the Austrian government allocates to housing, per America's lower income tax rates. But this second category of comparison just makes the Austrians look even all that more wiser. It makes what Americans are doing even all that more ill-advised, if not downright ridiculous.

The Americans may be kicking in less of their income to the federal kitty, but then the U.S. Congress still spends the money out of the kitty at about the same rate of GDP on housing as the Austrians. The U.S. government blows the tax money, mostly by handing it over to landlords and banks for high prices, not for investing in homes average people can buy or rent.

Kicker #3: The U.S. Sends Most of the Housing Tax Welfare to Wealthier People

On top of all of that, there's even more to this. We couldn't make this up if we tried. We would not make this up, even if we wanted to.

Yes, after Congress finishes up handing over tax money to landlords for

**Personal Federal Income Tax Rates
Austria[104] (in Europe) and the United States
Comparison in 2023 U.S. Dollars**

Austrians Pay No Property Tax on Homes or Apartments

Austria Income Bracket	Tax Rate	United States Income Bracket	Tax Rate
$ 0 to $11,748	0%	$ 0 to $13,850	0%*
$ 11,748 to $19,224	20%	$ 13,851 to $44,725	12%
$ 19,225 to $33,108	35%	$ 44,726 to $95,375	22%
$ 33,109 to $64,080	42%	$ 95,376 to $182,100	24%
$ 64,081 to $96,119	48%	$ 182,101 to $231,250	32%
$ 96,120 to $1,067,994	50%	$ 231,251 to $578,125	35%
$ 1,000,000 and up	55%	$ 578,126 and up	37%

The table has basic rates. A net tax rate depends on tax deductions, sales tax, local tax credits, and other variables in both nations. *Note: The U.S. standard deduction on 2023 returns is $13,850 for individuals, which makes the effective tax rate 0% below $13,850 of income, as is shown above. IRS tax information,[105] however, still refers to a 10% tax rate at the lowest income level, but that IRS statement is in effect null, as the deduction makes the effective rate 0% for people in the "10%" tax bracket. Thus, the table above changes the 10% rate to 0% as the effective federal rate. Tax on $13,850 of income may still be paid for Social Security (FICA) tax, Medicare tax, or state income tax.

high rents for our poorest of the poor, then there's more. (That's when even poor people could own a paid-for place, if it was modest, given some time.)

Then Congress hands out *even more* tax money to welfare payments (welfare = money taken and not repaid) for owners of upscale homes and condos to help pay their mortgages and property taxes.

The mortgage interest deduction and property tax deduction remains for households that itemize their deductions, mostly higher-income folks.

Many people who get the mortgage interest deduction are not millionaires, but millionaires get it. A home worth $5 million with a mortgage gets about $12,000 a year in welfare. Every year. For 30 years, or more. That adds up.

Most Americans don't understand that more U.S. federal tax spending on housing goes to welfare on higher mortgages, starting at $350,000 for singles and of $750,000 for couples, than on welfare on housing for poor people. Yes, that's fiscally correct, explained on p. 127.

The U.S. and Austria Have Comparable Economics and Demographics

Austria 's population and land space is similar to a major state in the U.S., such as the U.S. state of Georgia or Missouri. People in Austria spend on average 18% of their income on housing.[55] Now, that's a national 18% average. By being a national average it means that wealthier people pay less as a percentage of their income. But that's true on any income scale in any nation, for any one thing people buy. The people who make more on the income scale have more left over after making a payment on any one thing.

In Austria, entry level employees may spend 30% of income for housing. A wealthier household may spend 10% on housing out of that household's more ample income. Overall, the 18% national average shows a desirable result. That's not 18% out in the sticks only, that's 18% including Austria's busy cities, and the suburbs. That's with plenty of luxury mansions and luxury condos. That's perhaps better, in all seriousness, than anywhere else in the world, for what everyone's getting in Austria.

The comparison would be as if the whole U.S. state of Missouri had modestly priced homes available for all residents who needed a modestly priced home. That's a big state with the cities of St. Louis and Kansas City.

Or it compares with the whole state of Georgia in the U.S. Everyone's covered, including in a busy metro region with a large city, like Atlanta. Wouldn't that be something, our fellow U.S. readers? It's happening and working in Austria in Europe.

Following Austria's national example is directly relevant to any U.S. state, and to the whole United States. The nation of Austria proves that home prices don't have to be astronomical.[56]

Wouldn't Americans who are being priced out jump to get that deal? And strongly support it politically too?

Of course they would.

It's time to offer this to U.S. customers, and around the world.

It will take time, but start with one building, or one development, then another, and people will respond. Then another, and another. When it's a good deal, a good deal works.

In Summary: 5 Methods of Housing are in Use

In summary, this brings us to 5 categories of housing to contend with.

1. Market-priced owning (until you're priced out)
    costs 35% of income to start on a mortgage
    costs 15% to 60% of income in retirement after mortgage is paid off; higher as gentrification property taxes rise.
2. Market-priced renting (the rent trap)
    costs 35% to 60% of income because of possible gentrification effects
3. Renting with welfare (U.S. welfare): costs are split between the renter and the taxpayers, all going to the landlord
    Example of $1,200 U.S. monthly rental:
        senior retiree on $1,500 monthly Social Security
        costs $450; 30% of income from individual renter to landlord
        costs $750 of taxpayer money (Section 8) to landlord
            which keeps going up for taxpayers with gentrification effects
4. Affordability agreement owning (trust agreements worldwide)
    removal of gentrification effects
        costs 35% of income to start
        costs 15% of income in retirement with property tax cap (i.e., after mortgage is paid off),
        costs 20% to 40% of income, or more, in retirement with no property tax cap, depending on gentrification effects (i.e., after mortgage is paid off)
5. Affordability agreement renting (Austria and elsewhere, in trusts)
    removal of gentrification effects, assuming some property tax cap is in place
        costs 10% to 35% of income to start
        costs 10% to 35% of income in retirement

There are variations such as Singapore's method, and other refinements in western Europe. Japan allows new construction with few holdups, so housing is built in Japan near where the jobs are, which lowers housing prices.[57] Yet, this book is not a compendium of all housing methods, but a quick look at promising methods. It shows that where things are bad for average households, it doesn't have to be that way.

Chapter 7

Use Available Financing: The Math Works

What seems to get lost in all this discussion of real estate markets, interest rates, economic trends, bond risk, investor risk, income levels, and whatever else is involved, is this:

Paid in full is paid in full.

After a home or apartment building is paid in full, only basic insurance, property taxes, and maintenance remain. Those costs can be set up to be reasonable, to anyone, working or on a pension. That's Austria's secret to success, which really isn't secret, but just isn't well known to the rest of us.

Standard mortgages of 15 years, 20 years, or 30 years from private financing should suffice. The financing would be backed by land and buildings where people want to live. Such collateral, properly managed, reduces risk.

The renters or homeowners are very motivated to pay on time, in order to hang on to a reasonable price. Payments that are within their income won't strain them. After the mortgages are paid off, monthly payments for the homes and rental units can end up lower, since only upkeep and taxes are due, not principal and interest. For average folks, real estate can be stable, even as speculators continue to speculate, as they always will.[58]

Long-Term Financing Helps Spread Out Costs

With extremely high land prices, or with developments that are 100% at moderate prices, the extra upfront costs and lower monthly payments can be spread out longer than 30 years if needed. For economic stability for a nation, such scenarios ought to be worked out, not ignored. The conditions can be fair to all parties, including for home ownership and lower rents. One U.S. mortgage program already in use goes to 32 years or 38 years.[59] Many developments may avoid that, but it still beats high rent for 60 to 70 years.

For renters, as in Austria, even if it takes longer to pay off the land and building, during that time rents can be lower. That's when the apartment building is run under an affordability agreement contract, not run just for whatever-the-market-will-bear at the highest profit. The payments to investors and managers are agreed to by those who take the deals. If private parties take a pass, housing boards can proceed with management staff. Again, when the land and building are paid in full, the rent price can go even lower. When the bonds are paid in full, all bond risk for the investor and bond cost is eliminated.

Paid in full homes, condos, and apartment buildings are a great benefit to the users, who then pay only upkeep, as is done in Austria, at 10% to 35% of income usually. Those details are examined starting in note 60 on p. 147, continuing to note 66 on p. 148.[60]

Scarcity? Well, That Depends

The world is generally not short of investment reserves for a cycle of building starter homes and rentals and paying them off. The Wall Street Journal in an article used the phrase that investor Warren Buffett of Berkshire Hathaway was "hamstrung" with $100 billion in spare capital[61] to invest because he couldn't find, at the time, a suitable business opportunity for him. He held the investment capital in cash, or like equivalents.

That's $100,000,000,000 cash.

Being held, looking for investments.

That's just for Berkshire Hathaway, and that's often the case, as to the huge scale of money held by that one fund in cash or short-term notes. Investors, responsible for huge reserves don't buy willy-nilly, no matter how much they have on hand. Large totals are found if one adds up the money that investors hold in reserves.

Longer Terms, if Needed? Long Terms are Nothing New

Housing bonds discussed here have sold to investors and banks in Austria. Such financing is routine on rental buildings. Such bonds are worth considering even if it takes longer than 30 years. No one objects to a long-term method as a matter of course when people rent for 50, 60, or 70 years, when that's their only option. Don't apartment building owners count on the long term?

How many million are in a billion or a trillion?

In the U.S. it is counted as $1,000 million in $1 billion. A billionaire has $1 million x 1,000, usually in business assets.

For $1 trillion, it is $1 million x 100,000, usually cited for government budgets, or worldwide markets. Other nations may use different definitions of a billion for their currencies. Business assets held are not the same as spendable personal cash (see page 120). About wealth distribution see page 134.

Banks, lenders, and homeowners approve as homeowners refinance their homes, and extend their mortgage to 30 years again, after paying for 10 or 20 years, for a 40- or 50-year total. There are no objections. Or when a homeowner sells and moves, starting up another 30-year mortgage, after paying for 10 or 20 years, for a 40- or 50-year total. Many people go into their retirements with decades left on the mortgage. A reverse mortgage, which is commonly approved, adds even more years, pushing the carrying charges past 50 years, to 70 years or more, if you live that long.

Not that long terms are recommended, if the longer terms are not necessary or advantageous, but long terms are a norm, more so than an exception.

On units for purchase, to use affordability agreements with longer payback periods is perhaps possible. Some costs can carry forward, like selling a home with a balance still due on the mortgage. Owners cash out with some equity. The home can pass to an heir, even with some balance due. The heir can sell, pay the debt off if they have the means, or pick up the payments. Such transfers, between one qualified owner to another qualified owner can be anticipated and be part of the system.

A longer amortization schedule can provide profit for each owner involved, unlike high rents. This keeps equity and lowers payments. Re-amortizing the loan should be an option in retirement. Then, at some point, the land, construction costs, and interest costs are paid off.

If the longer terms are not necessary or advantageous, all the better. Having a property paid off sooner is great. Lower payments are great. The savings can be significant.

And another beneficial case is when rent is very low, like at 10% to 20% of income, as it is in Austria for many households. In that case, people can put a lot of money into savings, building capital and assets. Then the asset of home equity can be bypassed and people can still be prosperous.

Paid-in-Full Homes are a Good Problem to Have; Adjustments Can Work Out

There are many contingencies involved with affordability agreements. It involves pay scales, future sales prices, and inflation rates. The existing affordability agreement contracts in use around the world provide guidance and experience. Contracts could have hyper-inflation provisos for protection of the participants. We provide some discussion of these factors, but we won't attempt to move past the basics in this book. What about homes that are paid in full under affordability agreements? These could be passed on to an heir whose income is within the income bracket. See more on p. 147, note 62.[62]

When Income Goes Up

When income rises, procedures can be figured out. We should be so fortunate in the U.S., to have to debate about too many people having too low of housing payments.

In Austria, it's been working so well, that no one cares much when the renter's income goes up. The issue is debated now and then, but the rule in Austria remains that a lease option lasts a lifetime. You can always stay, even if your income goes up. Average households like the idea that higher-income people live in the building. The top 20% of households are not eligible for such contracts, but they usually want upscale units anyway, so they don't complain.

Austria has enough nice buildings under these contracts, so that:
- Middle-income people want to live there.
- Even some wealthier folks in the 60% to 80% income level choose it.
- There are enough units for everyone, without undue waiting

Certainly, when Austria's middle class and working class have more savings and spending money, rather than just blowing it on higher rent or on sky high property taxes, it seems to be working for that nation.

That scenario voids the welfare rut in the U.S., in whatever extent that it still exists. That rut is when personal income goes up, a person loses a valuable cash equivalent, so the person make no effort to increase personal income, not when it's a wash. The rut encourages people *to not* change their personal circumstances *to not* raise their personal income, but stay stuck in a rut, in a so-so apartment, even in a rough neighborhood.

People could come out of their ruts, with the money they build up if their rent is only 10% and 20% of their income; and if the rent stayed low as they worked more to raise income, and/or got better jobs.

The Austrian system gives an incentive to keep more of net money coming in. That's unlike the U.S. system. Where does the U.S. system send the extra money that people get from two jobs, or from overtime, or from getting a promotion? To the landlord or the lender for these infernal high prices.

A lot of U.S. people want to improve their lives and improve their neighborhoods. But they do not have the resources or time to pursue such good things. Once again, our fellow Americans, can we see how these issues coming up over and over, which get blamed on other factors, are in fact acerbated and enabled by the U.S. housing system. It may well be that primarily a key contributing factor has long been and still is the U.S. housing system, not the usual suspects. Let's look squarely at this.

If people can have a lower rental or purchase price,
> then they build up their own money, then they can benefit and
> > then society can benefit.

Financing Repayment is From Business Payrolls

Financing has a dedicated repayment stream from the payrolls of the U.S. business establishment of the U.S. economy, which provides the payroll because the business establishment needs the workforce. That's where the money really comes from, the business establishment, to the workforce, to repay the bonds. These bonds could sell.

Such housing-linked bonds are, in practice, free-market, private investment, primarily, not direct tax cash from taxpayers. The cash comes from private investors who buy the bonds. Bonds are paid back by business payrolls to private-sector renters and buyers. On the upfront cash, and on the repayment cash, it's private investment, not government funds. The housing bond is a conduit. Processing costs can be covered by fees from investors and the payments from renters and buyers.

Further, housing bonds are not general, generic bonds. They are special purpose bonds, with collateral of the land and in-use structures, thus are not really even comparable to the risk of general business or government bonds.

From now for the next hundred years, each generation of employees has to live somewhere, after all. Having a roof over your head doesn't go out of style or become obsolete, unlike other products will in the next 100 years.

Housing bonds should have rock solid protections against these bond proceeds or values being used or sold to pay any other obligations. See a discussion of bond risk in note 60 on p. 147.

Suggestions abound that national governments in conjunction with state and local governments increase the pace of this funding. Researchers Saoirse Gowan and Ryan Cooper suggest that the federal government issue housing bonds at the same rate of U.S. Treasury bonds plus a basis point (1/100th of 1 percent). They suggest that a federal incentive matching the equivalent amount of the Low Income Housing Tax Credit (LIHTC) could be included in the financing. These could be linked to local and state programs.[63]

Doing Something About Unfair Economic Inequality: More Studies? Or More Housing that People Can Afford to Buy or Rent? Call Now. Deals Are Waiting.

Who knows when housing inventory commitments like Austria's will take hold. In the meantime, here's something that can be done starting right now, if anyone wants to get going, in any nation. Angel investors, social investors, entrepreneurial incubators, investment funds, venture funds, think tanks, foundations, and major universities have staff and resources. Institutions conduct research on investment policy, stability for local and national economies, unfair economic inequality, economic disparity, disproportional disadvantage for some, and ways to improve equality of opportunity.

Perhaps instead of approving more staff time and money be spent on yet more study of lagging economics and economic inequality, a foundation or institution could allocate staff time and money to have a concrete effect on unfair economic inequality, in an area, city, or region. That's possible by funding new housing for purchase or rent at moderate prices, with affordability agreements for future generations. This could include any investor who wants to make a few honest bucks. This could include institutions whose investment managers are fretting over diminishing returns or volatility in other investments.

Investor cash or the foundation cash can combine with existing loan programs or investment capital funds, which usually have investment capacity awaiting. Los Angeles has a fast track for homes for lower-income buyers and renters. Within the U.S., financing options can be explained by the staff of any regional office of the U.S. Housing and Urban Development agency. The phone number of the office for each area is listed on the agency website. Call now. Funds and incentives are waiting. Some developers avoid any government programs and requirements, while keeping prices lower.[64]

The housing developments can turn a profit. The units or building can sell, returning the money to the organization, perhaps to be used again for the same purpose. The key is to have affordability agreements so the homes and rentals will stay at lower prices. Otherwise, the units just gentrify later. This boosts local economies, while reducing inter-generational economic disparity. This concretely helps people that have been unfairly discriminated against in the past. The disparity lowers as they build assets to match up to mainstream assets. This can continue, over and over, so only a portion of capital need be tied up.

Organizations, businesses, investors, and foundations could start making a real dent in unfair economic inequality, not just proselytize about unfair economic inequality. At lower prices, funds are available, as are customers.

That might help social improvement, more so than handing out money for more research on social improvement. Again, the projects can pay back the money, plus profit, which academic reports do not, usually.

Housing Activists Put the Cart Before the Horse

Is it correct to say that U.S. housing and property taxes are working well for average households? Is that the argument? That things are good for average folks with their take home pay, after housing payments and property taxes? Let's hear from the elected officials who say housing payments are a good deal for average folks. Who comes to mind? No one. They are avoiding this discussion, beyond approving extra funding into the existing system. They are running away from any hard decisions on this issue.

Tax money has been used in the U.S. as extra tax incentives to try to get someone to build homes to rent or sell at modest prices in the first place. That's since, besides some dips, it has been profitable for business people to invest in regular U.S. residential, commercial, or industrial real estate, or in the stock market, or the bond market, or in operating any number of other businesses. If it's optional, why bother with constructing starter homes? The developers did not bother with starter homes. And developers still won't bother with starter homes.

Requests for increases in tax money are the cart, put before the horse, an inventory commitment. The biggest market impact can be from the inventory commitment, followed by affordability agreements, not the amount of a bond fund or tax credit, even if higher. Having more financing or tax credits does not mean that builders will add homes at lower prices into their next subdivision. Or that housing boards will ramp up some big numbers. That's not happening, much, usually. Binding commitments are needed.

Incentives to Compete With Gentrification Usually Fail

Competing with gentrification with extra incentives alone as a method has failed to make big impacts so far around the world. Rental tax credits would just fund higher prices. In the U.S., the tax money goes through the Low Income Housing Tax Credit (LIHTC), or similar credits, which pad the numbers to try to entice developers away from higher profits.

Generally, tax credits do not to entice enough inventory away from the path of least resistance of gentrification. Adding a lot more tax money to the LIHTC kitty is a regular proposal before Congress.[65] If that happens, however, investors can still take a pass. Perhaps if a tax credit linked to low price inventory were much higher it would work. Perhaps that's a trade off that developers and taxpayers could embrace. Maybe that could boost ratios of inventory at lower prices in new development. It has not been working so far, however.

Unlike a voluntary use of a tax credit, an inventory commitment can require that homes be built at starter prices each and every year, by a local housing board, if no one else wants to bother. Employees still have to bother paying the rent, each and every year.

When some developers claimed they could not or would not build sensibly priced housing units in Austria, the local housing boards just said, fine, we'll buy the land and hire someone to do it. Housing boards put out the notices for the bids. With open bidding, it's still free enterprise. And lenders and builders signed up. Lenders and builders didn't do it for free, but made money. A deal's a deal, after all. Customers moved in and are repaying the cost of the developments, so taxpayers aren't being fleeced.

With private companies, an inventory commitment that includes starter prices is like having the electric companies and the water companies include average households, not price average households out of basic service.

Whatever will work, is whatever will work. Whatever might work has to pass in a legislature or in binding referendum.

But more tax credits may not even be needed, once inventory commitments and affordability agreements are in place. In Europe, the primary impetus for investors and banks who agree to finance the lower-priced inventory is to have a steady, predictable rate of profit for their investment, backed by great collateral, the land, building, and the income stream from employed tenants or mortgage holders. Condo buildings or single-family home subdivisions repay the capital in full with the last sold property. Bonds for units for sale can be short term, ending when all the units are sold. For apartment buildings, they can be longer-term, 10 or 20 years or more, depending on initial construction costs.

Any collateral has risk as market conditions can change, often rapidly. Some positive factors in favor of housing bond collateral for rental units and for units for sale under affordability agreements include:

1. People are motivated to pay in order to keep their good deal.
2. The payment amount is not a strain, given normal economic conditions. What about bad conditions? Well, with lower payments and more savings, households in affordability agreements may be in better shape to make it through extreme events, more so than highly-leveraged people, with high payments. And affordability agreements can have adjustments for extreme events and downturns, which keeps renters in the buildings, even at lower payments, which is better than empty units that contribute nothing. Housing bond holders can see some cash flow, while waiting for the downturn to ease. The goal isn't to beat the returns of the S&P 500, but that the apartment building bonds be paid off, so rents drop even further, to cover upkeep only.
3. In standard conditions, foreclosure risk matches general economic risk of the national economy. Foreclosures only occur when people don't sell; and then they walk away. Most homeowners sell first. Usually, the lender or bond holder does just fine, pocketing all that principal and interest paid, and mortgage insurance proceeds, to resell the home, in this case at the agreed lower price. Construction-only bonds have no foreclosure risk, (unless the homes don't sell after construction, and have to be rented), because risk to collateral transfers immediately from the construction bond to the mortgage lender. Bonds held until homes are paid off are in effect mortgages or mortgage bonds. Unlike households with high payments, households with low payments (and lower property tax bills) can more easily make payments in downturns, or use savings they've accrued by having low payments. For really bad times, all mortgages and bonds should have forbearance clauses for lower payments during the severe economic conditions, with the extra due added on at the end of a loan time table. That's like a standard refi, which extends the time table, and no one complains. And people can always sell (perhaps with profit), moving into rentals or with other family.

In summary, regular housing bonds with affordability agreements may meet the need, with the LIHTC or similar items, if needed, as society's stake in the investment. The rest of this chapter advocates cutting tax rates, which can be skipped if you want to jump to the next chapter, which explains affordability agreements in more detail.

Let's Avoid Using Tax Money. Instead Use Payback Money from Renters and Buyers. If 100 Homes are Going Up, Who Wants in on the Deal?

Perhaps relatively little tax spending will be needed, since renters and buyers are repaying the costs. So, let's say there is a definite commitment for 100 homes to be built at modest prices.

Companies will consider putting in bids on the project. Somebody has to build the 100 homes. Material will be purchased. Construction crews will be put to work.

And if no valid bids come in, then the housing board, (from the city, county, or state that needs the 100 homes) will have to adjust. Construction can proceed by the housing board hiring its own managers and construction crews, with open budgets, auditing, and accountability. That works on infrastructure projects. If someone can manage building the Brooklyn Bridge, Hoover Dam and the Golden Gate Bridge, someone can manage building some sturdy homes built to code. At lower prices that beat out the high prices down the street, there will be customers who buy or rent the 100 units.

Housing construction certainly needs competent supervision and workmanship. This is about building solid homes, or solid mid-rise buildings, with standard plans, nice landscaping, and pleasant facades. Construction of durable, nice homes can be properly managed, and any city, county, or state can hire competent managers, employees, and contractors to do so, then sell or rent the housing at a modest profit, or at cost. That varies by area business payrolls and demand. For rentals, if construction costs are high then it just takes longer for the renters to repay the costs. At lower rent prices, the renters won't complain.

For homes or condos for sale in the highest priced areas, adding extra units can cover costs. Or perhaps financing of some of the equity can extend past 30 years, while still leaving owners some equity to work with, for home equity loans, or for when they sell. Let's see what people prefer, perhaps, by offering it. Compared to being priced out, forced into high rent for 60 to 70 years, and getting nothing back, there may be some takers. In time, the costs are paid.[66]

Let's Reduce the Use of Tax Money

Right now society uses federal tax money at about 1% of GDP to cover some costs for U.S. homeowners and renters including high-income households as well as middle-class households, and low-income households (see pp. 129-131). There is additional state and local tax spending. So, realize that society does this now already, as decided by our elected officials since it is deemed to be in the interest of various citizens. So, some tax spending has precedence, but we propose a significant change in this thinking and in practice as follows: With new methods, the goal is: to use less tax money. It could be a lot less.

So homelessness doesn't go up, there is pressure to keep Section 8 for the bottom 2%, mostly seniors, not evict them into the streets. Such tax spending could go down if more people in more generations owned their homes free-and-clear. Seniors in paid-for homes (with property tax caps) won't need Section 8 to avoid eviction and foreclosure. Wealthier folks may still decide to not pay down a mortgage at 6% to the bank, to try to make 9% in stocks, but does some of your federal tax money have to help pay the bank's 6%? Households in starter units repay construction costs, so that tax spending, if any, can be repaid.

Households using lower prices can be more stable and productive so they pay more taxes into the government, while lowering tax spending on social instability. As more households are upwardly mobile, in the third generation, for example, even reliance on Social Security and Medicare can decrease, as people are able to pay for more of, or all, of their own retirements and health care premiums out of their 401(k)s, other investment income, or savings.

The government, i.e. the taxpayers, will make back the seed money over time. Voters and taxpayers can understand that logic and support it because:
- The goal is that no more tax money is needed on these housing developments; after principal and interest has been paid off.
- The goal is that employed households will generate tax revenue. The renters and buyers maintain upkeep.

The current government programs need to change, to stop the never-ending taxpayer cash flow to landlords and high prices. From page one, let's use (1) reasonable property taxes, (2) inventory, and (3) agreements for the future.

Remember, all those benefits may ensue from the inventory commitment primarily, without using tax money that's not repaid. If, however, some tax money isn't repaid directly, by end users, it could still be recouped in overall lower tax costs down the line.

The money spent on housing is recouped in the spin-off savings in other spending programs, which are substantial. Later the U.S. taxpayers save a lot of money by spending less on social instability:

- 911 calls
- paramedic calls
- extra police patrols
- court and local jail costs
- social workers
- public defenders
- probation officers
- state and federal prison costs
- foster care
- PTSD care
- school counseling
- educational remediation
- extra school security
- vandalism repair
- graffiti removal
- addiction rehab
- unpaid hospital bills
- emergency room costs
- welfare

These are the costs, year after year, generation after generation, of economic and social instability.

A dollar saved is a dollar earned, for governments too.

So, even with some tax money spent up front through lower-priced homes, the beneficial compounding effects later, over many generations, could total up to a substantial net gain for government, taxpayers, businesses, and citizens.

If land costs and the construction costs exceed payments at 30% to 35% of income of a region's average employees, then the first step is to extend the payments. Even if it takes longer, the construction costs are repaid. We've shown examples using exact, full-market prices from 2024 price sheets from new construction by regular builders with no social housing bonds and no taxpayer money (pp. 16-17), whereby the costs could have been covered.

But if society must cover some of the cost, that could be a reasonable investment for the public good. There is precedence. All tax money spent is to benefit society, businesses, commerce, and citizens, in every category, from stop lights, to schools, to armed soldiers and officers who defend citizens from harm. In economics, tax spending has boosted the nation's development with seed money for all manner of things, to the benefit of all of society. This included land grants for homesteaders, for railroads, and for state colleges. This included money for canals, bridges, roads, ports, and interstate highways. This included money for scientific research. Such seed money has been and still is in the public interest.

Primarily, housing renters and owners can pay back the costs and maintenance, in most calculations. That could also be aided by some seed money from society for a long-term, long-lasting public good.

Lower the Tax Rates

Lower housing prices for average people = lower tax rates for everyone?

Maybe. Let's recap the points made, to consider that tax rates for everyone can be lowered by this. Here's how:

(1) Tax rates can be lowered
  (2) when there is less tax spending,
    (3) on dealing with intergenerational social instability of
      (4) dysfunctional households and dysfunctional individuals,
        (5) when there are:
          (6) a lot fewer dysfunctional households and
            a lot fewer dysfunctional individuals,
            (7) because they grow up in, and live in
              (8) stable economics and stable social conditions
                (9) not unstable economics and unstable social conditions,
                  (10) from being broke, on average income,
                    (11) from high housing payments.

Maybe tax spending on social instability can go down, and maybe go down in big numbers. Stable entry-level employees can pay their own way in life, gradually building assets and savings, gaining stability, self sufficiency, and some measure of wealth.

It's worth examining the options and the mathematics of it in greater detail. Beyond the common sense economics of it, it's worth the social considerations, in order to reduce levels of dysfunction which bring so much pain and sorrow to too many people, when normalcy is possible.

Thus, having taxpayers contribute to a stable economy with a relatively modest amount of tax spending as seed money for new homes is not only fair, it may in the long run be fiscally conservative for taxpayers by lowering other tax costs and by launching millions of households into stability, whereby they contribute more in taxes. Then Congress can lower tax rates for them, and maybe lower tax rates for everyone.

Chapter 8

Add Affordability Agreements: Keep Prices Fair for Future Generations

The method is to sell or rent for less, on purpose. Who would sell or rent for less? On purpose. That sounds crazy. Yes. It does sound crazy. At first.

But, in a lot of areas, you're priced out otherwise.

To get a good deal now, you agree to give someone a good deal later.

This is already occurring. It's been in use in Europe for 100 years. It's used all over in the U.S. One example is in Manhattan, in New York City at Cooper Square, for privately-owned homes at lower prices. It comes with a decision to offer homes at lower prices for buyers and renters of average means, and keep the price low.

An affordability agreement is a binding sales contract or lease contract that keeps home prices manageable for the long term. To get a lower price, the average-income buyer agrees to sell later at a similar price to another average-income buyer, and so on. For average people, the price must remain lower, going up gradually, even when the wealthier will pay much more in the same area.

Then those buyers agree that they also have to sell at a similar price later on. And they choose it. That's right, choose it, as in, of their own free will, not out of a hurried decision, or because of any arm twisting. They can sell at any time. If they want, they can move. Many people conclude it's a good deal. Here's why. Many households cannot rent or buy in an area otherwise.

The best deals occur after the mortgage is paid off, for single-family homes, condos, and for apartment buildings. Then only maintenance costs need be paid. Then payments might be 60% to 70% lower. For renters and owners, the payment can drop in older age. Renters can save extra for upward mobility. Someone in the family can inherit a paid-for home, or cash from the equity at the time of the sale. A renter, with the huge savings from avoiding high rent over a lifetime, can build a nice amount in a 401(k) or other investments.

Would you like to inherit a paid-for home or condo, or a nice amount of cash from a parent or grandparent? Or would you prefer they pay high rent their whole lives, and remain broke? As things are, what will you end up with?

For buyers, to get in on a good deal they agree to give the next person a good deal too. That next person can be someone in the family or household. That way average buyers always have a chance. Could we get used to this idea?

For renters, they sign for a reasonable payment. The rent payment can go down even more when the building has paid off the mortgage. In that case, renters can plan for the lower payments in their future. Later generations in paid-for buildings will have the even lower rent payments right off the bat.

What other method will keep home prices within average wages for the long term? It's open for suggestions.

An old, standard market-based strategy is that older housing inventory is priced lower for lower-wage employees. In the past, that happened. Often now that has reversed, as older buildings are upgraded or replaced for high-end use.

The affordability agreement combines

(a) real estate proximity to jobs with

(b) wage-scale factors.

Nothing else does this, it seems. The current laissez-faire methods do not put homes at fair prices where workers need them, in the heart of a region with employment, in the midst of rising prices.

The affordability agreement takes a specific location and keeps some units at a moderate price. That price increases along with wage growth and currency inflation. Later, that price matches wage levels and economic conditions that occur later, to match what's considered a moderate price for the next-generations.

For a certain number of homes, it stops gentrification's fast price hikes, like from $200,000 up to $500,000, then to $800,000, then over $1 million. The reserved homes are for people at working-class and middle-class income. Middle-class homes could have more amenities and be priced higher under such agreements. In an example using 2024 equivalent prices, such homes could start at $250,000, rise to $300,000 over time, then to perhaps $400,000 years later, but wouldn't jump to $800,000 more quickly like under gentrification.

This already works for a lot of people in Europe and for some in the U.S. For examples see page 100. The practice has advocates around the world. It just takes funding, which can be drummed up, and customers, which may be there. It's only used, if it is needed.

People can still try the regular real estate market at any time. It's a free country. If people can buy in the regular market, they often should do so. The profit can be excellent. The fact that gentrification profit can be excellent does not take away from the logic for reasonable prices for average households.

The excellent profit of gentrification is exactly why starter units under affordability agreements are logical for people who are priced out from gentrification's excellent profit.

If demand for affordability agreements is not there, that's good news. It means the regular market is affordable. In Japan, for example, lots of new residential construction is priced for lower salaries.

In Chapter 2 we used the example of the Lincoln Park neighborhood in Chicago, which in 2024 is very wealthy. In 1960, when it was a poor neighborhood, what if some affordability agreements had started there? One couple, for example, like a janitor with a spouse or partner who is a dishwasher, could still own a home there, with the taxes adjusted to their starter-price value, which would be fair.

Would the rich folks now living in Lincoln Park have been hindered?

No.

Would an entry-level employee of any type who works in the area and was next in line to own a home in Lincoln Park for a moderate price take the deal?

Probably.

Lost Profits? Not If You Can't Ever Buy, Or Save Any Money

In busy regions, working-class households and many middle-class households would not be giving up windfall profits. That's because there is no way they could buy in the busy region in the first place, in order to see a windfall profit. In many areas of the U.S. they can't buy, other than through an affordability agreement. With one, they can quit renting now, buy now, and when they sell later, they get a reasonable profit. If their goal is to still strike it rich someday with a business, or in a career, and later buy into the regular real estate market, the affordability agreement doesn't prevent that. Nor for renters either, under affordability agreements. Renters can save a lot of money over time for upward mobility with affordability agreements, which they can't do with gentrified rents.

This is still classical Adam Smith capitalism, relying not on "benevolence" to get the deal done between buyers and sellers, "...but from their regard to their own interest," as with Smith's examples of the butchers, the bakers, and their customers.[67] This fits Ayn Rand's advocacy of self reliance out of self interest.

If conditions change, the affordability agreements can adjust. If demand for affordability agreements wanes, the empty units could convert to market rates. In either case, great.

People still have general housing risk when they buy under an affordability agreement which is just the same general housing risk as if they bought without an affordability agreement, so that's equal and fair. This is still a real estate decision and an investment decision in which people should prudently estimate what an area will be like in the future. They should estimate what will happen when they retire, or if they want to sell. They should plan for what the area will be like if they want to pass the home to their grandchild, for example. That's no different from regular home buying.

There's no guarantee in regular home buying that the value won't drop. In the 1950s, many steady U.S. working-class areas looked to be a safe investment for retirement 40 years later. Then in the 1980s and 1990s, many areas in the U.S. weren't at all like they were in the 1950s. Some had become upscale, but others had become troubled neighborhoods, with lower values. From younger age into retirement, conditions can change.

Advocates of renting instead of buying point out that renters can quickly leave neighborhoods that decline in value. Whereas, if one buys and continues to live there, at retirement the home value is lower.

Let's examine that point. Yes, on some blocks of Cleveland, or certain blocks in the Englewood neighborhood in Chicago, or certain blocks of Gary, Ind., or some blocks of Memphis, Tenn., or some blocks in Fresno, Calif., a home in 2020 was worth less, adjusted for inflation, than it was in the 1950s, 1960s, or 1970s. In 50 years neighborhoods may change further, or not.

Are such examples evidence that *most* people should continue to rent to age 85? Even if they can buy at some point with some effort?

How many areas have increased substantially in value, if one had bought in 1970, 1980, or later?

Most of the U.S.A.

Renters who moved away from Chicago's Englewood neighborhood, from Gary, Ind., from Memphis, Tenn., or from Compton, Calif., and still rent elsewhere still have no equity. And those who never bought in Chicago, Gary, Memphis, or Compton, but still rent there, well, they have no real estate equity either.

We know people who bought homes in such areas. Would they have done things differently in hindsight? Yes. They say that their main regret is that they did not buy in a nearby area that went up more in value. Some nearby areas went up a lot more. They do not say that buying in general is a bad concept.

They do not say that they should have kept paying rent at about the same monthly payment, to get nothing out of it. They say that they benefited from a fixed mortgage payment for a long term, excluding taxes. They have a paid-for home, even if it is at a lower value than they expected. They aren't paying rent or a mortgage in their retirement. They have equity, if they sell, or to borrow against, for end-of-life expenses. They still have a home to sell, or to place in their will for a child, who can live there, or rent it, or sell it.

The regular real estate market, anywhere in the world, doesn't change these types of risks or potential benefits. Unforeseen events and trends occur. Nothing's guaranteed. Until recently, downtown real estate values in the U.S. looked great, like a sure thing. Until COVID hit. Some homes in Cleveland might be a good investment over the next 50 years, as compared to the last 50 years. Or not. For home buyers, an affordability agreement doesn't change any of that basic, expected, well-understood risk. What it does is give a fair price to people to rent or buy of their own free choice, when otherwise the price in that area would be well beyond what they can afford on their income.

Untapped Equity Within the Equity/Affordability Paradox

In the U.S., there are a few do-gooder investors here and there, and a few land-trust properties. Otherwise, no one helps the average homeowner get or stay in an affordable home. Not even fellow average homeowners help, as they look ahead to sell for gentrified prices. Under gentrification, after the last working-class homeowner sells for a high price in that area, no working families ever return.

If average-income employees who buy for moderate prices agree to sell later to other average-income employees at similar prices, they gain only moderate profit. So what do they do about the extra equity if homes nearby go to higher prices? Just leave the equity? Maybe, yes. That's essentially what's happened in Austria under agreements that started some 100 years ago. Values rose a lot, but some properties remain the same, renting at lower prices. There is equity that isn't being cashed out, and won't be cashed out. It hasn't ruined anyone personally, nor ruined that nation's economics.

An owner who needs an affordability agreement option to buy in the first place is not losing equity, nor incurring an opportunity cost, because other than with this option, he or she would have no opportunity to buy in that area. You can't lose equity or opportunity that you would never have had in the first place.

We don't see a way to tap the excess equity in the current time, while keeping prices low for those specific buyers. We examined derivatives, but if some equity can't be transferred, it can't be in a derivative. That equity is on hold.

The on-hold equity could be tapped, if demand for affordability agreements wanes in a region, like with population dropping in the future. If no one wants that home at the starter-value price, the land and structure can be sold into other uses. So, in the really long term, perhaps no equity would be left out at all, for any of us capitalist purists who are concerned that no profit be left unturned.

So leaving some real estate equity untapped for a while might be the way it has to be. That could be in the self-interest of the entry level employees; and in the self interest of the middle class. It could be in the self interest of businesses who need employees who can afford to live nearby, especially small- and medium-sized businesses. This could be in the self interest of society.

Without an affordability agreement, such equity is only tapped by the first working family selling into gentrification anyway, and then the equity transfers forever to wealthier owners. In this new deal, wealthier owners won't even miss that equity from that property, because they'll buy something else.

At starter prices, people on average incomes can have a modest monthly payment, so there isn't strain. People now and in future generations can save to get ahead. Some people will be more ambitious, investing and prospering. If so, they might choose an upscale home, after selling the starter unit to a working-class buyer. Not only does one entry-level household, for example, escape paycheck-to-paycheck life, but the daughter or son can do better.

Development At Lower Prices. These Developers Are Doing It.

National Organizations

Center for Community Land Trust Innovation (International) This organization and its website have extensive information, manuals, books, contacts, and examples.
Canadian Network of Community Land Trusts https://www.communityland.ca
Community Land Trust Network - (United Kingdom) https://www.communitylandtrusts.org.uk
The Center for New Economics - (U.S.) https://centerforneweconomics.org/apply/community-land-trust-program/directory/
U.S. Department of Housing and Urban Development https://www.hud.gov
Local Housing Solutions (LHS) (U.S.) https://localhousingsolutions.org
Resident Owned Communities (ROC) USA https://rocusa.org
Grounded Solutions Network (U.S.) https://groundedsolutions.org
Shelterforce (U.S.) https://shelterforce.org

Examples of Successful Developments at Fair Prices

London, England: St. Clements Community Land Trust - https://www.londonclt.org/st-clements-community - **Canada:** Greater Vancouver Housing Corporation - Region of Peel (Toronto area) Non-Profit Housing Corporation - **California:** San Diego Housing Trust Fund - https://www.sdhousingfund.org - **Illinois:** Community Partners for Affordable Housing in Illinois - www.cpahousing.org - see home buying - community land trust
Maryland: Montgomery County Government - https://www.montgomerycountymd.gov/DGS/OPD/AffordableHousing.html - **Michigan:** Iron Mountain, Michigan Housing Commission - **Minnesota:** https://www.mncltc.org - **New York:** Cooper Square Mutual Housing Association & Cooper Square Community Land Trust, Manhattan, New York City, New York. - www.cooperquareclt.org - **North Carolina:** https://communityhometrust.org/listings/ - **Oregon:** Housing Works housing authority for Deschutes, Crook, & Jefferson Counties - https://housing-works.org/our-properties/ - **Texas:** Austin, https://www.guadalupendc.org - Houston, Row House Community Development Corp. https://www.rowhousecdc.org - **Vermont:** Champlain, https://www.getahome.org
Virgina - Arlington Partnership for Affordable Housing - https://apah.org

© 2024, photo by Lydia Deckert
In a very wealthy neighborhood, these are affordability agreement apartments, in Key West, Florida. This is near multi-million dollar homes, but the above apartments have low prices for local employees. This is the Roosevelt C. Sands, Jr. Affordable Housing Complex of the Housing Authority of the City of Key West.

Then the granddaughter or grandson may move into the middle class and upward into wealth. If so, then the original affordable home keeps passing along to another entry-level couple so a new family starts the good cycle again.

Or people can choose not to be particularly ambitious, but just live on average income with independence and dignity, while contributing to the economy and society. The method isn't widespread yet, but there are many examples (see the opposite page). Affordability agreements reserve equity for employees that they wouldn't have otherwise in busy areas, a significant piece of the pie for the workforce, which is lifetime ownership of homes. Or, at their choice, lifetime leases at low prices.

Part of the pie is significant capital reserved for the entry level workforce and the middle class. And the other part of the pie is for upscale buyers.

To each his own, and at least under affordability agreements, the entry level workforce and the middle class still have something to call their own.

This doesn't limit upward mobility or options, but rather enhances people's agency to retain capital out of earnings for upward mobility. Thus, there's no need to oppose development under affordability agreements as if the agreements limit people's options. Or as if equity capital will lag, when the world is awash in investment capital. The equity of upscale holdings will remain and can expand to what the market will bear.[68]

For new development like this, sellers of existing real estate get full market price for land and buildings. Just like a regular market sale, they sell, for full value, and they're out of it. It's up to the new owner to decide what's next. That is a free-market concept indeed. The new developer takes over, a private investor, or a local housing board. The intent is that some starter units will be included, so those terms are agreed to. This is where there is an opportunity cost to the new developer, compared to full-priced real estate, which is understood by the new developer. This is freely agreed to by any private investor, who may simply decline, and invest elsewhere in any other venture. A housing board, investing in effect on behalf of society, knows all the details as well.

Affordability agreements insure that basic economics do not exclude average households from prospering. Or should the housing system exclude ownership, or an ability to save any money, to those with average incomes? That's in effect what the U.S. system is doing to a lot of people. Affordability agreements have some counter effect against unfair economic disparity, potentially a highly significant effect. The level of initial distribution of income to the workforce remains a variable.

Most policy suggestions keep high rents or are temporary fixes, which gentrification compromises or renders useless. Social housing shouldn't exclude workers from owning, if they want to own. Usual suggestions seem insufficient without the three items from p. 1 of this book. We explain the limitations of other suggestions as follows: wage increases (p. 123), income supports (p. 53, p. 67), wealth taxes (p. 158), tax credits (p. 89), and mortgage interest credits (p. 125- 127).

Summary

As gentrification increasingly sets in across the U.S. and worldwide, workers and the middle class have only three possible cases regarding asset equity:
1. zero assets to inadequate assets, since they can't afford to buy any real estate; or save enough money to buy other meaningful assets
2. moving to a remote area where prices are low enough to buy or rent, but that depends on income available in remote areas, which may limit gains, or be a net loss
3. some home equity or savings to buy assets while living under affordability agreements, which offer
    - 3a. lower rents, especially after an apartment building is paid off. The low rents allow tenants to save significant money. The money can be invested, so a good retirement 401(k) is an option. It's like having a home equity equivalent. Children are sent off in life in better circumstances. Parents can help their young adult children with tuition, home down-payments, and the like, or
    - 3b. an option to buy a home or condo with lower monthly payments, especially after the mortgage is paid off. The home equity is available to the household, and to heirs

Objections Come From Perceptions of Bad Effects

Objections to starter prices come from perceptions of bad results from past mistakes. These mistakes can be fixed, as outlined in Chapter 5, starting on page 59. Let's change the mindset, so that affordability means nice homes at prices for the middle class. It can mean modest, nice homes for entry-level employees, all paid for out of wages, not welfare. Let's change the mindset so affordability means safe, secure buildings and safe subdivisions, with strong social settings, mixed into ongoing employment and business operations. City Point, 7 DeKalb Avenue, Brooklyn, N.Y., has 200 rentals at lower prices, mixed into upscale units, with businesses at the street level. Use a map app for a street view of this building. It looks great. And it has some units for working families.[69]

These Condos and Townhomes Could Sell Like Hotcakes

Units with such agreements could sell, as 7 DeKalb Avenue in Brooklyn indicated, with 87,000 applications for 200 units.[70] For a vote by the city council, county board, or state legislature, strategies include commitments for:
- enough reasonably priced units added, with ratios for each area, in high-rises, in mid-rises, in townhomes, and among new single-family homes
- enough reasonably priced units in high-rises and mid-rises added in commercial corridors, or
- enough reasonably priced units added in downtown and central core areas, or
- all of these.

For the majority of residents and businesses, this is in their interests, not at all risky radicalism. (What is risky and radicalism is exclusionary elitism.) Businesses get stable employees and more customers. Business owners recognize the benefits of having an economy that is hitting on all cylinders. Let's keep the economy going with reliable entry level employees, a workforce with money to spend, and a substantial middle class. That provides robust markets for sales. This isn't supposed to be a charity, but sustainable, profitable home building. It has the bonus of freeing up huge sums of money out of people's paychecks to pay for all the other products, services, investments, and savings that underly and gird up a sturdy, growing, well-balanced economy.

About Single-Family Homeowners

About single-family homeowners: They can be protected from encroachment for many decades because more housing can be provided in more single-family homes in expanding suburbs; and by more mid-rises and high-rises in the central core; and in commercial strips. Condos can go in the airspace above the stores on a busy block already taken up by stores. Some shopping malls are adding residential units.

Eventually in busy areas, a lot of single-family homes get replaced by larger buildings. Manhattan, New York City, for example, had a lot of single-family homes at one time. Homeowners are bought out one by one by developers to build mid-rises. Then mid-rises are bought out one by one to build high rises.

So society shouldn't be as fretful about single-family homeowners' sensibilities as much as some of them are. If the shift occurs to density, they get paid, often very well. They can move into any of the many single-family homes that are going up in suburban America. But if larger buildings take over, the difference should be that condos and rentals with lower prices are included. Ample acreage remains in the U.S. for tracts of single-family homes and townhomes.

Housing Patterns Will Change When Population Declines

This Manhattanization pattern and the suburban sprawl pattern will abate as world population levels off and then declines. The pattern for this is already happening. Birth rates are dropping in areas where education levels rise, among other factors. As birth rates drop, a nation's economy will shrink unless businesses add employees from nations with labor surpluses. Some areas, like those with democratic freedom for citizens, may retain status as desirable locations, and have growth. Where jobs and income are, price competition in housing depends on housing inventory.

Finally, worldwide total population will fall; perhaps around the turn of the century, 2100, maybe sooner, maybe later. By 2050 or sooner, lowering birth rates may affect employment and income at all levels, from janitors to scientists.

Things will be different with lowering population. Homes in some nations and areas, from the suburbs to the downtown high rises, might not have enough people who want to move in. A lot of tear downs of residential, commercial, and industrial use could occur, changing to parks, open space, or areas for homes with extra acreage. Perhaps people will have more wealth per capita. That would be good. The annual national wealth distribution pattern is another factor (see pp. 156-161). People might own multiple places to live, have larger spaces, and have vacation homes. Maybe more of the world's population can have paid-for housing by the time the total world population declines.[71]

Standard Sprawl and Sprawl with Urbanism Mixed In

The U.S. has ample land and airspace for expansion, as do many nations. New development can proceed in a smart, well planned fashion.

For the opponents of sprawl, well, you have won some converts. Units in denser new-urbanism developments in cities and suburbs usually have buyers and renters. In central Tokyo, for example, demand remains, while demand for homes in Japan's outer regions has dropped.

But polling and market buying shows that a large portion of people like single-family homes. They like driving a car instead of taking a bus or a bike. Suburban-style living, including a car, can include homes, townhomes, and condo developments that include some lower starter prices. U.S. development can have standard sprawl, and mix urbanism concepts into suburban settings. Already, U.S. suburbs are adding development next to train stops, and by highway on-ramps. Shuttle service can connect high-rise clusters and mid-rise clusters to commuter rail and public transit during rush hour.

Help the Lowest-Earning Employees Own a Home

Many people remain lower-rung employees into retirement, such as starting as a janitor and retiring as a janitor. They deserve security. This can be with low rent prices, as explained. Yet, owning should also be an option. Dishwashers and housekeepers, for example, could own modest homes, making a huge difference for them and for their children too.

But many lower-rung employees spend too many years in high rent, or never own at all, because for them, the amount to close on even an 3%-down FHA loan is daunting. To get to their jobs and to keep their jobs, the first priority is major and minor car repairs, on top of car payments, on top of full-coverage insurance and gasoline fill-ups.

Those items take a lot out of a housekeeper's net pay after high rent. Or they get one of those outrageous bills that U.S. hospitals regularly generate. That bill has to be paid off on time on regular payments or it ruins the credit score needed to buy.

It can take many years on a laborer's paycheck to save the thousands needed for a down payment and closing costs.

So they wait. They don't even check on home prices while they are younger. Years go by. Under the current system, they are then priced out.

It's not because the people who work as housekeepers, dishwashers, or similar lower-rung jobs are lacking integrity or focus. They have enough integrity and focus to work full time their whole entire lives.

Many pay rent on time, decade after decade after decade, being late now and then. Good grief, even a standard mortgage has a 15-day grace period each month and a lot of homeowners pay late a few days now and then, or regularly. That's accepted for 30 years on a mortgage. With rent, over 60 years, with $1,200 rent a month for a couple, for example, it totals $864,000. At $1,400 a month, a couple pays $1 million. (See p. 68.)

So we, as society, the system, can ask a couple to pay $850,000 to $1 million in rent over their lifetimes? That's fine. That's acceptable to everyone.

$1,000,000 in rent is OK. But for a $225,000 modest cottage home or condo, it's too much to think about, to help them buy that? Pause to consider the logic of that conclusion.

If someone's paying $1,400 in rent and those payments will rise further, probably by a lot, it is lower risk to get them locked into a fixed $1,200 mortgage payment. That's whom we should help. Then principal and interest are locked. If property taxes are capped at 2% increases, that's best. Insurance and HOA fees generally go up modestly under regular economics. First-time buyers programs can be responsible.

That said, if every home starts at $500,000, then even a $25,000 assistance program won't do much. Without prices, for example, matching what a Walmart full-time employee can afford to buy, then these programs, even as high as $25,000 are useless. Without starter inventory, and new or remaining inventory at starter prices on an on-going basis, the extra money just promotes the usual high prices, transferring that cash into the usual high prices.

There are warnings about first-time buyers like full-time employees stocking shelves at Walmart who don't make a lot, comparatively, to all other homeowners, Let's address that. This debate goes back decades to the issuance of the first 30-year-mortgages in the 1930s and 1940s. Some critics of lower down payments point to the low-documentation loans and the stated-income loans of the 2008 bubble and bust, which were ridiculous. (You could "state" your income, with no proof.) We note, as well, that most home buyers in the 2000 to 2008 price run-up had a lot more income than employees stocking shelves at Walmart.

The documentation requirements going forward for standard mortgages is very stringent as of 2024. Underwriters can identify reliable households.

All lenders require mortgage insurance, paid for by the borrower, no less, if the equity is less than 20%. Lenders are covered pretty well going forward.

Rather, a valid alarm to sound is how for many employees, the money to close on a home remains always several thousand dollars out of reach, as prices go up in the area where people work. Some people won't move up to manager, or get a degree. They'll remain at the level they're at, in retail, at a warehouse, at a restaurant, or in an office.

Are these full-time employees, with decades of work record, so risky? Or is it that this system gives them not an iota of time or thought? Who's being negligent here? The full-timers at Walmart? A middle-class office manager? Or is the U.S. system negligent in how it provides homes? The assistance can be paid back at $50 or $75 per month over time. Again, compare that to renting for 60 years.

Businesses could benefit by funding and promoting such programs, with an agreement that the employee will stick around a while. If employees have a homes nearby at lower payments, it could lower payroll costs and turnover costs for a company. If employees sell and move right away, the money would be paid back from the seller. Any assistance could be repaid, with interest. If the interest rate for the first time assistance is a little lower, a bank looses a little profit, but gets the full rate on the regular mortgage.

To improve the workforce, high school seniors should receive information about home buying, and about down payment assistance programs. Employers should include this information along with the 401(k) and other benefit information, as it is just as vital to the employee's well being as other items.

The Higher Concerns in National and International Macro-Economics

Let's see, what are the more pressing macro-economic (big picture) concerns for the U.S. and other nations:

(a) workforce instability?

(b) social instability?

(c) tens of millions of couples, families, and households all blowing $1 million on rent in a lifetime (see p. 68), ending up with nothing?

(d) or that banks and landlords don't have enough profit yet?

Housing insecurity produces bad results for families and society. Unless you're the landlord or lender.

Housing security is a bargain to any society and any nation, for the beneficial impact of freeing people from a lifetime of rising rent and paycheck-to-paycheck living. Lower-level employees and the middle class are worthy people who deserve manageable options.

Chapter 9

A Young Couple Gets Out of a Bleak Situation

Here's an example from a few years ago. This true story fits in well to conclude the first part of the book.

We personally know two young roommates who each have modest jobs. When we first met them, they were each earning the equivalent of $16 an hour in 2023 figures and lived, at that time, in a moderately priced region of the nation, Tucson, Ariz. The area had some homes at prices they could afford, but values were rising faster than the national average. At that point, they weren't trying yet to make it to professional or managerial salaries, and they may never try to do so. Yet they were optimistic and energetic in their demeanor. They showed up for work on time and did a good job. They had some fun, but lived frugally. One of them, for example, drove a 1980s VW bug, that she kept running with due vigilance, and regular tinkering under the hood.

But when it came to finances, their mood and outlook was bleak. They were always just over broke, or often behind. They had one of those huge medical bills, barely whittled down by a small payment each month. They just shook their heads as they looked ahead to decades of rising rents that left them with very little. In their minds, they were stuck in the 60-Year-High-Payment Plan

"Why don't you buy a house before the prices go up even more and you won't qualify?" we asked them.

"Are you kidding? There's no way, *no way*, we can buy a home," was the response.

We told them about one mortgage program, that of the non-profit National Assistance Corporation of America (NACA). We had to bring it up several times, in detail, before they decided to look into it. Still skeptical, they signed up for the free orientation.

NACA is a regular mortgage program, but one that tries to be patient in walking people through the process, while not being predatory or high pressure, so don't expect a quick return call from these folks. Using NACA, the couple bought a small home on a block that hadn't gentrified yet. Their house payment is lower than the rent had been. They're paying extra, to own it free-and-clear sooner. They might have a paid-for home at age 45. All on regular wages.

Now they can see a day with no rent payments and no mortgage payments. And that's with their same jobs, or similar paying jobs. While they are still fairly young, they will have no more mortgage payments, never another rent payment and some freedom and flexibility in life sooner, and in retirement.

Economic subjugation causes strains and pressures which cause people to end up in worse conditions. Debt may be ever-present. Assets are few to none. Strain pushes people, so they might cut corners in their career and finances, and make bad choices. Strain hardens feelings, spurring breakups and divorces that didn't have to be. Or the lack of any independence makes it all the harder to get out of situations that have turned sour, or worse. Even if the worst is avoided, a lifetime of subjugation prevents people from ever getting to where they really want to go in life, modestly or mightily.

After getting a foothold in the economy in a job or business, the steps for financial emancipation require some money left over after paying for housing. It's the first thing.[72] This household accomplished that. Then the step-by-step journey to independence helps provide a more content household to build upon.

It helps maintain healthy personal lifestyles, with time and resources to start personal relationships, build them up, and keep them healthy, for lifetimes. Stability nurtures better behavior in child rearing, in careers, in business, and expands options for good pursuits in time off of work. Stability promotes physical and mental well being. Stability helps people get somewhere in life, modestly, or mightily.

So, compare the two different possible lifetime paths for this one couple. They moved from one path, economic subjugation, to a wholly different path, economic emancipation. Their whole outlook and feeling about their lives has changed.

About six months after settling into the home, one of them said,

"Thank you so much. Thank you. Thank you. Thank you. Really."

She looked down, paused, and looked up.

"Seriously. This changed our lives. Thank you."

How important is a home? Even a modest one? Much more so than at first glance.

End of the Main Part of the Book

This finishes the main conclusions of this book.

A second part of the book examines other related factors in greater detail after the break pages.

Second Part of the Book

Additional Information

Chapter 10

Related Political Factors, Social Factors, and Economic Factors

Examples of Change in Political and Economic Power

In reviewing housing articles and books, and from interviews with people about housing, we noticed that the situation was often left in general terms.
1. People were unwilling to think through a step at a time, to see how a package of steps could work.
2. So, people concluded that there was no way to change things.
3. So, people won't even pause to think, that there might be options.
4. Then they accept the status quo, bad as it is, even for them.

In response we've offered specific options. Change can occur.

Some people are overly cynical because change often takes time. It's easy to point out how some things haven't changed, and that some people who benefit from the status quo will block change. So what else is new? That's not especially insightful, nor wise in any way that's useful to one's fellow human beings. Cynicism is not the same as being realistic. There's a vast difference. Being a realist is being smart and not being naive. Cynicism is too often a poor excuse for giving up, for lazy thinking, and for doing nothing, to one's own detriment. Cynicism is also used as an immoral justification to grab what you can, ignoring, or even harming, society, civilization, and humanity at large. These are serious stakes.

Wise realists avoid doing things to their own detriment. Realists are not naive as to what's going on. Responsible realists seek something better for themselves and others, while being realistic that it takes time and effort. To address this, we'll go over social and political factors for a bit.

Power is the Dispensation of Justice or Injustice

What is power? It is the dispensation of justice or the dispensation of injustice. All human interactions, of money, property, sustenance, pleasure, business, work, and relationships, fit under these two categories:

(1) the exercise of justice or (2) the exercise of injustice,
either of which is the exercise of power.[73]

Under liberty, we have freedom of thought, expressed in freedom of speech, press, and religion. In our interactions, (work, relationships, recreation, expressed thought, or religious worship) power is exercised, with justice or injustice.

Money is not power by itself, as it depends on context. Money can be powerless at times, and at other times money can purchase a means of influence. Here's an example of power as it regards money:

        One person makes $1,000,000,000   ($1 billion) a year.
        A second person makes $158,000   a year.

Who holds the most power between these two?

In a democracy, when the person making $1,000,000,000 a year, a billionaire, is found guilty of serious crimes, a judge making $158,000 decides the billionaire's fate, The billion dollars held no power. Power is held by society though government, subject to voters, dispensed by civil servants, like investigators and judges. In democracies, power to dispense justice falls to government.

Who Holds Power? And Why?

Who decides who runs the government?
    In democracies, it's from the total ballots on election day,
        by those who vote.

That's clear enough.[74] Politics determines economics. Conditions show who has power and who does not. The people treated unfairly are the ones who lack power. That's one summary analysis of causal socio-political factors of the variated equations of any economy's growth and income allocation. When the rich are rich, the middle class is stuck, and working families are broke, that's why. The wealthier exercise power through consistent voting. Candidates for the working families do not get enough votes. U.S. economics do not favor the U.S. middle class nor U.S. working families, because *that same majority of the people in the U.S. do not vote most of the time.*

Businesses complain of unfair special-interest costs. Officials could end such price gouging, but not enough people vote, so officials aren't accountable; except to special interests and those who benefit, i.e. the wealthier folks who voted. Businesses are dependent on officials which the wealthy select by their votes.

Economies in democracies evolved from the 1800s with many methods still in use, such as mechanized production, contract law, LLCs, trade treaties, and courts to settle disputes and fight fraud. Yet, people forget some of what changed:

1. Half of a nation's entire population, the women, had no right to own property, to speak in court, to sue in court, to vote, or the right of self defense from assault.
2. Factories used children from the 1800s to the 1930s, for 10 to 12 hours a day, and even adults got no overtime pay, no paid sick leave, no health coverage, no paid holidays or paid vacation, and no unemployment pay.
3. Up to around year 1865 or so, business owners had been legally allowed to beat workers, even to death, and keep workers against their will. That is, if you were an indentured worker, a serf, or a chattel slave, as was in use in Asia, Australia, Europe, the Middle East, Africa, South America, and North America.[75][76]

All those things did change. That was not how things had to be. So societies did conclude that agreements about what is right and wrong could overrule the rate of profit. Would that be correct, as well, for how to provide housing?

The Status Quo

People try to benefit from existing conditions, to get by or do better. They generally do what's easier, so that's the status quo. It includes *all of* the conditions, with inertia from lack of thought and effort by people, who are busy with what concerns them, continuing on by inertia. Who needs to control us? Nobody. We control ourselves, all by ourselves, doing the usual, as usual. Problems remain because of a *lack of control* of complications involving millions of people. It's left as is, since few people attempt change. Change, however, does occur. The U.S., for example, set up a democratic republic which has lasted more than two centuries, no simple matter. The U.S., for example, worked out of the Great Depression and helped win World War II, for example. George F. Will , wrote,

> "Government, unlike an economic market, has responsibilities. It has a duty to look down the road and consider the interest and needs of citizens yet unborn. The market has a remarkable ability to satisfy the desires of the day. Government has other, graver purposes."[77]

Elected officials have this grave duty, and can be known for standing up for the people. Or they can join the forgotten caretakers who "also held the office." Mayor Blah, Governor Blah, Senator Blah, Minister Blah, or President Blah.

Wealthy citizens know the vote determines who runs a democracy, so they vote. Working-class people, instead of voting, choose a self-defeating, self-fulfilling prophecy of do-nothing pity. Here are the steps: They say,

> "Why should we vote, since no one in the government cares about us?"

Then they do not vote. Then that is what happens:

> No one in government cares about them.
> Because they do not vote.

The non-voter instigated this, by not voting, not others, nor government. The non-voting adults are not in a superior status, but instead end up powerless over government, by their own illogical, misinformed refusal to vote.

The West European Employees Who Vote Get the Best Benefits

European middle-class and working households get a better deal than we do in the U.S. (And the wealthy in Europe still want for nothing.) That's since:

> The average-income European adult votes, most every time.
> The average-income U.S. adult most often does not vote.

In Europe, average employees vote regularly, so they get results. The proof is there, that voting decides the results. Things aren't perfect in democracies and change takes time, so to get results, you must vote, time after time, your whole life. Would you prefer a dictatorship? Try one of those, where you will participate for sure, like do what the dictator says, or else

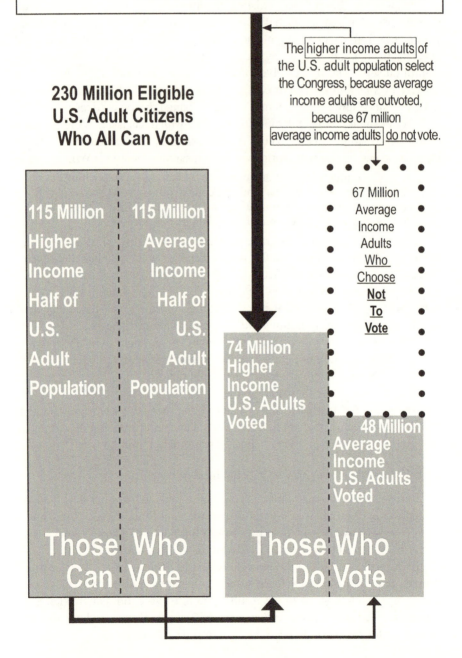

U.S. Voting by Household Income

(a) The population with lower income mostly decides not to vote.
(b) The population with higher income mostly decides to vote.[108]

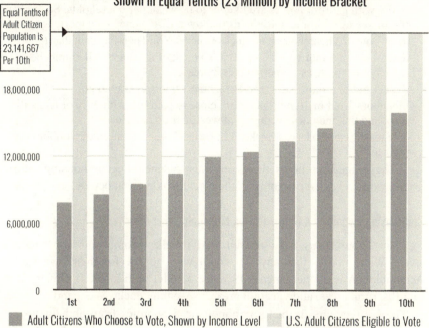

U.S. Adult Citizen Population Eligible to Vote (230 Million) and Voting Turnout in 2018 Midterm Election (non-presidential) Shown in Equal Tenths (23 Million) by Income Bracket

Equal Tenths of Adult Citizen Population is 23,141,667 Per 10th

■ Adult Citizens Who Choose to Vote, Shown by Income Level   ▨ U.S. Adult Citizens Eligible to Vote

Income Brackets by Tenths of Population	Household Income 2018	Adults in that Income Bracket Who Chose to Vote	Equal Tenth of U.S. Adult Citizen Population of Eligible Voters 2018 Midterm Election
1st	$1,000 to $14,629	7,868,167	23,141,667
2nd	$14,630 to $25,601	8,562,417	23,141,667
3rd	$25,602 to $37,002	9,488,083	23,141,667
4th	$37,003 to $50,000	10,413,750	23,141,667
5th	(Median) $63,179	12,033,667	23,141,667
6th	$63,180 to $79,542	12,496,500	23,141,667
7th	$79,543 to $100,162	13,422,167	23,141,667
8th	$100,163 to $130,000	14,579,250	23,141,667
9th	$130,001 to $184,292	15,273,500	23,141,667
10th	$184,293 and up	15,967,750	23,141,667

The U.S. Housing Balance Sheet: It's Lousy for Average Households

It's often cited that about 65% of U.S. households are home owners. That sounds great. At first glance. But it's deceptive. Here are the statistics.

- The figure of 65% of people being home owners is mostly those who owe a bank for a home. It's co-owned by the bank. If they sell, they borrow again.
- Of all households that own, 70% to 80% owe money on a mortgage. The 20% to 30% with paid-for homes are likelier to be wealthier households. So, perhaps 90% of average-income households that own, owe money on a mortgage.
- About 1 out of 3 households rent, stuck on the 60-Year-High-Payment Plan (p. 34).[78]
- About 4 out of 5 mortgages owe 60%, so most of them are well entrenched in a high payment plan, as property taxes increase.
- About 1 out of 3 mortgages owe 80%, an even longer way to go.
- Only about 1 out of 10 mortgages are close to paid off, with 20% or less still owed, and that includes averaging in wealthier households.[79]
- More middle class folks can't make the 25% to 35% cost-to-income cutoff for loan approval.[80]

For average households, that is one lousy balance sheet for housing security for the world's largest economy in the world's oldest democracy.

The Housing Inventory: A Gentrification Monopoly Takes Over

More households have moved into middle-income and upper-income levels, with success that anyone would want to see for their own family. Accumulation is mathematical. It's more people, with more. It affects cities, suburbs, rural areas, and vacation areas, as wealthy enclaves expand.

These effects are de facto monopolistic economics from and for upscale residential use. The sheer buying power of the upscale users, combined with a lack of inventory at lower prices, leaves median-income buyers and entry-level buyers unable to compete. What countervailing effect can stop gentrification?

It seems as if the only solution available to offset this monopoly effect of upscale buying power is through the power of required action. That's how any other monopoly is dealt with in a democratic free market. Nudges for voluntary action won't do much. That doesn't work for other violations of monopoly, does it? A suggested nudge? If another way to widespread change in housing in our more immediate lifetimes is available, what is it?

The spatial, geographic aspect of housing makes a huge difference. Thus the monopoly in upscale pricing can't have a solution under usual antimonopoly laws against:

- one company, as in the old Standard Oil Company case, or
- against a group of companies in a typical price-fixing case.

Housing's upscale monopoly is solved with starter homes, regardless of which companies build them. The free market should offer multi-generational economic emancipation, excluding no one. Starter homes interrupt a monopoly of high prices, which is sabotaging free market economic emancipation.

Raise the Wages? If You Can, So What. Wages Won't Beat Gentrification

About housing, raise the wages, we hear. That's with higher wages, higher tax credits, or higher levels of government assistance. Yet, prices then overtake the extra pay, even the higher pay of union employees and middle-class managers gets taken from them. That's not an excuse for low wages, but these are different categories;

(a) wage raises, and (b) housing inventory

(a) wage raises won't fix (b) housing inventory

As housing prices rise, wage increases, higher tax credits, and more welfare are just more money transfers from the employer or the taxpayer, through the worker, dissipating into gentrification effects or to the landlord. Businesses and unions should lobby for more starter homes and apartments, as payroll costs and wage increases go to real estate profiteering. All that money, moved over.[81]

Letting corporations with record profits pay low wages is not the intent. Yet, just pointing out that some corporations made record profits does not cover all aspects of this. Employee-owned companies successfully distribute all profit to workers. Even then, of any and all profits, if paychecks were to go up, so would housing costs. So after housing, still, what's left of household income?

Lowering housing costs forthrightly boosts employee net income. That lowers payroll pressure on businesses. Both conclusions are accurate, regardless of other ratios of pay. Of course income distribution is important. Economists and officials, however, can't agree on what's best. Some conclusions are listed on pp. 156-161. Proper distribution and reasonable costs *in the first place* eliminate _re_distribution altogether. What's proper in the first place, is the debate. In that, how do you cut the biggest cost, that of housing? But, back to wages.

Owners pay the workers more only when they have to, generally, in two cases, usually: (1) When they can't get enough employees to show up, or
(2) When a minimum wage is raised, or a benefit is added.

And those depend on many factors: Such as, (a) who is in charge of a legislature, (b) which depends on elections, (c) which depends on voter turnout. Then, wages are affected by (d) labor availability and (e) participation rates, and (f) immigration labor levels, and (g) hiring demand, depending on (h) economics nationally, which depends on (i) the global economy, which depends on (j) interest rates, (k) energy costs, and other things (l, m, n,o, p...) to (z), and more.

To recap, if you want to raise wages, have at it. Yet, be warned: if you succeed in raising the wages, yet only do that, and ignore housing. So what.

Yes, that's right. Respectfully and regretfully, so what. So what if wages go up? Or there's a new tax credit? Or there's an income supplement? After housing costs, so what. So what's going to prevent the price of housing from going up even more? That's what's going on. When pay goes up, landlords have been raising prices on workers and business payrolls for centuries, What's going to change the landlord's price increases?

The Facts Are In: Half of the People "Own Virtually Nothing"

(a) "The most striking fact is no doubt that...half of the population own virtually nothing...."[109]
(b) "In inheritance from parents ...50 percent receive virtually nothing...."[110]
(c) 40% of U.S. households have $0 net worth.[111]
(d) "... most people do not accumulate financial wealth on a working income."[112]

These reports come from economists James K. Galbraith (d), Thomas Piketty (a) & (b), Edward N. Wolff (c). Many U.S. people, however, Galbraith notes, have housing assets; and U.S. people access immense amounts in Social Security, Medicare, and Medicaid.[113] Economist Martin Feldstein also noted government benefits as U.S. income.[114] Feldstein then touted education. Yes, education can move entry-level staff up. But entry level staffers are needed, or they're not on the payroll, are they? Education won't alter those job duties and for many people, it's their level. They deserve dignity for a lifetime of work.[115]

However it's added up, for many people, assets are meager. So, from 1820, to 1920, to 2020, if half of all people in the world own next to nothing, as Piketty concludes,[116] then that's something to consider. After 200 years, that's a downer.

Piketty suggests that $r > g$ (r = return on capital investment, g = growth of a nation's economy, its gross domestic product).[117] Since good investors often make good profits, why wouldn't capital returns often exceed, in percentages, that of general economic growth? Even in Piketty's statistics, however, Noah Wright sees where $r < g$ from 1920 to 2000.[118] Galbraith asks whether:

(A) a higher split for the wealthy slows growth, as Nancy Birdsall posits, or
(B) a higher split for the wealthy speeds growth, per supply-sider Kristin Forbes.

Robert E. Lucas, Jr. surmised that growth is the best means to having plenty for everyone.[119] Galbraith finds that the available data cannot determine beyond doubt how distribution affects growth. "But there is, he writes, "...compelling evidence" that inequality lowers performance and "...that rising inequality is a sign of trouble...."[120] Wall Street veteran Robert Rubin finds that even with growth, higher inequality is counterproductive.[121] Sohrab Amari, Michael Lind, and Joseph Stiglitz stress similar conclusions. Yet, any government ignores the Laffer Curve at its peril, whereby taxation drives out business. But, with too small a tax base, government spending via excessive bonds and money supply led to hyperinflation wreckage in Germany and Venezuela. Oh well, it's always something.

So, can investors *always* create never-ending profit, if they just need not pay any tax for a government? No, someone must still buy their products. And is anarchy (no government) good for business? Well, for cartels, it is. Or can investors always ignore the status of the workforce? (Customers with no buying power are good for business?) Economics has 3 modes; (1) growth (2) even level, or (3) contraction. Always and evermore, in either (1), (2), or (3), economics is about distribution of the production and profit.

From the distribution, can average people make it through old age? Or end up broke? CEOs and shareholders profit from low-paid workers, who then need taxpayer welfare for sustenance, i.e., privatized profit with socialized costs. Wasn't free enterprise supposed to provide bountifully to all? Or must taxpayers (government) provide workforce sustenance? Which was which, again? As to who is getting the best deal, or a raw deal, neither conservative Sohrab Amari, nor liberal Thomas Piketty are waiting for more statistics. Amari blasts the results as "Tyranny, Inc."[122] Piketty derides the "patent" "short-sighted egoism" of "dominant classes."[123] He means that the wealthy are dominant, now, that is. Yet, the middle class and working families can dominate voting, to determine power, when, and if, they actually vote (pp. 120-121).

Whether $r > g$, $r = g$, or $r < g$, more people could have assets and cushion from lower housing costs, moving trillions from landlords to the people (p. 129).

What's going to build anything other than higher-priced housing? Nothing on the docket right now. Help is not on the way. Even in trendy higher-wage areas, how are the average professionals, managers, and employees doing? How's life, after astronomical housing expenses, being trendy and broke?

Payroll Costs for Businesses

Businesses struggle to meet payroll costs. Why do workers seek higher pay, ready to leave for another company? The reason is the real estate market, which may be affecting payroll pressure, more so than other usual factors. The companies in the S&P 500 index employ only 17% of U.S. workers.[82] So 83% of employees work at small and mid-sized companies, not the giant ones with the record profits that you hear about in the media and from politicians on the campaign trail. Can smaller companies match high home prices?[83]

So about wages, it's not always the job market that's causing instability, but rather, the cost of housing. So, offer housing within current wage scales.

A List of Current U.S. Housing Programs (costs listed from 2018 pre-pandemic budget[84])

1. Tax exemption on home profit for higher-income homes, $23 billion.
2. Tax exemption on home profit for middle-class and entry-level homes, $21 billion.
3. Property tax credit for more expensive homes, $6 billion.
4. Mortgage interest deduction for more expensive homes, $37 billion.
5. Public housing: $7.5 billion, both in cities and in small rural counties.
6. The Low Income Housing Tax Credit (LIHTC) $9 billion.
7. Property tax caps: Many governments don't have them, or they are very limited, thus failing to protect many households from having to sell.
8. Government Section 8 rent vouchers, $21.4 billion. This program reaches only 2% of households, those with the with lowest income. [85]
9. First-time home buyers down payment assistance is usually local, like $1,000.
10. Mortgage Credit Certificate (MCC): This small program is rarely used. It's for lower-income loans and poor areas. It is not the mortgage interest deduction #4.
11. Free-market affordable land trusts and home trusts are excellent, but hardly used.

Usual federal tax spending (non-pandemic) on homes for lower- and moderate-income households is 00.3% of real GDP, i.e. 3/10ths of one percent.[86] A rent tax credit would hand taxpayers money to landlord profits. It won't lower prices, but might raise prices, since the landlords pocket the cash.

Who Gets Most of the U.S. Federal Tax Welfare Spending for Homes?
Homes That Cost $750,000 for Couples & Homes That Cost $350,000 for Singles

The wealthier households get substantial direct federal subsidies. In fact, they get most of the federal housing welfare money. That spending *does not* produce self-sustaining sensible prices. For example here are 2018 federal spending totals, which are pre-pandemic, pre-inflation.[87]

$37 billion - the mortgage interest deduction only for upscale homes
$22 billion - the exemption on profits on upscale home sales
$ 6 billion - the deduction for property taxes on upscale homes, and
<u>$ 4 billion</u> - the deduction for property taxes on vacation homes
$69 billion - in total to wealthier homes.

This full welfare on mortgage interest per home for 30 years for millionaires can go as high as $416,425; on a 5% mortgage, for example, at the 37% tax rate. With welfare for property taxes, it totals about $520,000. (See p. 127.)

The Ineffective Use of U.S. Tax Money

The U.S. splits most housing tax money between two ill-advised things:

Ill-advised thing #1: The highest housing welfare spending is for upper-middle class people and millionaires on mortgages for their homes, which transfers the money to banks. Prices go up. Average folks remain broke.

Ill-advised thing #2: A high rent trap is maintained by which landlords collect from seniors on Social Security and other lower-income households, and with U.S. welfare cash transferred to landlord profits. The seniors or other households shell out 30% of their income and the taxpayers shell out the rest. Both the taxpayers and the households stay in a high rent trap, year after year.

Free Market Failure in Housing

We are free-market advocates, straining to find free-market solutions. The U.S. market hasn't added units at lower prices to meet demand. Free market theorists predict that markets will meet the need, just wait and see. After all this time, let's see it. Will quick, low-cost building permits increase inventory of starter homes in busy areas? No. Not without a commitment for more starter units. As things stand, a quick permit will be used for, likely, higher-priced units. Any type of zoning can include employee housing, on single-family lots, in townhomes, in mid-rises, and in high-rises. Even mansion zoning areas have employee units included for needed staff, to offset commutes.

Tell Congress What You Think
And You Can Request A Response
(These options will change with website updates)

To contact your member of Congress
Go to www.house.gov
On top right, use FIND YOUR REPRESENTATIVE
Follow the directions

To contact your U.S. Senators
Go to www.senate.gov
See Find your Senators
Choose your state, click Contact: Follow the directions

If you need a plus 4 for the zip code, check at the post office, or use United States Postal Service, www.usps.com - use Quick Tools - Look Up a Zip Code - Find by Address

Reversing Landlordism is a Revolution Worth Trillions

A top economist, formerly with the World Bank, who also won a Nobel Prize in economics, was asked some years ago to identify a main economic problem to fix worldwide. He pointed out good old-fashioned landlordism. That conclusion has a lot of substance to it.[88]

From the feudalism of the middle-ages of year 1523 to year 2023, the landlord still reigns, or the landlord's close associate, the lender.

After 500 years, that's a lack of progress in the economics of humanity, wouldn't you say? Many people now live as the economic equivalent of landless feudal peasants. They trade their labor for a whole, entire lifetime to stay under the landlord's roof or the lender's roof.

Federal Taxpayer Welfare For Millionaire Home Owners
Welfare = Money Given and Not Repaid

Eligibility Requirement: Mortgage balance of $750,000 for a couple
Mortgage balance of $350,000 for a single.

Lower balances are generally not eligible for this welfare program, unless all itemized deductions exceed $25,900 for a married couple, or $12,950 for a single. Millionaires and up can also receive this welfare. Bear in mind that many other households with incomes closer to the middle-class level also may receive the mortgage interest deduction, which doesn't seem so unfair. Yet, should millionaires be getting this?

Welfare Program #1: Total up to $400,000 or more total over 30 years
The Mortgage Interest Deduction:

Homeowners first choose to pay the interest to the bank, but that decision is affected by the guaranteed rebate on taxes of about $10,000 per year. Many people might choose to not pay banks some or all of this $10,000, if they weren't reimbursed by the $10,000 in welfare. With lower interest payments as the mortgage is reduced, this total in welfare might total about $150,000 to the home owner in 30 years, the figure used above. If the mortgage never drops below $750,000, which it might not on a multi-million dollar home, the full welfare for 30 years for millionaires is $416,425; on a 5% mortgage at the 37% tax rate. With Program #2 (below), it totals about $520,000.

Welfare Program #2: Total $100,000 total over 30 years
The Property Tax Deduction

Upscale owners get another $2,000 to $3,500 each year in federal welfare to help pay their property tax bill.

$3,500 annual tax reduction
x   30   number of years
= $105,000

(This is at 30 years of living in the home, but it can go longer.)

Grand Total: $500,000 of welfare <u>or more</u> over 30 years for the millionaire, on a personal home

They have no guarantee beyond this month's payment. With a mortgage, they can sell, but they need another place, which is more expensive.

So they get a new mortgage with a new guarantee to be kicked out, if they don't pay next month. Renters can't sell anything, but the furniture, before they get kicked out. These are cases of being the equivalent of a landless peasant.[89]

Many people use about half (or more) of the capital earned in their lifetimes of work, to pay for where they live to the landlord or lender, just as in past centuries. Sure, the places are nicer, with some carpeting, TV, and Netflix.

Yet the economic status is that of not owning the land and unit free and in full, in which they live. Their status is that constant toil, each week, each month, each year. Even in retirement the payment is constant and sizeable. It's required every month, every year, without end, to their deaths. They are never free from this yoke. It's a status of a landless peasant.

Residential real estate worldwide is 80% of the value of all real estate, with business real estate at 20%. Homes in recent totals are worth about $250 trillion. (Business real estate is worth around $75 trillion.) This immense residential total shows the trillions in dollars that average people are paying to the profit, mostly, of others.[90] A lot of residential value is in luxury mansions, to be sure, but that's beside the point of how many trillions are sucked up from average employees and retirees by banks and landlords. That's from business payrolls, to remind the business owners and stock holders of where their money goes.

Instead, however, the system could provide that people, by age 55, either own their homes free-and-clear; or they can have had modest rents; so they have savings and assets. Worldwide, such changes would shift trillions of dollars to the ownership and control of entry level employees. That's a monumental change in stability and wealth. That's a revolution, yet accomplished calmly, if the pieces are put in place.

Who is Controlling Whom? Usually, Nobody. The Lack of Control Creates Problems

As home prices rise, no lower-priced units are being added. But on whom do we pin that blame? Not on people who are minding their own business, buying a nicer place. Thus, there's no conspiracy among upscale buyers or upscale sellers to target entry-level employees for harm or neglect. It's just not the upscale buyer's or seller's direct responsibility to take care of entry-level employees. Like if you move to a nicer place.

It's not that modern democratic societies want to ruin people's daily lives. Or are "controlling" average people, who need no controlling at all, as they control themselves just fine, as they work to get by and pay their bills.

Yes, some limited number of people are criminal or conniving as they unfairly control a situation to make a profit. Those types of people fit the "controlling" category. These range from small-time ripoffs, to big-dollar insider traders, to extensive criminal operations of drug cartels.

Reversing Landlordism for Better World Stability

1

Landlord & Bank
Housing Assets

Owned Free and Clear
Current World
Housing Holdings

Middle Class &
Working Family
Housing Assets

Trillions of Dollars

$ Not much

2

Landlord & Bank
Housing Assets

Use Monthly Payments to
Gradually Transfer Most
Ownership of Homes &
Apartment Buildings from
Banks & Landlords to
Middle Class &
Working Families

Middle Class &
Working Family
Housing Assets

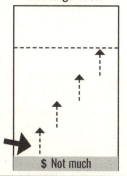

Trillions of Dollars

$ Not much

3

Landlord & Bank
Housing Assets

The Result:
A Revolution in Stability,
Patiently Accomplished

Middle Class &
Working Family
Housing Assets

$ Enough Left
To Live
Quite Well

Trillions of Dollars

But those criminal types are not controlling *all of* society and *all of* the economy, but rather they are controlling only *the affected* people they are stealing from, or *the affected* market they are manipulating. That's until the victims wise up, or the perpetrators are eventually reported and prosecuted, usually, in democracies. (In dictatorships or cartel areas, customers shut up and pay.) Also, in functioning democracies, a business can try to gouge customers for a time in its limited market share, which then comes to light, and corrective measures proceed, like customers quit buying there, or the business is sued.

⮕ When **one (1) problem** comes up,
there is no evidence that in modern democracies like the U.S., a single pervasive group controls all 330 million people, and every dollar of the trillions of dollars that the U.S. population spends, in transactions with millions of U.S. businesses, to control:
every aspect of the whole broad status quo,
every business sector,
every competing business,
every decision of
every customer in
every town, every city, and every state,
every year, every month, every day, every hour, every minute,
every single action,
just to create one specific problem,
  so that people in the group can:
profit from people affected by that one problem, all on purpose;
    and do the same for the next one problem, all on purpose,
      and the next one problem, and the next one problem,
        to include all of the problems of the entire nation,
          to make a buck,
            because they have no other possible way to make money,
              which is why that problem exists,
⬅ which is the **one (1) problem** someone brought up. ⬅

That's the sequence of events in a democracy that must occur in order that "everything" in life is being "controlled" by "them," and that "they" could fix everything, but they won't on purpose because "it's all about the money."

If your conclusion to every single complex problem is
  "They could fix it, if they wanted to,"
    perhaps you might reread this chapter and reconsider your logic. If someone you know has that conclusion about every complex problem, do not just nod in agreement at that statement.

At the least, a logical reply is,
  "Well, it's not that simple. What would fix it?"

Another logical reply is,
  "What are you going to do about it?"

If you do nothing, well, then no one cares. If it's criminal, report it. If it's fraud, file a fraud complaint. To do something about general matters, vote, at the least. And, in addition, in five minutes time or so, send your mayor, Congressman or one of your U.S. Senators an email suggestion. Government officials can affect things. They care about voters' opinions. Perhaps you have a solution. That screen is found in a web search (see p. 126).

In reality, the status quo in any one situation involves a large amount of inertia, which is lack of thought, lack of planning, lack of effort, and lack of action, by huge numbers of people, since they're busy with other things. Thus inaction combines with all the other factors to end up with how things are, which is the status quo.

Populism's Roots: Anxiety

All capital is threatened by social instability. When people know that they aren't getting ahead, it stokes hard feelings. It's exhausting living on edge. People get cynical, not caring, stuck in hopelessness, and dysfunction.

People in one group blame their hardships on people in another group. But anyone in any group, wouldn't have nearly as much financial stress to begin with, living in a paid-for home, or with rent at 10% to 20% of a paycheck.

Employees, business owners, unions, and others are missing the fact they all struggle to meet the high cost of living and operating in the U.S., and other nations, because of the high cost of housing

There is tremendous support for sensible home prices. But, because someone has to connect the economic dots, the attention moves elsewhere. Officials skip the root problem, and blame the lack of progress on corporations, or the 1 percent, or other politicians. But what demands average people's largest monthly payment? The real estate market.

When people have no way to get ahead, they give up, don't care, and aren't involved. Having a way to get ahead is how to convince people to improve themselves, and care, and be involved.

Less Strain Can Decrease Criminality

In working-class neighborhoods, economic unease brings conditions that can bring out the worst-case results, when people, seeking money to ease the strain, turn to money from the wrong people. That's a topic beyond the scope of just housing, but yes, there is a clear, undeniable cause and effect, because high housing costs contribute mightily to economic unease.[91]

How are we supposed to keep youth from the cartels, when the cartels offer a better deal to the working class than what standard economics offers?

The basic economics are all wrong for working families.

They are aware of the situation.

"They" Could Fix It, If "They" Wanted To

For any one problem, it requires immense and sustained effort. The effort must be paid for. About this, we have all heard it said, "They could fix it if they wanted to." Who are "they"? The wealthy? The governments? Let's examine both assertions. The vast majority of the world's money is tied up in:
  (a) ongoing business operations and assets,
  (b) ongoing government operations and assets, and
  (c) cash flow and assets of the billions of the world's population used for food, commuting, utilities, and shelter.

Thus all of this money *is not* available to fix problems, because it's already being used, right now. It's spoken for.

"They" are the Wealthy, and They Could Fix Every Problem, If They Wanted To

For one rich person, one company, or one bank, even the richest of them, each has enough available cash to buy only a limited number of other companies at any one time. Most companies must keep their cash on hand to operate. Even the #1 largest corporation will run out of cash to fix all world's problems. Then with no cash for regular business operations, it is bankrupt, good for nothing. Oops.

Millionaires, and billionaires have their wealth mostly held in business operations, as in line (a) above. To get such money they must sell the business to another business owner for cash, to spend to fix a problem. For *all* the wealthy to fix *all* the problems, they must *all* sell their businesses, since all the problems are all present at the same time, like right now, as you read this.

That becomes unrealistic, if not impossible. If every business is being sold, there's not enough other corporations with the cash to buy and keep those businesses open. Nor can the less wealthy people buy all the businesses from all of the wealthy. All the world's businesses could still try to solve all the world's problems by using cash on hand and selling assets for cash, with the cash going to problem solving. That shuts down all the businesses. All of them. So no one has a job. No one. That's a problem. So, that won't work.

To fix problems, can the wealthy use personal money? Somewhat. That's done by many. Yet they haven't succeeded, because their personal funds are not enough money. Even if they all chip in almost all the personal cash that they have from selling business assets, it's likely not enough. Or even close. Facebook's Mark Zuckerberg dropped $100 million to help the problems in just one (1) town in just one state, one time. Problems remain in that town. He hasn't tried that again. Andrew Carnegie of U.S. Steel had one of the largest fortunes in human history after he sold his business assets in his old age. Carnegie spent nearly all of it on society's problems. His foundation has some money left, enough for some earnings each year to spend a bit more. It's been a drop in the bucket for world problems.

"They" are the Government, and They Could Fix Every Problem, If They Wanted To

People saying "They could fix it if they wanted to" include governments. Let's take a look. Governments run what is set up so far, from stop lights to the army. For money to fix new problems, some or all current government operations must cease for funds to fix the other problems. Or government must get money with new taxes. How much will you pay in new taxes? Or which stoplights will you remove? Or how much of the U.S. Army will you cut?

So, the statement that "they" can fix whatever "they" want to, is not so easy to prove. If people say that, don't nod and agree, but say "It's not that simple."

Change involves local, national, and international factors. Any governmental or corporate office will consider your specific suggestions.

When legitimate economics are skewed, here's what happens:
1. Saving money and owning assets are necessary to gain upward mobility.
2. There is no shortcut for regular people with regular paychecks.
3. Empowerment means having assets.
4. The housing system in many nations prevents this, causing strain.
5. Legal, legitimate, peaceful means to assets is lacking.
6. So people consider other means.

Labor is Capital's Only Customer: The Roots of Economic Unease

Labor is capital's only customer. The holders of capital would do well to remember this. Labor is ultimately the capitalist's only source of more capital. Some capitalists mistakenly conclude that their returns on investment are high above any connection to the middling commoners. Boutique venture capital firms boast about yield opportunities in innovative niches of this sort, or from favorable derivatives of that sort. Which means, they try to make a profit on something. Which flows from sales or arbitrage of products or services. Even the fanciest, luxury products or the highest tech services rely on buyers whose income comes from businesses. The businesses rely on the whole economy, which relies on sales to the base mass of the people, which is labor. Labor is capital's only customer.[92]

Yes, Employees Can Control All Production & Get All The Profits. Employee-Owned Corporations Do That. The Owners Don't Object.

It's a free country. You start a business to make money. Economics starts with that. You decide how to spend the profit you make. Or you wouldn't start the business, would you? You can sell shares in your business. If so, you have a corporation. Shareholders decide what to pay themselves and what to pay employees. Owners and corporations often use profits on their dividends, stock buy-backs, and high executive pay, not on employee pay raises.

What if someone did the opposite of that and paid employees _all of the profit?_ That is going on as you read this, including in the U.S.A., with employee-owned companies. Workers control production. That's the classical definition of socialism, in case some democratic socialists hadn't noticed. Labeling aside, the result is yes, workers are in control of production, and distribution of profits, while protecting individual private property (like employee income), within capitalist free enterprise, without central planning.

See www.nceo.org for information. The firms can pay employees more.

The new owners won't object. It's those same employees.

It's the _same_ products, at the _same_ retail prices, with the _same_ profits.

It's _not_ the same _distribution_ of the profits, is all. To set these up, there is cash flow to pay back loans at a profit to any investor, foundation, or pension fund. For ambitious go-getters, to fight exploitation of workers, this method does a lot. After the loan is repaid, the same money can convert another company, and another. And another. The workers of the world await. These examples show why it's much easier for critics of economics to complain about the economics, than it is for critics to provide the means to fix the economics. If you start a business, how much profit (capital) will you pay your workers (labor)?

Selected Bibliography

These works relate to housing or economic stability, selected for relevance for readers seeking more information. Not each was cited. Some sources cited, such as news articles, are not in the bibliography, but are cited in the notes. We offer a summary of each book. In the bibliography, citations from the books use "(p. 1)" to indicate the page in the work itself.

Amari, Sohrab. *Tyranny, Inc.: How Private Power Crushed American Liberty - and What to Do About It.* New York: Forum Books. 2023.
  Amari identifies private-sector "... tyranny: ... the power of the asset-rich few..." which should be "... met by the countervailing power of the asset-less many...," via greater political participation (pp. xxiv-xxv).

Atkinson, Anthony B. *Inequality: What Can Be Done?* Cambridge, Mass and London: Harvard University Press, 2015.
  Atkinson wrote, "... the redistribution of wealth is as much about the encouragement of small savings at the bottom as it is about the restrictions of excesses at the top." He notes that increased wealth for the 99% came "... notably, but not exclusively ..." from housing assets (p.155). This supports the idea that housing assets can contribute to an adjustment in asset accumulation.

Austen, Ben. *High-Risers: Cabrini-Green and the Fate of American Public Housing.* New York: HarperCollins, 2018.
  Austen chronicles U.S. public housing, calling for high funding levels for housing programs.

Auten, Gerald and David Splinter. "Income Inequality in the United States: Using Tax Data to Measure Long-Term Trends." www.davidsplinter.com (Sept. 29, 2023).
  Auten and Splinter state that net income after taxes and benefit payments shows all income groups rising since the 1960s and with the wealthier dropping a bit since 1980.

Berger, Alan M., Joel Kotkin, and Celena Balderas-Guzman, eds. *Infinite Suburbia.* New York: Princeton Architectural Press, 2017.
  The authors note worldwide suburbanization (p. 10), and a desire for ownership (p. 58). Yet, still there are dense urban units successfully in use, as in India's Navi Mumbai (p. 399).

Bruegmann, Robert. *Sprawl: a compact history.* Chicago: University of Chicago Press, 2005.
  Bruegmann compares development patterns. Sprawling Houston, Texas, for example, has better commute times than pro-transit Portland, Ore. (p. 274.)

Boushey, Heather, J. Bradford DeLong, and Marshall Steinbaum, eds. *After Piketty: The Agenda for Economics and Inequality.* The Belknap Press of Harvard University Press, Cambridge, Mass. and London. 2017
  This book has essays on national income distribution, with a response from Thomas Piketty.

Davis, John Emmeus, Line Algoed, and María E. Hernández-Torrales, eds. *Impactful Development and Community Empowerment: Balancing the Dual Goals of a Global CLT Movement.* Madison, Wisc.: Terra Nostra Press, 2021.
  Davis, Algoed, and Hernández-Torrales present good news of developments worldwide with thousands of homes and apartments at fair prices using community land trusts (CLTs).

Desmond, Matthew. *Evicted: Poverty and Profit in the American City.* New York: Crown Publishers, 2016.
  Desmond recognizes the entry level workforce as an "... intertwined ..." economic component (p. 316-317) of society, worthy of housing with a societal commitment.

Dougherty, Conor. *Golden Gates: Fighting for Housing in America.* New York: Penguin Press, 2020.
  Conor examines gentrification effects, recognizing " ... people whom the private market won't take care of ..." (p. 233). Mixed solutions are most likely to work (p. 232).

Ehrenhalt, Alan. *The Great Inversion and the Future of the American City.* New York: Crown Publishers, 2016.
  Ehrenhalt sees a move of the wealthy into cities, the working class outwards, and the middle class seeking suburbs of a "... midlevel urban experience..." not "...l ong ... commutes" (p. 226).

Ellickson, Robert C. *America's Frozen Neighborhoods: The Abuse of Zoning.* New Haven: Conn. and London: Yale University Press, 2022.
  Ellickson has a full history of U.S. zoning, with analysis. He states that "An invisible hand does not assure the optimality of..." either total population, density, or the density pattern (p. 245).

Emanuel, Rahm. *The Nation City: Why Mayors Are Now Running the World.* New York: Alfred A. Knopf, 2020.
  Emmanuel is correct that local governments have substantial power to create livability.

Fischel, William E. *The Homevoter Hypothesis: How Home Values Influence Local Government Taxation, School Finance, and Land-Use Policies.* Cambridge, Mass. and London: Harvard University Press, 2001.
    Fischel documents that homeowners have higher rates of voting and political participation.

Florida, Richard. *The New Urban Crisis: How Our Cites are Increasing Inequality, Deepening Segregation and Failing the Middle Class — And What We Can Do About It.* New York: Basic Books, 2017.
    Florida is an urbanist. He suggests mixed use with mid-rises (p. 193). He supports, citing Robert Sampson, wrap-around programs for neighborhood revitalization (p. 207).

Fuerst, J. S. *When Public Housing Was Paradise.* Westport, Conn: Greenwood Publishing Group, Inc., 2003. (Urbana, Ill., University of Illinois Press version, 2005).
    Fuerst documents that U.S. public housing was highly desirable when first it was developed.

Galbraith, James K. *Inequality: What Everyone Needs to Know,®* New York: Oxford University Press, 2016
    Galbraith wrote in 2016 that data was limited and that highly definitive conclusions weren't warranted. (See the 2023 work by Gerald Auten and David Splinter which states that net income data (after taxes and benefits) allows such conclusions, which they proffer.

Giridharadas, Anand. *Winners Take All: The Elite Charade of Changing the World.* New York: A Borzoi Book Published by Alfred A. Knopf, 2018.
    Giridharadas argues for political participation to strengthen democracies, rather than expecting wealthy elites to fix the world's problems.

Husock, Howard. *America's Trillion-Dollar Mistake: The Failure of American Housing Policy.* Chicago: Ivan R. Dee, 2003.
    Husock finds about every mistake made in government housing policy and implementation. Husock points to good results in the Charlotte, N.C. region, and in the work of Habitat for Humanity. We note that Habitat's homes gentrify, as later the homes are sold for profit, or owners are priced out by property taxes. Habitat is not a long-lasting, nor intergenerational, inventory program at low prices.

Hunt, D. Bradford. *Blueprint for Disaster: The Unraveling of Chicago Public Housing.* Chicago: University of Chicago Press, 2007.
    Hunt shows the history of public housing; from success with middle-class residents lined up to apply in 1949 (p. 60) to when employed workers left public housing.

Jacobs, Jane. *The Death and Life of Great American Cities.* New York: Vintage Books, 1961.
    Jacobs advocated a mix of building types, uses, and income levels. (Property taxes based on income level may be needed for that, we note.) Jacobs was dismissive of suburban homes, which many prefer. She suggested a public subsidy to match rents (which, we note, subsidizes gentrification).

Knowlton, Christopher. *Bubble in the Sun: The Florida Boom of the 1920s and How It Brought on the Great Depression.* New York: Simon & Schuster, 2020.
    Knowlton cites a Florida housing boom and bust, along with housing prices from 1923 to 1927 as important factors prior to the Great Depression, while only 1% of Americans owned stock.

Kotkin, Joel. *The Human City: Urbanism for the Rest of Us.* Chicago: B2 Press, 2016.
    Kotkin states that 80% of U.S. jobs are outside of urban core downtowns (p. 184). Thus, Kotkin is correct that the suburbs and rural areas must be part of any housing program.

Lehmann, Nicholas. *The Promised Land: The Great Black Migration and How It Changed America.* New York: Alfred A. Knopf, Inc., and Toronto: Random House of Canada Limited, 1991.
    Lehmann's U.S. history covers events to year 2000 which led to current conditions, through a detailed examination of the politics in neighborhoods, towns, and cities.

Lind, Michael. *Hell to Pay: How the Suppression of Wages is Destroying America.* penguinrandomhouse.com: Portfolio, in imprint of Penguin Random House LLC, 2016.
    Lind promotes a living-wage/insurance premium model without welfare (like from the 1940s to 1980s U.S.) rather than low-wages with welfare (p. 183).

Madden, David and Peter Marcuse. *In Defense of Housing.* London and New York: Verso, 2016.
    Madden and Marcuse write that rather than it being the government which is "... meddling ...," it is private developers who are "... using government to reproduce residential inequalities" (p. 143).

Mallach, Alan. *The Divided City: Poverty and Prosperity in Urban America.* Washington, D.C.: Island Press, 2018.
    Mallach's history of development promotes use of the social compact to improve, as did Singapore, which "... in 1965 had fewer assets than most American industrial cities have today" (p. 290).

Meltzer, Allan H., *Why Capitalism.* New York: Oxford University Press, Inc., 2012.
    Meltzer presents a case for democratic republics with free-market economies.

Moskowitz, P. E. *How to Kill a City: Gentrification, Inequality, and the Fight for the Neighborhood*. New York: Bold Type Books, 2018.
   Moskowitz senses that more U.S. people are favoring inclusion of the average households, and urges the foundational work " that preceded other changes such as in civil rights. (pp. 216-218).

Phillips, Shane. *The Affordable City*. Washington, D.C.: Island Press Books, 2020.
   Phillips reviews policies and proposals worldwide, with a lot of detail about the cascading complexity of housing development. Phillips favors letting users decide what they value, such as separated micro-units with kitchens and bathrooms, or units with shared kitchens (p. 206).

Piketty, Thomas.
   A Brief History of Equality. Cambridge, Mass., and London: The Belknap Press of Harvard University Press, 2022.
   Time for Socialism: Dispatches from a World on Fire, 2016-2021, Yale University Press, New Haven, Conn., and London, 2021.
   Capital and Ideology. The Belknap Press of Harvard University Press, Cambridge, Mass., and London. 2020.
   Why Save the Bankers? And Other Essays on our Economic and Political Crisis. Houghton Mifflin Harcourt, Boston and New York, 2016.
   The Economics of Inequality, The Belknap Press of Harvard University Press, Cambridge, Mass., and London, 2015
   Capital in the Twenty-First Century, The Belknap Press of Harvard University Press: Cambridge, Mass., and London, 2014.
   In each work, Piketty focuses mostly on overall distribution of income, production, and asset accumulation. He gives sparse attention to the effects of real estate in net asset distribution and accumulation. He does sum up housing well with, "The fact that rising housing values explain a large fraction of rising capital / income ratios in recent decades ... is not particularly good news for inequality dynamics. ...high housing values make it difficult for new generations with limited family wealth to access property" (p. 658, Boushey, DeLong and Steinbaum). Piketty suggests asset taxes.

Ricardo, David. *Principles of Political Economy and Taxation*. New York: Barnes & Noble Books, 2005. First published in 1817.
   Ricardo has a chapter on Taxes on Houses (pp. 142-145). He warns that "... unequal taxation ..." on homes "... would surely be very unjust ..." (p.144), citing Adam Smith in agreement. Ricardo writes of " ... many years of toil ... " to own a home, and that "... security of property ..." "... should ever be held sacred ..," " best dealt with by "... qualities of the soberminded proprietor ..." rather than in "... the hands of those who possess more of the qualities of the gambler ..." (p. 145). He quotes Smith who notes that two factors of high real estate prices are those of "... mere vanity and fashion ..." (p. 143). From the 1700s and the 1800s, we find that Adam Smith and David Ricardo, two founding fathers of capitalist analysis, warn us of excessive gentrification.

Rolnik, Raquel. *Urban Warfare: Housing Under the Empire of Finance*. London: Verso, 2019.
   Rolnik documents the politics, laws, and history of residential real estate, worldwide, for centuries, focusing on finance. She calls for an increase in public housing.

Ross, Andrew, *Sunbelt Blues: The Failure of American Housing*. Metropolitan Books: New York, 2021.
   Ross examines the robust economy of Osceola County, Florida, where housing eludes many (p. 5), who need "... a government response far beyond ..." current methods. Ross supports land trusts, co-ops, rent control, and social housing, but concludes that lower costs in health care and college will also be necessary for average households to be more stable (p. 206).

Rothstein, Richard and Leah Rothstein. *Just Action: How to Challenge Segregation Enacted Under the Color of Law*. New York: Liveright Publishing Corporation, 2023.
   Richard Rothstein and Leah Rothstein ask that people overcome feelings of "... their helplessness ..." that it is " ... pointless to try ... " to implement change. They argue that incremental successes to complete daunting tasks can overcome opposition to change (pp. 252-253).

Ryan-Collins, Josh, Toby Lloyd, and Laurie Macfarlane. *Rethinking the Economics of Land and Housing*. London: Zed Books, 2017.
   Ryan-Collins, Lloyd, and Macfarlane link the lack of average housing to financial instability and lower investment and productivity (p 1). Solutions require democratically-controlled policy mitigation (p.12), through "... large-scale investment in affordable housing, like that of the Korean Land Corporation in South Korea, not just more profit-driven, pro-cyclical private sector development" (p.222). Community land trusts are one option, now " ... often at too small a scale ..." (p. 221).

Sendra, Pablo and Richard Sennet. *Designing Disorder: Experiments and Disruptions in the City*. London: Verso, 2020.
   Sendra and Sennet ask that real estate use includes the entry level employees and middle class, like in the Garment District in New York City, rather than the new upscale-only Hudson Yards.

Sennet, Richard. *Building and Dwelling: Ethics for the City.* New York: Farrar, Straus and Giroux, 2018.
Sennet cites lovely development that works well enough, but doesn't meet the state of the human mind and spirit as the most important thing to people, as they dwell in their neighborhood. What looks great, can leave people unhappy, while what looks jumbled, might be what makes people happy. He states that the laboring class "...pays too much of its income for a place to live...."

Shaw, Randy. *Generation Priced Out: Who Gets to Live in the New Urban America.*
Oakland, Calif.: University of California Press, 2018.
Shaw chronicles U.S. housing programs, development, and related politics. He recommends development be linked to more housing at lower prices. Dense zoning with sparse affordability, he writes, spurs gentrification. He notes that voting power can improve housing for the majority.

Schuetz, Jenny. *Fixer-Upper: How to Repair America's Broken Housing Systems.*
Washington, D.C.: Brookings Institution Press, 2022.
Schuetz has a comprehensive study of U.S. housing conditions, with political and social factors. She points to middle-class and upper-class objections to workforce housing, along with inertia of businesses and governments. "... renters do not have a voice in government" (p. 163). "Change is hard. People grow attached to their homes and neighborhoods as they are now-- or as they were in the past.... Even for people who struggle ... the prospect of change can be frightening: things can always get worse." (p.166). For "meaningful progress", "there must be some accountability to higher levels of government..." (p. 34), with "exclusionary behavior" on housing getting "sturdy" penalties, such as withholding state and federal funds for schools or roads (p. 143).

Smith, Adam, *An Inquiry into the Nature and Causes of the Wealth of Nations.*
Introduction by Mark G. Spencer. Hertfordshire, England: Wordsworth Editions Limited, 2012. First published in 1776
Smith wrote that the employed classes should be "tolerably well... lodged" (p. 83), not overworked (p. 87) and such policies would be "just and equitable, but it is sometimes otherwise..." (p. 148). like when businesses pay only "...the bare minimum to prevent undernourishment..." (p. 71) Also see Ricardo, David.

Sowell, Thomas, *Social Justice Fallacies.*
New York, Basic Books, an imprint of Hachette Book Group, Inc., 2023. Copyright 2023 by Thomas Sowell.
Sowell examines how different outcomes end up in societies with a stated goal of equal opportunity. He examines common assumptions of logic. He cites evidence that disproves the assumption. Which isn't to say that the proof might not still be out there, but what's been given so far lacks logic. He may leave the next items unstated, leaving you the reader to determine what other factors cause the outcome. It's refreshing, in a way, to be left scratching your head, after Sowell shows that the evidence cited to prove the cause of an outcome, *does not* prove the point. Sowell avoids one-upmanship, showing a respectful concern for society that is worth emulating. [Please remember to understand the distinction between a fallacy and a falsehood. A fallacy is an error in logic, which well-intentioned people can make. A falsehood is a proven and known fabrication of facts, a lie, which is another matter.]

Stein, Samuel. *Capital City: Gentrification and the Real Estate State.* Verso, London, New York, 2019.
Stein writes "... human beings will always resist regimes in which land ownership gives a small number of people enormous power of the lives of all others. People will fight back, and I believe that we will win" (p. 12). He supports private ownership under affordability agreements, citing Cooper Square in New York City, and efforts in Paris and San Francisco, whereby the cities act as the developer (p. 164).

Stiglitz, Joseph E.
People, Power, and Profits: Progressive Capitalism for an Age of Discontent. New York and London: W. W. Norton & Company, Inc., 2019
The Great Divide: Unequal Societies and What We Can Do About Them, New York and London: W. W. Norton & Company, Inc., 2015.
In *The Great Divide*, Stiglitz finds concludes that highly unequal distribution of economic profits " ... creates downdrafts ..." (p. xvii) and that there is a link between distribution rates and economic performance. When more profits are allocated to top earners, who then sit on the cash, or park it assets such as luxury real estate, then aggregate demand drops; thus inequality slows growth, posits Stiglitz. As evidence, he points to the U.S. tax cuts under President George W. Bush, and the lack of growth afterward. Stiglitz warns that unfettered markets, rather than resulting in fast, regular growth, can instead result inefficiencies such as monopoly and theft, when government/societal oversight is faulty.

Taylor, Keeange-Yamahtta. *Race for Profit: How Banks and the Real Estate Industry Undermined Black Homeownership.* Chapel Hill, N.C.: The University of North Carolina Press, 2019.
Taylor provides a detailed history of U.S. residential real estate practices and trends. Past practices included racial prejudice and racial segregation. When such practices continue, such factors loom

for further remediation, as Taylor documents. Taylor supports housing not based purely on profit. Taylor questions "a social order that makes the quality of one's life and the substance of one's citizenship contingent on the possession of private property" (p. 262).

Tighe, Rosie J. and Elizabeth J, Mueller, eds. *The Affordable Housing Reader.* New York: Routledge, 2013.

Tighe and Mueller provide a large compendium of research on housing, of some 550 pages.

Trounstine, Jessica. *Segregation by Design: Local Politics and Inequality in American Cities.* Cambridge, United Kingdom: Cambridge University Press, 2018.

Trounstine promotes vigilance and enforcement for proper laws and practices against unfair discrimination.

Will, George F. *Statecraft As Soulcraft: What Government Does*
Cambridge, United Kingdom: Cambridge University Press, 2018.

Will provided a classic clarification of political economy:

"The market has a remarkable ability to satisfy the desires of the day. Government has other, graver purposes."

In addition, he wrote, "Government, especially conservative government, exists not to serve individuals' immediate preferences, but to achieve collective purposes for an ongoing nation. ... In any society scope must be given, and in liberal democratic societies ample scope has been given, to the egoistic motives of ambition and accumulation. The political system must also incorporate altruistic motives. ... that express the community's acceptance of an ethic of common provision." (p.120).

Notes

Citations to works in the Bibliography use the author's name and year of publication. Some notes are in smaller point size to save space.

(1) See "Municipal Property Tax Caps in Chicago - A preliminary policy brief." Researchers: Zarek Drozda, Benjamin Guzman; Concept: Troy Deckert. (https://www.pauldouglasinstitute.org/Publications/Municipal-Property-Tax-Caps-in-Chicago.)

(2) Any inventory standard ratios could adjust to regional prices. A main point of this book is that without requirements and enforcement, change in inventory will not occur. Many housing analysts also state this conclusion, or write in favor of inventory adjustments, at the least. For example, see pp. 43 and 143 of *Fixer-Upper: How to Repair America's Broken Housing Systems*, (Schuetz, 2022). This detailed analysis states that for "...meaningful progress...", "...there must be some accountability to higher levels of government..." (p. 34), with "...exclusionary behavior..." on housing getting "...sturdy..." penalties, such as withholding state and federal funds for schools or roads (p. 143). Accountability means requirements, and penalties means enforcement. See also notes 8 and 11.

(3) A provision for hyperinflation could be added to protect bondholders. For this contingency, payments could be suspended in times of hyperinflation, until a currency is reset and stabilizes. The danger to bondholders is that bonds are paid off early with hyper-inflated currency that is still the legal tender for repayment of the bond. In other words, a 30-year mortgage should not be paid off with nearly worthless, inflated currency.

(4) The expense threshold of 30% for lower-income brackets is responsible, although wealthier households may by choice spend more, while still having enough to comfortably meet other expenses, concludes the U.S. Census Bureau, in a report by Mary Swartz and Ellen Wilson in 2006 (https://www.census.gov/housing/census/publications/who-can-afford.pdf). For ordinances, and rules on housing, the level could go to 35 percent. That would not strain as many middle-income households, but could strain lower-income households more, although that level is better than the even higher percentages that many households are at.

(5) "Nearly 90,000 applications for affordable apartments at City Point in Downtown Brooklyn," by Lore Croghan, Brooklyn Daily Eagle, March 16, 2016. (https://brooklyneagle.com/articles/2016/03/16/nearly-90000-applications-for-affordable-apartments-at-city-point-in-downtown-brooklπyn/) as cited in "Social Housing in the United States," by Saoirse Gowan and Ryan Cooper of the People's Policy Project (https://www.peoplespolicyproject.org/wp-content/uploads/2018/04/SocialHousing.pdf), downloaded July 9, 2019.

(6) Seattle seeks 6,000 new affordable units in 10 years under the Mandatory Housing Affordability (MHA) law. See the MHA overview at https://www.seattle.gov/Documents/Departments/HALA/Policy/MHA_Overview.pdf.

(7) The City of Seattle's household's number 304,157 in the U.S. Census 2016 estimate (https://www.seattle.gov/opcd/population-and-demographics/about-seattle).

(8) Legal scholar Richard Ellickson writes about zoning changes to allow an option for an additional 10%, not an actual commitment to build 10% of units, as we advocate. He gives examples of state requirements of 10% as a starting point for multi-family housing of 16 units per acre "...in relatively central locations...," with "...reasonable design requirements. ... Households of modest income deserve this reform." Ellickson suggests that "...stiffer preemptions come readily to mind..." for "...the development of missing middle housing...." (pp. 224-224, Ellickson, 2022).

(9) The City of Seattle's household's number 304,157 in the U.S. Census 2016 estimate (https://www.seattle.gov/opcd/population-and-demographics/about-seattle).

(10) For 3-story or 5-story mid-rises, the International Building Code was simplified. Using the basic IBC requirements lowers costs. The first floor or two can be a deck of concrete, with wood-bearing walls for 3 to 5 stories (p. 57, Ellickson, 2022).

(11) Housing analyst Andrew Ross points out two examples (p. 210, Ross, 2021) of extensive areas which could add housing in commercial strips and avoid most nimby opposition, both with good transit options for employees: (a) along Route 192 in central Florida's Osceola County, and (b) the 43 mile commercial corridor along northern California's El Camino Real from San Jose to Daly City. For the San Jose area, Ross cites the work of Peter Calthorpe and Joe DiStephano in Urban Footprint on Aug. 17, 2018 (https://urbanfooprint.com). Calthorpe and DiStephano conclude that 750,000 units can fit in the Silicon Valley commercial airspace.

(12) A paradox is that when prices drop in real estate downturns, often a concurrent overall downturn means job losses and/or income loss for many average-income people. If so, many average-income households cannot buy, even at lower prices. Wealthier investors with ample cash then stock up at lower prices.

(13) p. 200, Ellickson, 2022.

(14) In New York City a developer had a project at 28% lower-priced units. When the city council wouldn't approve it in 2023, suddenly 50% at lower-prices became profitable for the developer. The development is on Bruckner Blvd, in the Bronx, in New York City, New York. See the articles (https://www.bxtimes.com/bruckner-rezoning-proposal-uphill-climb/) and (https://therealdeal.com/new-york/2022/10/06/council-developers-strike-deal-in-controversial-throggs-neck-rezoning/) viewed Dec. 12, 2023.

(15) The reality of needing commitments for starter housing inventory isn't lost on policy experts. It's often, however, addressed by broad statements which are shorter on specifics. Brookings Institution scholar Jenny Scheutz wrote "To make meaningful progress on increasing the supply of moderately-priced housing, there must be some accountability to higher levels of government (either state or federal)" (p. 34, Schuetz, 2022. See also pp. 142-143, Schuetz, 2023). In the bibliography, some of Schuetz's suggestions are covered. Sohrab Amari wrote that market failures should be "... met by the countervailing power of the asset-less many." (pp. xxiv-xxv, Amari, 2023). In using the words *countervailing power* Amari recognizes the need for policy commitments.

(16) It's viable to discuss these conditions in terms of benefits to all groups in society because surveys, sociology studies, and psychology studies have determined that individuals and groups, from the working class to the business owners, want to pitch in to solve problems if they conclude that their contributions will be matched by others. One Wall Street insider, Robert Rubin, wrote this about income inequality, "I now believe income inequality is counterproductive to our society even if it is accompanied by broad growth," p. xxi, *The Yellow Pad: Making Better Decisions in an Uncertain World*, by Robert E. Rubin, 2023, Penguin Press, New York.

(17) Regarding economic and social stability, analyst Sohrab Ahmari cites the example of U.S. conservatives, centrists, and liberals, who together concluded in the 1930s that an economy which handed "... unrestrained power ... " to big business had led to " ... turbulence and speculative chaos." Those leaders then increased " ... workers' countervailing power: the indispensible lever for improving the lot of the asset-less and for stabilizing economies..." (pp. 193-194, Ahmari, 2023). A step in this, again, is starter homes and reasonable rents as a policy, to increase the economic agency and power of employees.

(18) "How Housing Policy Hurts the Middle Class," by Michael Miliken, Wall Street Journal, March 6, 2014, p. A17. Miliken cites CLSA Asia-Pacific Markets. In a related example, a direct link between high housing costs and poverty is found in England. See the report by Rebecca Tunstall et al, of the Joseph Rowntree Foundation; (https://www.jrf.org.uk/report/links-between-housing-and-poverty).

(19) There are many writings on the issue of economic stability. (Search Amazon.com for books on "economic inequality.") A Wall Street leader, a senior partner at Goldman Sachs and former U.S. Treasury Secretary is Robert Rubin. His book is *The Yellow Pad: Making Better Decisions in an Uncertain World*, 2023, Penguin Press, New York. He wrote: "... helping ... low-income communities reduces public costs in the long run, boosts productivity, and increases social cohesion" (p. 208).

(20) From "The Rotting of the Republican Mind: When one party becomes detached from reality," by David Brooks, New York Times, Nov. 26, 2020, (https://www.nytimes.com/2020/11/26/opinion/republican-disinformation.html?action=click&module=Opinion&pgtype=Homepage)

(21) See the report "2022 International Transactions in U.S. Residential Real Estate," p. 12, from the National Association of REALTORS®, https://cdn.nar.realtor/sites/default/files/documents/2022-international-transactions-in-us-residential-real-estate-07-18-2022.pdf

(22) Housing analyst Andrew Ross wrote that new housing could include varied types for all income levels and household types (p. 214, Ross, 2021).

(23) p. 5, ibid. Ross writes that the U.S. should "... secure decent housing as a basic guarantee for all ...." Ross cites U.S. President Harry Truman, who in 1947 called for housing at a reasonable price to be considered a right. (See Housing and Rent Act, www.trumanlibrary.gov.) Many writers, analysts, and officials have called for a housing commitment.

(24) Income Scales

Societies accept wage differences for different types of work. A doctor is paid a higher wage than a janitor. That is considered fair, generally. The incomes are thus by definition unequal, but the different pay, is considered fair. There are thus two categories to understand:

(a) differences of income (the standard wage scale, for example, for a janitor, and a doctor), and

(b) unfair inequality of income.

Every nation has a wage scale, from janitors to doctors, for example. Incomes are not equal, so that is technically "income inequality," although income differences between a janitor and a doctor are accepted as fair, generally. So, a national wage scale is one topic, which is the term (a) income inequality, like between different jobs.

This is different from another category, which can be termed "unfair economic inequality." The category (b) is *unfair* economic inequality. The unfair economic inequality topic refers to when some people within an income scale have inadequate living conditions. It doesn't mean that a doctor and a janitor should expect equal income. The term "unfair economic inequality" is often reduced to just "economic inequality," for shorthand, but category (b) includes "unfair" which is different than category (a) which could technically mean only different income for different jobs in a fair manner.

Expecting equal income for each job would be the definition of strict "economic equality," which is a whole other category, which we will label category (c). Strict economic equality is communism, with no differences in pay, regardless of job duties, or business responsibilities. Under economic equality, a janitor and a doctor are paid the same income. An example would be that everyone gets the same pay rate, drives the same-sized car, and lives in the same-sized house, and eats the same basic foods, with no extras, and no expensive items included. Strict economic equality, communism, hasn't worked out well, yet, on a sustained level, long term, when tried.

Another related topic is "equal opportunity" within a national wage scale and a national economy, which for this explanation will be category (d). In a free enterprise democracy, with equal protection under the law, there is equal opportunity to learn skills, start businesses, to compete for job openings, and to compete for business contracts. That is the ideal of free enterprise, also called democratic capitalism. Unfair discrimination is against the law, providing equal opportunity. Not everyone will choose to be a doctor, but the opportunity is equally available to attend school, from beginning levels up to be a doctor, if a person can perform the duties required. So there are not equal outcomes expected or guaranteed (because not everyone has equal ability to perform a doctor's job requirements). But equal opportunity if available for those who can perform the duties required, if they so choose to go that route. That's the idea, at least. The ideal falters when unfair discrimination still occurs, and enforcement against unfair discrimination is lacking.

In the economic cause-and-effect of a truly free economy, businesses that resort to unfair discrimination and exclude fair opportunity to everyone, will end up losing money in a free market. Such businesses lose money from losing the best available staff and losing the best business innovations, because of their unfair discrimination. Unfair discriminators lose in a free economy. "Market forces penalize discrimination and reward inclusion," wrote economist Phil Gramm in the Wall Street Journal. (https://www.wsj.com/articles/the-gender-pay-gap-is-a-myth-that-wont-go-away-1f0e3841.)

In summary, here are descriptions of these different, though related, categories:

(a) economic inequality, which is different pay for different job duties and responsibilities.

(b) unfair economic inequality, meaning inadequate pay even with work full time.

(c) exact economic equality, in which everyone is paid the exact same income for full time work, even doing different work.

(d) equal economic opportunity, with open, fair competition among willing sellers and willing buyers, willing employees and willing employers, but with different pay for different work.

(25) The original text is from Jewish writings of Biblical Hebrew of the Ktuvim, the book Qōheleth. This is also in Ecclesiastes, Chapter 4, Verse 1 of the translation of the English King James Version of 1611.

(26) See the report by Rebecca Tunstall, et. al., of the Joseph Rowntree Foundation; (https://www.jrf.org.uk/report/links-between-housing-and-poverty), under key points in the summary.

(27) See "The Cult of Tesla," by Youkjung Lee, with Robbert Fenner and Esha Dey, Bloomberg Businessweek, Aug. 29, 2022, p. 21.

(28) From interviews with Miami residents conducted by the authors in 2022.

(29) Demographers reported the following about a survey in 2020. "For example, Democrats and Republicans, who don't follow politics closely believe that low hourly wages are one of the most important problems facing the country. But for hard partisans, the issue barely registers," We group this concern about wages directly into the concern about households getting by, which is largely driven by housing, as the concern starts with the highest expense, housing cost. It found that those concerned about wages, thus households getting by, were the 80% to 85% of people who did not follow politics closely, i.e. average people. Among " ... political junkies ... " only 15% to 20% of people, the issue was not a high concern. This group (the political class, the insiders, the media, government officials and the 15% of people who argue about politics) were not concerned, but 85% of the nation is highly concerned.

They also note that only 10% of Twitter (which changed in 2023 to X) users account for 97% of political tweets, while 90% of Twitter (X) users are concerned about other things. The research was done at Northwestern University (https://www.ipr.northwestern.edu/documents/working-papers/2020/wp-20-35.pdf). The summary quotes are from Stony Brook University by associate professors Janna Krupnikov and John Barry Ryan in their article "The Real Divide in America Is Between Political Junkies and Everyone Else," Oct. 20, 2020, New York Times, https://www.nytimes.com/2020/10/20/opinion/polarization-politics-americans.html?smid=em-share.

(30) Pew Charitable Trusts, *Americans' Financial Security: Perception and Reality* (Philadelphia: Pew, March 5, 2015. This report is cited on p. 14, *The Great Risk Shift: The New Economic Insecurity and the Decline of the American Dream*, by Jacob S. Hacker, 2nd Ed., 2019, Oxford University Press, New York.

(31) See p. page 14. The top 40% for both owning and renting average 16%. The figures did not break down the percent of owning and renting for each income bracket, which we have yet to do. That may be available elsewhere. The low 20% for both owning and renting avg. rental avg. is 57%, but since a lot more of this income bracket likely rents (at a 63% avg.) than owns (at a a 51% avg.) a 60% estimate is given in the description on p. 36.

(32) Regarding U.S. property taxes, the Lincoln Institute of Land Policy and the Minnesota Center for Fiscal Excellence has published:

50-State Property Tax Comparison Study: For Taxes Paid in 2022, August, 2023 (https://www.lincolninst.edu/publications/other/50-state-property-tax-comparison-study-2022)

The Lincoln Institute of Land Policy also publishes an annual review of U.S. property taxes: "Comparing Property Tax Disparities in America's Largest Cities," in Land Lines Magazine.

(33) A study by Cook County Treasurer Maria Pappas shows that property tax rate increases were triple the regular cost-of-living increase, a 99% increase for taxes over 20 years, compared to a 36% increase for regular expenses. And that's just the average. In gentrifying areas, we expect that the increase would be much worse. As reported in the Chicago Tribune, Oct. 26, 2020, "Feel like your property taxes are climbing higher than your other bills? New 20-year study shows you're right" (https://www.chicagotribune.com/politics/ct-cook-county-property-taxes-maria-pappas-study-20201026-sguyjshaafdl3kl3ub5tmxen3e-story.html).Regarding property tax caps, a 2023 report by New York City housing official Carmela Quintos examines a staggered method to caps in her report "Transitioning Out of Capped Property Assessments: The Value Recapture Approach, Working Papers, August 2023" on the Lincoln Institute website (https://www.lincolninst.edu/publications/working-papers/transitioning-out-capped-property-assessments).

(34) p. 13 Ryan-Collins, et. al (2017). Josh Ryan-Collins, Toby Lloyd, and Laurie Macfarlane write, "We argue that there is a paradox at the heart of landownership. The spread of ownership of land has ... democratised power and spread wealth; yet, we argue, it equally has a tendency towards concentration and monopolisation of resources via excessive rent extraction with increasingly negative economic impacts at the aggregate level .... Landed property can thus be thought of as both 'freedom and theft.'"

(35) In a home under an affordability agreement, yes, there is still one controlling factor, the sales price later, which is limited to the price that can be paid by another working-class buyer or middle-class buyer. So, yes, there is that one restriction. But in such a case, without the agreement, the citizen couldn't have bought the home anyway. So the purchase was by a willing citizen choosing the limitation later, to their benefit in their lifetime, so they could be more independent in a home they could afford and pay off.

(36) "Elizabeth Warren's Ambitious Fix for America's Housing Crisis," by Madeline Carlisle, Sept. 25, 2018, The Atlantic, https://www.theatlantic.com/politics/archive/2018/09/elizabeth-warrens-fix-americas-housing-crisis/571210/

"Imagine a Renters' Utopia. It Might Look Like Vienna: Soaring real estate markets have created a worldwide housing crisis. What can we learn from a city that has largely avoided it," By Francesca Mari, May 23, 2023, New York Times Magazine.

(37) "Imagine a Renters' Utopia. It Might Look Like Vienna: Soaring real estate markets have created a worldwide housing crisis. What can we learn from a city that has largely avoided it," By Francesca Mari, May 23, 2023, New York Times Magazine.

(38) "Elizabeth Warren's Ambitious Fix for America's Housing Crisis," by Madeline Carlisle, Sept. 25, 2018, The Atlantic, https://www.theatlantic.com/politics/archive/2018/09/elizabeth-warrens-fix-americas-housing-crisis/571210.

(39) Adding 30 million new starter units for 60 million households will affect the prices of the existing inventory that those 60 million households would have used otherwise. The effects can be estimated, such as fewer households doubling up. As examined in our chapter on Austria's system, one effect is that the high priced inventory will come down in price, as it did in Austria, compared to other European nations. Any nation, and its investors, can manage under that effect. If landlordism doesn't bring as high of investment profits, other investments beckon. Again, the U.S. Constitution does not have a provision guaranteeing a rate of return on investment, only the freedom to invest, under conditions set by free and open elections of willing citizens.

(40) The Leviathan goes local, is how Robert C. Ellickson describes localized power in development decisions (p. 1, Ellickson, 2022). Ellickson's addition to Thomas Hobbes' work is apt.

(41) Housing analyst Jenny Scheutz wrote "Local labor markets function better when housekeepers and baristas and grocery store workers can live within reasonable proximity of their jobs, even though those workers will never be able to compete for housing against hedge fund managers and technology magnates"(p. 78, Schuetz, 2022).

(42) Realize that federal education funding goes to low-income school districts to help with social remediation through literacy improvement. Federal education funding does not go to wealthier school districts usually, except for programs targeted to lower-income households, such as school lunch

funding. This is true of much of state education funding as well. Wealthier citizens pay more into the federal and state school funding via income tax and sales tax, which then helps low-income students. A property tax fund also could be established to pay for school districts without enough funds. Each property tax bill could pay into a state school fund, which would go to low-income school districts.

(43) "From Rats to Rainwater, a Tour of New York Public Housing," by Howard Husock, Wall Street Journal, June 6, 2018, p. A11. See also, " ... one criticism rings at least somewhat true - past public housing perpetuated the concentration of poverty," p. 19, "Homes for All: The Progressive 2020 Agenda for Housing," by Peter Harrison and Henry Kraemer, Data for Progress, 2020, (https://www.dataforprogress.org/homes-for-all) viewed July 26, 2023. Here Harrison and Kraemer point to pockets of poverty, though in other conclusions they are in contrast with Howard Husock. Harrison and Kraemer favor an increase in social housing.

(44) See "Imagine a Renter' Utopia: It Might Look Like Vienna," by Francesca Mari, May 23, 3023, New York Times Magazine.

(45) Housing economist John Emmeus Davis, writing in 1994, reports that ... most of the nation's 3,060 public housing authorities are well operated and all guarantee perpetual affordability for the units under their control," p. 9, *The Affordable City: Toward a Third Sector Housing Policy*, edited by John Emmeus Davis, 1994, Temple University Press, Philadelphia, Penn. Davis cites the following works: (1) "Public Housing: The Controversy and Contribution," by Rachel Bratt, in *Critical Perspectives on Housing*, edited by Rachel Bratt, Chester Hartman, and Ann Meyerson, 1986, Temple University Press, Philadelphia, Penn, pp. 335-361; (2) *Rebuilding a Low-Income Housing Policy*, by Rachel Bratt, 1989, Temple University Press, Philadelphia, Penn; (3) "From 'Projects' to Communities: How to Redeem Public Housing," American Prospect, no. 10 (Summer, 1992), pp. 74-85.

(46) Legal scholar Robert C. Ellickson points out, "Prospects of gain may tempt a homeowner who is neither a classist nor a racist to support exclusion" (p. 10, Ellickson, 2022). "Residents' devotion to the welfare of their children powerfully influences zoning outcomes." (p. 11, ibid). Ellickson cites "The Effects of Exposure to Better Neighborhoods on Children: New Evidence from the Moving to Opportunity Experiment," by Raj Chetty, Nathaniel Hendren, and Lawrence F. Katz, 2016, American Economic Review, vol. 106, p. 855.

(47) Personal safety and protection of property is intertwined into housing wealth, valuations, and use. Suresh Naidu, an international affairs analyst and economist at Columbia University in 2023, touched on these relationships in "A Political Economy Take on W / Y," an essay in *After Piketty: The Agenda for Economics and Inequality* (Boushey, et. al, 2017). "The stock of housing wealth capitalizes not just amenities and agglomerations, but also local politics. Because it is the perception of security that matters for the promises of future income enshrined in assets, laws and policies, to alter those perceptions become political demands" (p. 120 Boushey, et. al. 2017).

This is further described as "financialized claims on a forthcoming stream of revenue— the result, not of lengthy accumulation, so to speak, but of political control of the future," by J. Bradford DeLong, Heather Boushey, and Marshall Steinbaum in an essay in the same book (p. 12, Boushey, et. al., 2017).

(48) To fully include all the percentages of housing available: Is it fair to include crime-ridden blocks as a valid part of the housing inventory for entry level employees? It would be the most fair to working families to exclude counting in the inventory of apartments and homes in the areas where parents fear criminal recruitment or delinquency around their children. That is not a small percentage of existing housing inventory priced for working families in the U.S. and in many other nations.

(49) Luxury living shouldn't push everyone else around, to the point of it being detrimental to everyone else. One can find many conclusions from some of the wealthiest capitalists that the most recent disparity levels in distribution of production and income are not wise, as of publication in 2024. The statements recognize the recent disparity levels as being worthy of some type of corrective action, as follows:

(1) Billionaire investor Warren Buffett stated

"The rich people are doing so well in this country. I mean, we never had it so good. It's class warfare, my class is winning, but they shouldn't be." See an interview with Warren Buffett by Lou Dobbs of CNN. "Buffett: 'There are lots of loose nukes around the world,'" By Lou Dobbs, CNN, June 19, 2005; Posted: 12:32 a.m. EDT (04:32 GMT) (https://www.cnn.com/2005/US/05/10/buffett/index.html.

(2) Billionaire Melinda French Gates was asked, "Do you believe the tax code should be changed in ways that address some of the enormous economic disparities in this country?" She replied,

"Bill and I completely agree if you're wealthy in this country, you benefited from the system, you benefited from the amazing infrastructure of the United States, and so you have an obligation to give back. And we don't have a tax policy that is appropriately taxing the wealthiest. I'm not an expert on tax policy, but I will say this: A lot of wealthy people are making a lot off of their capital gains, versus their ordinary income. And I think that's one place we ought to look at tax policy." ("https://www.nytimes.com/2020/12/04/business/melinda-gates-interview-corner-office.html) So, Melinda French Gates acknowledged the disparity in U.S. the living standards in a context specifically about taxation of "the wealthiest." Such tax rates are not appropriately high enough, in her conclusion. She includes her own billions, so she can't be accused bias against billionaires. So Melinda French Gates supports one active measure to adjust distribution, that the wealthiest can help disparity by paying some more of their profits for the U.S. government infrastructure and services their businesses use, and we all use.

(3) The CEO of the largest bank in the United States, thus one of the world's leading capitalists in 2024 is Jamie Dimon, CEO of Chase Bank. He stated:

"So the bottom 20% of America have not done particularly well over the last 20 years. Incomes barely went up. They're actually starting to go up for the first time in almost 20 years. Remember, suicide, fentanyl, crime, inflation, there are a lot of negative effects. Some people can't get mortgages, can't buy their home. Their jobs are still paying, you know, I think 25% of the jobs in America pay $15 or less. So, yeah, there's a part of society who's kind of struggling, there's part of society who's not (struggling) and I think that's a different issue, about how we deal with the policy. But you know, you can see why that has people upset." "... I'm like a full throated, red-blooded, patriotic, free enterprise capitalist and I'm unabashed and unashamed. I also acknowledge that we've left part of society behind. There's nothing wrong with acknowledging it and trying to do something about it." (The citations above were transcribed from "Jamie Dimon on the Economy, Geopolitical Risks and AI: Full Interview," by Emma Tucker, Wall Street Journal, April 25, 2024, a podcast interview, at minutes 2:07 and 31:05.)

(4) Billionaire venture capitalist Vinod Khosla was interviewed by Anand Giridharadas, who wrote:

"The thing that could stave off social unrest, he (Khosla) said, is 'if—big if—we do enough redistribution, if we handle minimum standards of living for everybody where they work when they want to work, not because they need to work.' He knew that such redistribution could cost people like him dearly, in the form of higher taxes. But it was a good investment, he felt. 'To put it crudely, it's bribing the population to be well enough off,' he said. 'Otherwise, they'll work for changing the system, okay?'" (p. 58, Giridharadas, 2018).

(5) One entertainment industry millionaire pledged to not buy any more clothing for the rest of her life.

Jane Fonda, of the Hollywood Fonda family (of Hollywood starts Henry Fonda, Jane Fonda and Peter Fonds) will use the apparently significant amount of clothing she has already purchased over her lifetime of wealth; "Jane Fonda Swears Off Shopping By Announcing Her Last Clothing Purchase," by Carly Ledbetter, Nov. 11, 2019, Huffington Post.

(50) Europe does have some rougher neighborhoods, such as Mollenbeck in Brussels, Belgium, but the per-capita crime rates in these areas are lower and the overall ratio of the entry level employees that is exposed to violence is much lower in Europe than in the U.S.

(51) Housing in Austria, Europe:

See "Vienna's Affordable Housing Paradise: Public housing is the accommodation of last resort in the U.S. Not so in Austria's capital city," by Adam Forrest, July 19, 2018 (https://www.huffpost.com/entry/vienna-affordable-housing-paradise_n_5b4e0b12e4b0b15aba88c7b0).

See also "Vienna's Unique Social Housing Program," (https://www.huduser.gov/portal/pdredge/pdr_edge_featd_article_011314.html), as of Sept. 1, 2019.

See also Public Radio International, "Why rich people in Austria want to live in housing projects," by Denise Hruby, Oct. 26, 2015, (https://www.pri.org/stories/2015-10-26/why-rich-people-austria-want-live-housing-projects).

See also "Social Housing in the United States, by Saoirse Gowan and Ryan Cooper of the People's Policy Project (https://www.peoplespolicyproject.org/wp-content/uploads/2018/04/SocialHousing.pdf).

See also https://www.alt-erlaa.at which is a website for some of the residential buildings in Vienna. It's in the German language, but some browsers offer a translation. In any language, by clicking around the website, you will find photos of the buildings and facilities, including rooftop swimming pools, indoor tennis courts and much more.

(52) In one affordable building, "It's been home to local sports superstars like soccer icon Hans Krankl, high-ranking politicians and labor union heads. Even a former president's daughter chose social housing over a posh First District penthouse," reports Denise Hruby of Public Radio International in "Why rich people in Austria want to live in housing projects," GlobalPost, Oct. 26, 2015 (https://www.pri.org/stories/2015-10-26/why-rich-people-austria-want-live-housing-projects)

(53) "Social Housing in the United States, by Saoirse Gowan and Ryan Cooper of the People's Policy Project (https://www.peoplespolicyproject.org/wp-content/uploads/2018/04/SocialHousing.pdf), downloaded July 9, 2019;

(54) See the appendix.

(55) See "The Austrian System of Social Housing Finance," by Dr. Wolfgang Amann and Alexis Mundt, 2013 (http://cms.siel.si/documents/170/docs/socialhousing-finance-amman-mundt.pdf), see p. 22, Sect. 5, Conclusion; In Austria, with " ... high standards in quantity and quality ..." the average expense on housing " ... is not more than 18 percent of household incomes."

(56) See "The Austrian System of Social Housing Finance," by Dr. Wolfgang Amann and Alexis Mundt, 2013 (http://cms.siel.si/documents/170/docs/socialhousing-finance-amman-mundt.pdf), see p. 22, Sect. 5, Conclusion; In Austria, with "high standards in quantity and quality" the average expense on housing "is not more than 18 percent of household incomes."

(57) We refer to Japan as having ample new housing. We note that housing expert Jenny Schuetz found that this factor has effects. She wrote, "In housing markets with ample new construction, the highest-income households move into newly built homes that are the top of the housing food chain..." leaving older homes for "... middle- and lower-income households" (p. 29, Schuetz, 2022). Note that Schuetz has the condition of "ample" new construction, which in which "ample" would mean enough construction so that the older homes do indeed remain for use by low-income households. But that condition is not met under gentrification, even with a lot of new construction, when the new construction is only 5% to 20% starter units, if any.

(58) Historically, the housing inventory for the entry-level workforce has had similar problems to those in 2023. There were speculative mortgages in the lead-up to the 2006 real-estate bubble and bust, and other busts. An example was in the growing economy in 1923 to 1927. Average households had paychecks coming in, times looked good, and people signed up for mortgages and leases that they later couldn't maintain. See Knowlton, Christopher, *Bubble in the Sun: The Florida Boom of the 1920s and How It Brought on the Great Depression* (p. 330), in the bibliography.

(59) This is the U.S. Department of Agriculture home mortgage program.

(60) Long Term Bonds

Economist Steffen Wetzstein discusses and supports long-term financing in "Access to Affordable and Adequate Housing is Perhaps the Social Problem of Our Generation," by Dr. Steffen Wetzstein, on Housing Europe blog, at http://www.housingeurope.eu/blog-1283/access-to-affordable-and-adequate-housing-is-perhaps-the-social-problem-of-our-generation on the Housing Europe organization website. Further examination is recommended by Oxford Professor of Economics John Muellbauer, who points to the work of Dr. Josh Ryan-Collins, Toby Lloyd, and Laurie Macfarlane in their book, "Rethinking the Economics of Land and Housing" (see bibliography), which points out "For example, social housing assets generate revenue directly from the rental income of future tenants - revenues which cover the cost of the original construction and ongoing property management," among other points in pages 219 to 222 of their book. The government of England has been paying on the same bonds, essentially, with no default by rolling them over for more than 300 years. In addition, the United States has been paying on the same bonds, in effect, rolling them over with no default since 1835, for nearly 200 years. Bonds from England and the United States are benchmarks, which investors, buy regularly on 30-year terms.

Bonds for basic residential real estate units could be structured to rely on moderate income levels for solvency. Ratios can mix in development, with 90% upscale and commercial to 10% average-income, or a 50-50 split, or whatever. In a recession, bonds for average-income housing might remain solvent, or recover better than commercial bonds, or notes on higher-end use. In mixed use, perhaps some provision for the average units can be included, so those people keep their homes at moderate prices, even if commercial or high-end use defaults. A U.S. Treasury bond default is possible, given the high level of U.S. debt. If people quit buying U.S. t-bills, the wide range of bond holders, from large funds to other governments, would wait for their payments, and make do. This is all the more reason to have more people living in paid-for apartment buildings and paid-for homes.

(61) Wall Street Journal, "Buffett Note Highlights Stock Risk," by Justin Lahart p. B10, 2-25-2019.

(62) Affordability Agreement Contracts

Affordability agreements have been in place for decades in land trusts around the U.S. and around the world, and in Austria, in a higher ratio, with success. Various conditions would be accounted for in the contracts, as is occurring. These include: (a) Sub-leases could be rented to a household that's within the income levels of the agreement. (b) Temporary increases in household income can be allowed, such as employment bonuses, investment profits, or inheritances. This lets people strive for upward mobility and not immediately have to limit their income to keep their unit. If a person seeks a promotion or better job with a much higher salary, and gets it, a transition period can be worked out, before the person must move. Fraud protections should be in place. (c) A person's assets could rise with an inheritance which is put into retirement funds, but which doesn't make their regular annual income go up. (d) For homeowners or condo owners, increased income could be allowed to pay down debt on the house faster. (e) The owner of a paid-in-full home could use a reverse mortgage. (f) The home can pass to heirs who can live in it, sell it or rent it, if the users are within the income levels of the agreement. If the heirs are wealthier, the home is sold with the proceeds going to the heirs. Higher income levels can be dealt with.

(63) "Social Housing in the United States, by Saoirse Gowan and Ryan Cooper of the People's Policy Project (https://www.peoplespolicyproject.org/wp-content/uploads/2018/04/SocialHousing.pdf). See the section on "Housing America", sub-section: "1. Building Houses," second paragraph.

(64) See https://www.msn.com/en-us/money/realestate/why-private-developers-are-rejecting-government-money-for-affordable-housing/ar-BB1k0b9O.

(65) An example is the American Housing and Economic Mobility Act, as reported in "Elizabeth Warren's Ambitious Fix for America's Housing Crisis," by Madeline Carlisle, Sept. 25, 2018, The Atlantic, https://www.theatlantic.com/politics/archive/2018/09/elizabeth-warrens-fix-americas-housing-crisis/571210/, downloaded Feb. 2, 2019.

(66) Longer-Term Mortgages.

With high land and labor costs, it's possible that upfront costs could exceed what would be a fair mortgage payment of 30% to 35% on a household income of entry level employees. But society should not give up on these employees owning a home. It's unconscionable to make no effort to help a household of two full-time employees, a couple, for example, or two roommates, to avoid a lifetime of rent paying up to $1 million, to end up with no equity, for all that expense. With that goal, here's one idea:

For a home for $300,000 in 2023 figures, perhaps to keep the payment lower, a couple might be able to only pay off $225,000 of the principal by the 30-year mark. They still owe $75,000 in older age. They could then re-amortize to a lower payment with the existing lender or other lender for more years, 10 or 20, for example. The monthly payment is much lower in older age, and it's still a pay-as-you-go method that needs no welfare. That's still better than renting for 60 years and ending up with nothing. Or if they are able, regular payments could pay off the remainder sooner. Writing in 2023, there is a 32-year mortgage and a 38-year mortgage that is offered under a U.S. USDA federal program in rural and suburban districts, for example, so there is precedence. There is precedence when people refinance, extending terms out again to 30 years. The lender receives proper interest rates. Even if the couple still owes, the payment is lower than regular high rent. The couple has equity. The couple has a value to pass along to heirs, or to sell. Another scenario is that the couple rents in an affordability agreement their whole lives, which means they're never priced out, and can save for other assets for retirement.

(67) See p. 19, Smith (1776). Adam Smith wrote, "It is not from the benevolence of the butcher, the brewer, or the baker that we expect our dinner, but from their regard to their own interest. We address ourselves, not to their humanity, but to their self-love, and never talk to them of our own necessities, but of their advantages."

(68) World Wide, Investment Money is Available

The world wide pool of investment capital is huge. At times of low interest rates, some investment capital has even been parked in bank notes with negative interest rates. Yes, a negative interest rate was selected, by free choice by investors. That's essentially a savings account paying interest to a bank to keep the money, for that fee, in a national currency that is deemed fairly trustworthy, like the German mark or the Japanese yen.

In another example, the billionaire investor Warren Buffett, for example, was described by one economic writer one time to be "hamstrung" with $100,000,000,000 ($100 billion) in business cash to invest, but at the time he didn't like the available investments, so was saving the cash in his business accounts (Wall Street Journal, "Buffett Note Highlights Stock Risk," by Justin Lahart p. B10, 2-25-2019).

The Lack of Access to Capital

What's at dispute is access to the capital. When people question the availability of investment capital, we point out that it's a question of ratios. Lack of access to capital, like a small business loan, is often a complaint in why people lack empowerment. The Grameen Bank and other micro lenders give loans to the poorest of the poor for a new business. Often it worked, and also many people failed. In some cases, the loans were an a huge burden. Some people even committed suicide from the social shame of business failure. Access to capital was ruining some people's lives. They would have done better with their regular source of income, than starting ill-advised businesses. Still, micro lenders still do meet a need of small loans at reasonable rates, which is proper. In the U.S. and elsewhere local credit unions are ready to hand out loans, even very small loans of just a few thousand dollars, within reason. So, access to capital is available to prepared people, but that doesn't automatically bring sustainability. Without available markets, applied capital creates overproduction. That's why a lot of money is held in reserve.

(69) "Nearly 90,000 applications for affordable apartments at City Point in Downtown Brooklyn," by Lore Croghan, Brooklyn Daily Eagle, March 16, 2016. (https://brooklyneagle.com/articles/2016/03/16/nearly-90000-applications-for-affordable-apartments-at-city-point-in-downtown-brooklyn/) as cited in "Social Housing in the United States," by Saoirse Gowan and Ryan Cooper of the People's Policy Project (https://www.peoplespolicyproject.org/wp-content/uploads/2018/04/SocialHousing.pdf).

(70) ibid.

(71) Declining World Population

As education levels rise for women, they choose to have fewer children, and some choose to have no children. Two of the world's largest, modern economies by GDP, China and Japan, now have declining populations. Only couples with 3 or more children cause population to increase. When 2 adults replace themselves with 2 children on average, the population neither declines nor grows, but remains the same. As more people remain single, and as more couples only have 1 child or no children, population declines. The world-wide average is heading for declining population. As world population declines, will economic growth continue per capita? Open space and wilderness may increase. The future will be here soon enough, in either case.

(72) Our point is within the context of economic advancement being made after a person has entered the economy properly, being trained or educated to their level of ability. Many people with a degree are still broke after paying high rent, for example.

(73) Power Reveals

Historian Robert Caro correctly concluded that power reveals intent. It is dictatorial power that corrupts. Power can be used against corruption. The incorrect political science phrase "Power corrupts and absolute power corrupts absolutely" uses a rhetorical method of having an absolute statement, such as "He *always* does that," or "She *never* does that," thus the phrase has that fundamental problem of a flawed logic to start with. Like other rhetorical absolutes, it leaves only one condition open to possibility, dismissing all other possible situations, which in most cases is illogical and intellectually dishonest in political discourse. (Such absolute statements also generally are not fair in other disagreements either, like with your family or friends.)

Furthermore, the original phrases referring to power and corruption in fact were not such rhetorically absolute statements in the same sense, so the phrase is a misquote as well. The underlines are from us. William Pitt of England, stated "Unlimited power is apt to corrupt the minds of those who possess it," and John Acton of England wrote "Power tends to corrupt, and absolute power corrupts absolutely. Great men are almost always bad men" (https://literarydevices.net/absolute-power-corrupts-absolutely/).

These statements all have qualifiers, "tends to," "almost," and "apt to." The statements are better summarized as warnings of the temptation of people in power to abuse their power. That's true, even of anyone's boss at work, or in a family situation. Yet, millions of people, including many of very high office, use power justly. The first U.S. president, George Washington, stood for elections, and let the voters decide. He later turned over power to the next person elected, to the astonishment of the English king, and other monarchs and dictators. Washington held power, but didn't let it corrupt him. It is a choice to use power corruptly, not a certainty. Using power honestly, within the rule of law, accountable to voters, is a choice.

People should also remember to view power as a force for good when power is used to dispense justice, protect the innocent, and hold accountable those guilty of injustice. The incorrect phrases imply that power in and of itself is bad, which is the farthest thing from the truth when power is used for good and for justice.

Thomas Hobbes wrote of this in his arguments for the rule of law under a strong central government, to protect the individual from " ... a great deal of grief." "Where there is no common power, there is no law, ..." but "... force and fraud ..." rule the land (p. 81, Giridharadas, 2018).

European sociologist and political scientist Max Weber explored a just government's monopoly of violence to enforce the rule of law. Using power for justice is proper. Sociologist Steven Pinker showed the civilizing effect when central governments reduce everyday violence, crime, and tribal warfare per capita. Government replaces vigilante retaliation with lawful courts for justice and due compensation.

(74) An example of voter influence is seen the New Jersey Supreme Court Mount Laurel decisions. Although the New Jersey Supreme Court provided rulings by which local and state government should act to provide starter home and apartments, because of how voter turnout occurs, the status quo has remained in place; to not produce more starter units. Since one set of voters who do not want more starter units are the ones that vote more often, versus renters and entry-level employees who vote less often, the status quo remains. Elected officials in New Jersey respond to the voter pressure they feel, not to the rulings of the Supreme Court of New Jersey, nor to the large number of people, who sit at home, not voting. Analysts Richard Babcock and Fred Bosselman write, "In the current political posture, neither the communities nor the state legislatures will undertake this disquieting job [of reforming exclusionary practices] unless the courts compel them to do so" (p. 233, Ellickson, 2022).

(75) World Business Use of Human Trafficking

A wide range of U.S. media coverage and U.S. academic examination is available regarding the egregious extent of U.S. slavery. Further coverage is also available regarding the oppression and murder of African American people and the oppression and murder of their advocates which continued widely into the 1900s, up to the 1970s. In the U.S. this is because of the lack of enforcement of equal protection under the law. Since the 1970s, white supremacist violence and oppression against African Americans has decreased in some estimates, but remains, as exemplified by the 2020 choking murder of Michael Floyd, a Minneapolis, Minnesota African-American citizen, by a member of the Minneapolis police force. The conditions of 2023 are addressed in the book *Walk the Walk: How Three Police Chiefs Defied the Odds and Changed Cop Culture,* by Neil Gross, 2023, although this is but one book among many publications, articles, and documentaries on the topic of social conditions in the United States regarding African Americans, and other social minority groups of the U.S. See a few of these books listed on p. 62.

To the U.S., the Trans-Atlantic Slave Trade Database totaled 305,000 from Africa of people trafficked to the U.S.,[a] (citations are at the end of this note) which is about 2% of the trans-Atlantic trafficking listed in that database table. Other estimates are higher, such 10% of the trans-Atlantic slave trade going to the U.S. Estimates vary, but the pattern of estimates are in generally similar in ratios. By the 1860s, decedents of the trafficked 305,500 people in the U.S. grew to 4 million people,[b] when the U.S. outlawed slavery. For comparison, Brazil imported about 10 times more slaves from Africa, 3,521,975, [c] than did the U.S. The descendants in Brazil were 1,600,000 still in slavery in 1860, (p. 57, Piketty, 2022).

Worldwide 34,500,000 people or more were trafficked and used for labor in all continents in the 1500s to the 1900s, according to a BBC estimate published in 2001.[d] This doesn't include east Asia, which also practiced forced labor, but "... slaves usually made up a small portion of East Asia's population," according to *The Encyclopedia of World Slavery,* which estimates that generally 10% or less of the population in east Asia was under some form of forced labor. [e] By 1500 serfdom had almost completely disappeared in China (p. 52, Piketty, 2022). In earlier years, from 1000 to 1499, *The Encyclopedia* estimates that 5,020,000 people were taken from Central and Southern Africa in trans-Saharan trade for forced labor in North Africa or shipped abroad.[f]

In 98% of the trans-Atlantic trafficking of 12,521,337 people, the complicit businesses were in Europe, the Caribbean, and South America, [g] per the Trans-Atlantic Slave Trade Database. The French and British West Indies, for another example, had 1,250,000 people enslaved in 1780, which ended by 1860 (p. 57, Piketty, 2022).

In other parts of the world: 17 million people were trafficked from 1500 to 1900 along the Indian Ocean coast, in the Middle East, and in North Africa. Another 5,000,000 people were trafficked to further parts of the world east from Africa through the Red Sea, the Indian Ocean, and the Sahara desert, according to the BBC report. [h]

African-American scholar Henry Louis Gates, Jr., notes that governments, kings, queens, tribes, and factions captured and trafficked nearby people, or sub-segments of their own populations, then transported and sold the captives at ports, for example. ("Ending the Slavery Blame-Game, by Henry Louis Gates Jr., April 22, 2010, https://www.nytimes.com/2010/04/23/opinion/23gates.html).

Regarding an example of the world's accepted business practices and morality, it is relevant that indentured servitude and chattel slavery was accepted world wide on a huge scale. That was a grim economic decision made widely around the globe. The percentage rates of profit determined the torture and murder rates of workers by businesses, run by people in all continents, consistently for centuries. "That's just how things are," many people said. Those business shareholders and owners were abject barbarians. Those societies were barbaric in their conduct. Finally, in the latter 1800s, the moral decision took priority over the economic decision. It did not have to be how things were.

    a. From the Trans-Atlantic and Intra-American slave trade databases (https://www.slavevoyages.org/assessment/estimates), select Trans-Atlantic, Estimates, years 1501 to 1875 totals estimate, column 6, U.S.A., 305,326.

    b. Results from the 1860 Census, (https://web.archive.org/web/20040604075834/http://www).civil-war.net/pages/1860_census.html).

    c. Trans-Atlantic databases, see a. (https://www.slavevoyages.org/voyage/database#tables) select Tables, see years 1501 to 1875 Broad regions of disembarkment, column 6, Brazil, Totals 3,521,975.

    d. "Focus on the slave trade," BBC News, Sept. 3, 2001 (https://web.archive.org/web/20170525101036/http://news.bbc.co.uk/2/hi/africa/1523100.stm). The figures reported to each region total 34,500,000.

    e. *p.* 240, *The Encyclopedia of World Slavery, Vol. 1,* Junius P. Rodriguez, general editor, ABC-CLIO, Inc, Santa Barbara, Calif., 1997.

    f. pp. 647-648, *The Encyclopedia of World Slavery, Vol. 2.*

    g. Trans-Atlantic databases (see a.) (https://www.slavevoyages.org/assessment/estimates), select Trans-Atlantic, Estimates, years 1501 to 1875 totals estimate, column 9, Totals, 12,521,337.

    h. see d. above, BBC News.

(76) In the U.S. in the 1860s and 1870s, opponents of chattel slavery were murdered, African-American, men, women, and children of the parents, and murdered whites who opposed slavery. At that time the Republican Party of Abe Lincoln and Ulysses Grant of the 1860s and 1870s was **not** the political party of the Ku Klux Klan and other white supremacists, but rather the Republican Party of that time stood for full and unhindered voting for African Americans.

Historian Ron Chernow writes, "One district attorney in Mississippi despaired when five of his main witnesses were murdered. 'I cannot get witnesses as all feel it is sure death to testify before the Grand

Jury," he wrote." Chernow cites a letter from Mrs. S. E. Lane to President Ulysses Grant which stated that she and her husband were "true and hearty Republicans ... but Sir, we are in terror from Ku Klux threats & outrages ... our nearest neighbor—a prominent Republican now lies dead— murdered, by a disguised Ruffian Band, which attacked his House at midnight a few nights since his wife also was murdered ... & a daughter is lying dangerously ill from a shot-wound—my Husband's life is threatened ... we are in constant fear & terror ...." (p. 702-703, *Grant,* by Ron Chernow, 2017, Penguin Press, New York).

(77) We first found this quote from George F. Will at www.AmericanCompass.org, to give that organization credit. P. 120, *Statecraft as Soulcraft: What Government Does,* by George F. Will, A Touchstone Book Published by Simon & Schuster, New York, 1983.

(78) From "More U.S. Households are renting than at any point in 50 years," by Anthony Cilluffo, Abigail Geiger and Richard Fry for FactTank, 07-19-2017 by the Pew Research Center, https://www.pewresearch.org/fact-tank/2017/07/19/more-u-s-households-are-renting-than-at-any-point-in-50-years. The figure 36.6 percent was rounded down to 36 percent for our calculations.

(79) From "How Many Homeowners Have Paid Off Their Mortgages," by Mona Chalabi for FiveThirtyEight, 12-11-2014, by ABC News (https://fivethirtyeight.com/features/how-many-homeowners-have-paid-off-their-mortgages). From "More U.S. Households are renting than at any point in 50 years," by Anthony Cilluffo, Abigail Geiger and Richard Fry for FactTank, 07-19-2017 by the Pew Research Center, https://www.pewresearch.org/fact-tank/2017/07/19/more-u-s-households-are-renting-than-at-any-point-in-50-years. The figure 36.6 percent was rounded down to 36 percent for the calculations. With a renters total of 36 percent from Pew Research, (36 percent renters leaves 64 percent as owners, with 30 percent of owning households with no mortgage = 19.2 percent (64 x .30) of all U.S. households, so 36 percent rent, 19 percent are paid for and 45 percent still have mortgages; 36 percent + 19 percent + 45 percent = 100 percent of U.S. households. When one sees citations that 30 percent to 35 percent of homes are paid for, it seems that citation comes from the overall mortgage pool, and that doesn't exclude mortgages on single-family homes or condos that are rented out. Furthermore, of the pool of paid-for homes, most are probably wealthier families, and may include homes that are second homes of wealthier households, so it leaves most working-class and middle-class people without paid for homes, though we have not attempted to find those specific statistics.

(80) ibid, with the 1st quintile at 66%, the 2nd quintile at 38% and the 3rd quintile at 26% for an average of 43% (43.3% rounded down).

(81) Yes, the money is not really "gone" but is now being used or saved by landlords, banks, and real estate investors. The use of "gone" is used in relation to the business owner spending money on payroll, and the employees who gets the paycheck. For these businesses and employees, the money is indeed not available for their future use, thus is gone, for them.

(82) ibid.

(83) The early rent regulations of New York City were supported by "the city's industrial capitalists, who saw rising housing prices as a source of pressure on wages." p. 161, *Capital City: Gentrification and the Real Estate State,* by Samuel Stein, 2019, Verso, London, New York.

(84) See appendix.

(85) Many analysts also make this point about Section 8. " ... Section 8 housing which is privately owned but rents are subsidized through a voucher system. The private landlord can charge higher rents, but residents are guaranteed the right to remain in their homes and at a rental cap of 30 percent of their monthly income. The taxpayer picks up the difference between the new, higher market rate and the 30 percent cap of the existing tenant." (p. 17, cited below). "Directly subsidizing renters is not without policy risks. Absent external cost controls like rent stabilization or abundant housing options, greedy landlords would have a perverse incentive to massively raise rents in perpetuity and capture untold sums of public money." (p. 22, "Homes for All: The Progressive 2020 Agenda for Housing," by Peter Harrison and Henry Kraemer, Data for Progress, 2020, (https://www.dataforprogress.org/homes-for-all) viewed July 26, 2023).

(86) Federal programs did not reach 77 percent of low-income renters in a 2013 tally, with 23 percent reached, as reported in "Low-Income Housing Policy," by Robert Collinson, Ingrid Gould Ellen and Jens Ludwig, National Bureau of Economic Research Working Paper 21071, April 2015., pg. 2 (https://www.nber.org/papers/w21071). Our statistics of federal spending come from "Analytical Perspectives, Fiscal Year 2020 Budget of the U.S. Government", U.S. Government Publishing Office, Washington, D.C., 2019, ISBN 978-0-16-095073-5 (https://www.whitehouse.gov/wp-content/uploads/2019/03/spec-fy2020.pdf), pp. 176, 179, 242, 244, and 245. See a spreadsheet of the costs in the appendix. To make a policy conclusion, the statistic of the percentage of population is compared to a percentage of the GDP or the federal budget for housing. Yes, such rhetoric can be used for any budget item, like a military defense budget, which may be 1% to 2% of GDP, but is designed to protect 100% of the people. While recognizing this statistical reality, such comparisons are valid in housing, considering the effects on half or more of the population of many nations.

(87) The statistics of federal spending come from "Analytical Perspectives, Fiscal Year 2020 Budget of the U.S. Government", U.S. Government Publishing Office, Washington, D.C., 2019, ISBN 978-0-16-095073-5 (https://www.whitehouse.gov/wp-content/uploads/2019/03/spec-fy2020.pdf), pp. 176, 179, 242, 244, and 245. For 2016 and 2017 figures, see p. 141 from "Analytical Perspectives, Budget of the U.S. Government,

Fiscal Year 2018," U.S. Government Publishing Office, Washington, D.C., 2017 (https://www.whitehouse.gov/sites/whitehouse.gov/files/omb/budget/fy2018/spec.pdf). A $10 million cost of the HUD SHOP program came from the HUD website totals for 2018. (https://www.hudexchange.info/programs/shop/). For Austrian tax spending categories and totals see, "Housing subsidies and taxation in six EU countries," by Robert Wieser and Alexis Mundt, Journal of European Real Estate Research, Vol. 7, No. 3, 2014, pp. 248-269, © Emerald Group Publishing Limited, as provided by Alexis Mundt to Troy Deckert and Lydia Deckert, Oct. 2019. All the same housing categories are included, including mortgage interest deductions, tax exemptions on capital gains of home sales, tax exemptions on bond income for housing bonds, use of bond proceeds for housing, (discussed in Austria's case as supply side support), and direct payments for people's housing through tenant/owner subsidies. See also "The Austrian System of Social Housing Finance," by Dr. Wolfgang Amann and Alexis Mundt, 2013, (http://cms.siel.si/documents/170/docs/socialhousing-finance-amman-mundt.pdf) who write that in Austria, ..."the major players are non the less the markets. This report shows that for-profit bank and private financing mixes in and is repaid by renters and homeowners, not at all a wholly tax-subsidized operation, as Americans might imagine.

(88) p. 158, *The Best Democracy Money Can Buy*, by Greg Palast, 2004, A Plume Book, Penguin Group, New York, NY. The economist is Joseph Stiglitz. Stiglitz was born and raised in Gary, Indiana. Paul Samuelson was from Gary. Samuelson won the Nobel Prize in Economics.

(89) This comparison between a landless worker of 2023 and a landless peasant in the year 1523 is comparable in some ways, though not wholly equal in all conditions. Both workers must have had to work each month, mostly every day, to retain a roof from the landlord (or the lender in 2023) over their heads. If the work was not performed over the whole of the lifetime, month by month, the roof is not provided. The 2023 worker has some freedom to labor for a different landlord or lender. Still, there is no respite from work each month, nor independence, nor wealth, not in most nations. Life spans are longer in 2023, for additional years of laboring, not additional years of leisure, for those in landless status.

(90) Of the $250 trillion total of residential properties, much of the value is in luxury units. That fact does not alter the condition of many working families, who out of the money they pay in, don't even get to the point of having a modest home like $200,000 paid in full (partly because so few are available for sale), until old age. These are general figures, which can be found in internet searches. The International Settlement Bank has figures.

(91) Analyst Sohrab Amari writes that "... broad social consensus..." of the 1950s "...rested, at least in part, on rising living standards for working class and lower-middle-class Americans that purchased their "buy-in" to the system." He warns in 2023 that, in the U.S., "the right would prefer to altogether ignore economic equality's role in stabilizing culture" (pp. 184-185, Amari, 2023).

(92) Regarding the very wide macro-economic topic of the relationship between capital and labor, we note this conclusion for your consideration:

"Labor is prior to and independent of capital. Capital is only the fruit of labor, and could never have existed if labor had not first existed. Labor is the superior of capital, and deserves much the higher consideration. Capital has its rights, which are as worthy of protection as any other rights."

The author was Abraham Lincoln, from his 1861 state of the union address. (https://www.gutenberg.org/files/5024/5024-h/5024-h.htm).

(93) See the report "Income in the United States: 2023: Report Number P60-282," by Gloria Guzman and Melissa Kollar, Sept. 10, 2024, from the U.S. Census online Resource Library (https://www.census.gov/library/publications/2024/demo/p60-282.html).

(94) The term *working families* generally refers to households that are reliant on wage labor and that are below the middle class level. We use it in that context. The term does not mean to exclude the middle class and wealthier households from being involved in work for their income levels. Many people in all the different levels of income work diligently, often many hours per week above a standard 40-hour work week.

(95) See the book *Analyzing US Census Data: Methods, Maps, and Models In R*, by Kyle Walker, 2023, Routledge (www.routledge.com) and the "tidycensus" R package.

As of the publication date, we did not find the phrase "the gentrification curve" in a published work, or such statistics presented in a curve identified with gentrification effects. We thought of this phrase and prefer this phrase and the use of a statistical curve specifically to describe the data of housing costs compared to household income, as percentage. These data were compiled from U.S. Census data independently by the authors using tidycensus with www.walker-data.com. Our data includes renter and homeowner cost burdens. This includes those holding mortgages and those not holding mortgages. The code weighted.mean was used in PUMS. We note that we don't consider mortgage holders as full homeowners, as they owe the lender in most cases, thus are joint owners of the housing equity, with the lenders. The cost burden for the relatively fewer households (as a percentage of population, though the total is in the millions of households) who own their homes free and clear as compared to their income level is another clarification, which we have not attempted, yet.

That we found, similar data were published in three other works with different statistical totals and ratios than compiled by us. These other works showed their different statistical totals and ratios using different representations via bar graphs.

One report was by Jenny Shuetz in "Cost, crowding or commuting? Housing stress on the middle class," Section 2, May 7, 2019, at www.Brookings.edu (https://www.brookings.edu/research/cost-crowding-or-commuting-housing-stress-on-the-middle-class/), downloaded March 27, 2020. This report includes renters and homeowners, from data from the 2012-2016 U.S. Census American Community Survey.

A second report we found is from the Joint Center for Housing Studies of Harvard University, "America's Rental Housing 2020," copyright 2020 by the President and Fellows of Harvard College, Marcia Fernald, editor, downloaded Jan. 9, 2023 (https://www.jchs.harvard.edu/sites/default/files/Harvard_JCHS_Americas_Rental_Housing_2020.pdf). This report covers renters only. In the report on page 29, is Figure 30, Low-Income Renters Spend Disproportionately Large Share of Their Incomes on Housing, Transportation, and Energy Costs, Average Share of Household Income (Percent), which has a bar graph with data from U.S. Housing and Urban Development and from the U.S. Census American Housing Survey for 2017.

The third report is "The State of Nation's Housing 2023," copyright 2023 by the President and Fellows of Harvard College, Loren Berlin, editor, page 37, downloaded Jan. 9, 2023, Figure 26, "Across Income Levels, Cost Burden Rates Increased for Renters in 2021, Share of Cost-Burdened Renter Households (Percent)," with data from 2019 and 2021 U.S. Census Bureau, American Community Survey 1-Year Estimates, for renters only (https://www.jchs.harvard.edu/sites/default/files/reports/files/Harvard_JCHS_The_State_of_the_Nations_Housing_2023.pdf.).

(96)   The income brackets used during the writing of the book, in 2023 were those available at that time which were for Table B19080 2021, published by the Census at these levels for household quintiles: $1 to $28,262, $28,263 to $54,441, $54,442 to $87,037, $87,038 to $140,307, and $140,308 above. (https://data.census.gov/table?q=B19080&y=2021). In other sections of the Census website, income quintiles for 2021 have modest statistical changes in the estimate. On the Census website as of Oct. 2024, the publication date of this book, see U.S. Census Table A-4a for 2021 at (https://www.census.gov/library/publications/2022/demo/p60-276.html) These updated reports have been adjusted, as stated by the report's authors, but are not statistically different, as follows, "Real median household income was $70,784 in 2021, not statistically different from the 2020 estimate of $71,186 (Figure 1 and Table A-1)." The quintile brackets in the updated report for A-4a are a at: $1 to $28,007, $28,008 to $55,000, $55,001 to $89,744, $89,745 to $149,131, and $149,132 and above. Our PUMS analysis was undertaken during the book's 2023 main writing using tidycensus. It used the Table B19080 figures, which also differ by similar amounts to other Census tables. Given the national scope of about 120 million households, some 24,000,000 households per quintile, the percentages should not be statistically significantly different, per the Census report's authors as shown above, so another PUMS analysis was not taken for the book's publication date. The changes for the lower income brackets, were by only by a few hundred dollars annually. In the time frame since our analysis was processed for the 2021 data, in 2022 and in 2023 housing prices rose in the U.S. significantly. In 2024, a record high median price of a home in the U.S. was reached, and the home mortgage interest rate doubled from about 3% to 6%, so the percentages might be worse for lower-income and average-income households per the time of our PUMS analysis, not better.

(97) ibid.

(98) ibid. Economists have been comparing income brackets, with some adjustments and differences between the U.S. Census, the U.S. Congressional Budget Office (CBO), and the Auten Splinter report (See Bibliography, Auten). We used the Census table B19080 2021. The brackets in the CBO report do have a higher income total for the two lower income quintiles, from adding in Medicare as in-kind income, corporate taxes paid by employers for employees per capita, and welfare (means-tested) payments. The CBO income brackets don't vary as much from the Census for the top income brackets and the middle income bracket is listed nearly the same. Using the CBO brackets would perhaps put the lowest quintile at around 50% of income to housing, still a high burden. The gentrification curve wouldn't be as steep with the lowest income quintile at 50% for a cost of housing, but, that's little consolation to full-time employees who still pay half (50%) of their income to housing. And that's the national average, including areas with few jobs, and lower costs, not what people pay in busy areas where jobs are being created, where people want to live to get ahead, and where housing demand is highest, which is true for Census brackets as well. To remain consistent, we had to select one set of brackets to use, so we used Census table B19080 for 2021 with Census costs of housing reported for 2021 in Census codes GRPIP and OCPIP.

Economist Austin Clemons researched the differing income brackets offered as discussed in his article "New research doesn't overturn consensus on rising U.S. income inequality," published by the Washington Center for Equitable Growth, Jan. 10, 2024 (https://equitablegrowth.org/new-research-doesnt-overturn-consensus-on-rising-u-s-income-inequality/). About the CBO brackets, he wrote:

"Finally, to create its 'income after taxes and transfers' concept, the Congressional Budget Office subtracts federal taxes paid, which includes individual income taxes, as well as corporate taxes and federal excise taxes on items such as gasoline and alcoholic beverages. Some individuals who receive refundable tax credits, such as the Earned Income Tax Credit, could see their income increase in this step. Once taxes are subtracted, means-tested transfers, including Medicaid, the Children's Health Insurance Program, SNAP benefits, and others, are added."

"To be sure, the CBO income concept includes some things that most people probably don't think of as income. Medicare and Medicaid are not cash income, for instance, and corporate taxes are not something most workers consider to be part of their incomes. But, generally speaking, it is fairly clear why these items are included when studying the concentration of income in the U.S. economy."

The main debate among researchers has not been about any findings of a large change in the income bracket amounts in net dollars, but whether the top brackets were gaining an unfair share of national income, compared to the middle class and lower-level employees. Some economists concluded that was the case, while the Auten-Splinter report found a modest drop in the share of the top income brackets, mostly in discussion of the top 5% and top 1%. Therefore, the B19080 brackets used for percentages of household income compared to cost of housing show the broad general trends we were aiming to convey. These are the effects on net income for working families and entry-level employees of housing, in percentages, compared to the middle income and higher income brackets, for which the Census data gives reasonable measurements of such trends.

For readers who tout the Auten-Splinter data and conclusions, we note that the income brackets used for our PUMS analysis are very close to the Auten-Splinter data. We did not find in Auten-Splinter reports a quintile income bracket provided, but found income statistics in two Auten-Splinter tables, which generally match the income data used from the Census table A-4a, Table B19080, and other Census reports. Please see for 2019 income, Figure B7 on p. 60 in Figure B9 on p. 61 of the Auten-Splinter Online Appendix, Income Inequality in the United States: Using Tax Data to Measure Long-Term Trends, by Gerald Auten and David Splinter, May 22, 2024 (https://davidsplinter.com/AutenSplinter-Tax_Data_and_Inequality_onlineapp.pdf). In B7, income shares of the bottom income bracket (quintile) are shown at about 5%. This matches Census reports closely, which in various years around then are about 3% for that bracket. Thus if both Auten-Splinter and the Census have the bottom quintile at around 3% to 5% of the income share, then the annual income bracket would also be generally close as well. B9 shows the real income after tax transfers for the bottom 50% of income brackets in 2019 at $29,000 annually, which matches generally with the brackets from the Census in Table B19080 2021 we used, which showed $28,261 for the bottom 20% quintile for 2021. Table B19080 has the bottom 40% at $54,4400 annually for 2021. So the Auten-Splinter Table B9 averages a lower after tax transfer income than shown in TableB19080 for 2021, which we used as the latest data available during the book's writing. The years are close, from 2019 to 2021, so that a general comparison is valid. This shows that the Auten-Splinter data regarding income brackets at the bottom level generally matches Census income data at least for general income bracket information. This is for comparing income to housing expenses to obtain a general picture. The Auten-Splinter Using data or Census data as best we can determine in comparing these reports, show the same general income amounts. The main point that some economists and journalists point to in the Auten-Splinter reporting is that the top 1% and top 5% levels dropped modestly in shares of national income. And that was a modest drop. Auten-Splinter reports didn't change the general income brackets in a statistically significant manner compared to U.S. Census bracket reports, as best we can determine from the limited references in Figure B7 and B9 in the Auten-Splinter data appendix.

(99) The publicly distributed **price sheets** were obtained by the authors by personal visits to the builder's sales offices on Oct. 9, 2024, and are on file with the publisher. Because the price sheets and the corresponding website views are under copyright law permission protections by each builder, the publisher chose not to attempt to cite the specific builder's price sheet material under copyright, which would have needed permission of each builder. The publisher expected that these corporate builders most likely would not grant permission for their corporate names and price sheets to be cited in a commercial book such as Priced Out, published by an unaffiliated corporation, Public Policy Press. Such corporations are not expected to want to be affiliated with this commercial book, and with the recommendations the book makes. Such price information, square footage, and the base home amenities were information offered openly to the public in the advertised prices and itemized property and construction descriptions given to buyers and to prospective buyers, basically any member of the public, who asked for the information at the sales offices, as the authors did.

Confirmation of Oct., 2024 base prices can be made, if confirmation is desired. The base prices are standards that do not include extra add-ons, which are common to U.S. corporate builders and can be estimated with approximate accuracy. These can be verified by prices of the homes on the blocks and streets identified below. The sales prices have add-ons in most cases, to be subtracted out to confirm base prices. The prices are found in those deeds and mortgages to the properties, which sold in October of 2024 or thereabouts, which are public information in the public records of Pinal County, Arizona. In addition, websites such as www.Realtor.com and www.Zillow.com cite these public records to provide sale prices of homes, which are generally available to the public, showing, square footage, amenity add-ons, sales date, and sales prices. Since we used a mid-range base price, the estimate is still fair as it wasn't the lowest price offered per sq. ft., (around $155 per sq. ft.) so the example price could include usual add-ons. Examples are also given for fully finished home prices in the comparisons. These sale prices can also be confirmed as explained above.

The streets and ranges of blocks shown and cited in the examples given are: In the City of Coolidge, Arizona, Pinal County, Arizona, the west 1600 and west 1700 blocks of Inca Lane are used for the photos and the first builder's example ($162 to 223 per sq. ft.). For the second builder's example were actual move-in completed homes (12 homes offered on Oct. 11, 2024) at prices from $155 per sq. ft. (2,127 sq. ft. for $328,990) to $173 per sq. ft. (1,650 sq. ft for $284,990) on the west 1300 to 1400 of Hopi Drive, Toltec, Drive, and Pelayo Street, and the west 1600 to 1700 Laguna Drive. For this example, the average price per sq. ft. for the 12 homes was $165 per sq. ft., so that was used. Based on similar tax and property insurance bills of newer single family homes in the area, a tax bill of $1,100 annually was used (remember please that some Arizona property taxes are lower than many other states) and $1,100 annually for the insurance was used for the studio. For the cottage, annual bills of $1,200 for taxes and $1,200 for insurance was used. HOA fees are extra, but for information purposes, are about $45 to $50 a month for new home subdivision in this area.

(100) Photo by Harald Schilly, Atzgersdorf, 1230 Vienna, Austria - panoramio (3).jpg Created: 2 March 2014, This file is licensed under the Creative Commons Attribution-Share Alike 3.0 Unported license, https://creativecommons.org/licenses/by-sa/3.0/ CC BY-SA 3.0.

(101) Photo by Harald Schilly, Atzgersdorf, 1230 Vienna, Austria - panoramio (3).jpg Created: 2 March 2014, One of the housing buildings, with church in the foreground. This file is licensed under the Creative Commons Attribution-Share Alike 3.0 Unported license, https://creativecommons.org/licenses/by-sa/3.0/ CC BY-SA 3.0./

(102) Photo by Thomas Ledi, CC BY-SA 4.0, File: Wohnpark Alterlaa Dachblick von Block C1.jpg Created: 2016-11-01 13:00:01. A view from block C to block B, with block A in the background. (Wohnpark Alterlaa Dachblick von Block C1 Im Vordergrund die Wohnparkkirche. Dahinter Block B.) This file is licensed under the Creative Commons Attribution-Share Alike 4.0 International license, https://creativecommons.org/licenses/by-sa/4.0.

(103) Photo by Thomas Ledi, File: Alterlaa Schwimmbad (hinterer A- Block).jpg Created: 26 June 2011, Rooftop swimming pool. This file is licensed under the Creative Commons Attribution-Share Alike 3.0 Unported license, https://creativecommons.org/licenses/by-sa/3.0/deed.en CC BY-SA 3.0.

(104) From the Austrian Ministry of Finance, Tax Book (Steuerbuch) English version downloaded Feb.10, 2023. from https://www.bmf.gv.at/en/current-issues/The-2022-Tax-Book---Tips-for-Employee-Tax-Assessment-2021.html then download: https://www.bmf.gv.at/dam/jcr:c6cc0ce1-f260-4bd8-9435-e86cf31fe08b/Steuerbuch2022-en-v03-barrierefrei.pdf. Tax rates in the United States are from the IRS website as of Feb. 10, 2023 https://www.irs.gov/newsroom/irs-provides-tax-inflation-adjustments-for-tax-year-2023. The currency conversion was done on the website: https://www.xe.com/currencyconverter.

(105) ibid.

(106) Economist Michael Lind concludes, "The greatest hoax of our time is ... that bargaining power has nothing to do with pay." (pp. 1-2, Lind, 2023.) Lind sees 2023 U.S. practices as unduly favorable to owners, not employees. Another example on the other end of the ratio is presented by Holman W. Jenkins, Jr., who notes that outside recruits for top corporate jobs don't have the jobs yet, thus corporate boards "couldn't have been in the pockets of executives they had yet to hire." ("Capitalism Works, Says ChatGPT," by Holman W. Jenkins, Jr., Nov. 21, 2023, Wall Street Journal.)

(107) From authors' data analysis of U.S. Census data for voting matched to income brackets, from the Voting and Registration Supplement to the Current Population Survey and U.S. Census income quintiles Table B19080) adjusted into population tenths.

The Census voting was self-reported by citizens when asked. Actual voter turnout matched to income is a method to find this more precisely. We examined this, but the data sets don't match, very precisely. There is voter precinct turnout data, which is very precise, but the boundaries don't match well with Census tracts data, which is also fairly precise.

Because it is people saying whether or not they voted to a Census canvasser, the Census turnout report may overstate turnout in lower income areas, from what we've seen of actual precinct turnout records of voters. Turnout is usually lower in lower-income areas, than in middle-class and wealthy areas. In addition, from directly working on voter registration and ballot petitioning, we have seen that when people are asked by canvassers if they are currently registered to vote, up to 50% of people may say yes, when, in fact, they were not registered. The Census survey may also understate high-income turnout, from what we've seen in precinct turnout, which is usually very high in the wealthiest areas. A comparison, for example, is turnout in Kenilworth, IL, a highly wealthy area (but small in size for easier comparison) in suburban Illinois, with Robbins, IL, a very low income area (but small in size for easier comparison) in suburban Illinois. (We have been to both Kenilworth and Robbins many times, on working on elections in those areas. That would be more precise, and could be expanded for increased sampling, but requires further research. Voter turnout can be measured at the block level from municipal or county records to match to Census tract income, but that requires matching the individual voter turnout for citizens on that block to get a block turnout total. See https://www.census.gov/content/dam/Census/library/publications/2021/demo/p20-583.pdf

(108) ibid.

(109) p. 257, Piketty, 2014.

(110) p. 983, Piketty, 2020.

(111) See Tables 1 and 2, "Recent Trends in Household Wealth in the United State: Rising Debt and the Middle-Class Squeeze–an Update to 2007," by Edward N. Wolff, Levy Economics Institute of Bard College,

Working Paper 589 (2010), cited on p. 166, Galbraith, 2016. Wolff puts the total share of net national wealth of assets minus liabilities at 0.2% for the bottom 40% of households, which Galbraith calls " ... effectively zero ... ", and which seems like a fair description, at that rate.

(112) p. 133 Galbraith, 2016.

(113) pp. 3-4, Galbraith, 2016.

(114) See, "Piketty's Numbers Don't Add Up, Ignoring dramatic changes in tax rules since 1980 creates the false impression that income inequality is rising," by Martin Feldstein, Wall Street Journal, May 14, 2014. On another point, Feldstein took issue with Piketty's math. In 1980 and 1986, U.S. people moved income around to use the new lower tax rates. Piketty counted the moved-around money as new wealth, which Feldstein concludes it was not, which may be likely.

(115) Whatever the conditions are, there is a national wage scale, with a minimum, at any given time, always. Martin Feldstein suggested a mix of welfare payments into the minimum wage ("A Hype-Free Way to Help Low-Wage Worker: Minimum-wage hikes are job killers. Better to integrate earnings at the current rate with welfare payments," by Martin Feldstein, Dec. 12, 2013, Wall Street Journal). This safety net idea has taxpayers subsidizing the profits of business owners by taxpayers adding extra dollars to the wages for food and expenses. This is rather than sufficient wages being paid out of the profits of the free-enterprise economy. In 1937, the U.S. Supreme Court pointed this out when upholding minimum wage laws. "The exploitation of a class of workers who are in an unequal position with respect to bargaining power, and are thus relatively defenseless against the denial of a living wage, is not only detrimental to their health and wellbeing, but casts a direct burden for their support upon the community. What these workers lose in wages, the taxpayers are called upon to pay. The bare cost of living must be met." See U.S. Supreme Court, West Coast Hotel Co. v. Parrish, 300 U.S. 379 (1937), decided March 29, 1937 (https://supreme.justia.com/cases/federal/us/300/379). In the past, one example had been full-time Walmart employees who qualified for welfare food stamps.

Feldstein writes (cited above),

"Higher wages that are not the result of greater productivity force firms to raise prices to cover their costs...."

A more complete statement, rather, is: Higher wages that are not the result of greater productivity force firms to (a) raise prices to cover their costs *or to* (b) lower profit to the firm's owners. Profit is planned, or the business would not start operations. The question is the level of profit and its distribution. Case (b) is possible, unless there is not enough profit to even pay the sustenance of the owner, as well as the sustenance of the worker. Looking again at Feldstein's statement, notice how the level of profit to owners is left out of this math equation.

(116) p. 33, Piketty, 2022.

(117) Overall Economics

pp. 358-376, Piketty, 2014. We bring this topic up to highlight housing as a factor of middle-class and working-class cash flow, savings, and wealth, not to try to deconstruct the world's economy as Thomas Piketty and others are working on. Below are citations to some of the conclusions, some in disagreement with Piketty, and others who lean towards Piketty's conclusions. Such scope is beyond our limited research resources for this housing book. We offer only a short set of observations as follows.

The debates between economists and policy makers on distribution of income is immense. Economist James K. Galbraith, has surveyed the available worldwide research on income distribution for decades, with analysis and research of his own, backed by resources from of one of the world's major universities, the University of Texas. Galbraith concludes that the debate still lacks enough raw statistical evidence to make full conclusions. (See p. 124 in *Priced Out*.) Many people are working on the data, so hopefully clarity will emerge about where the money is going. Then the task would remain to come to a fair, prudent conclusion on distribution.

National Income Distribution: Income Inequality Levels: Fair? or Unfair?

Among reports of better or fair results for U.S. employees are:

(1) "Income Inequality in the United States: Using Tax Data to Measure Long-Term Trends", by Gerald Auten, Office of Tax Analysis, U.S. Treasury Department, and David Splinter Joint Committee on Taxation, U.S. Congress, Sept. 29, 2023 (https://davidsplinter.com/AutenSplinter-Tax_Data_and_Inequality.pdf) - "Concerns about income inequality emphasize the importance of accurate income measures. Estimates of top income shares based only on individual tax returns are biased by tax-base changes, social changes, and missing income sources. This paper addresses these shortcomings and presents new estimates of the distribution of national income since 1960. Our analysis of pre-tax income shows that top income shares are lower and have increased less since 1980 than other studies using tax data. In addition, increasing government transfers and tax progressivity have resulted in rising real incomes for all income groups and little change in after-tax top income shares."

(2) "The Myth of Income Stagnation," by Michael R. Strain, Dec. 15, 2022, Project Syndicate: The World's Opinion Page. Strain writes, "According to the conventional wisdom, ... income has not increased

for decades ... " yet Strain points to "... significant consumption gains ... " in 2022, compared to 1992. "Could this material progress really have coincided with stagnating incomes? ... Fortunately, we can find clarity in statistics released last month by the nonpartisan Congressional Budget Office - the referee in US economic policy debates - which confirm that the conventional wisdom is off base" (https://www.project-syndicate.org/commentary/myth-of-us-income-stagnation-by-michael-r-strain-2022-12). Strain writes, "According to the CBO, median household income from market activities – labor, business, and capital income, as well as retirement income from past services – was not stagnant from 1990 to 2019. Instead, after adjusting for inflation, it grew by 26%. This is in line with wage growth. By my calculations using Bureau of Labor Statistics (BLS) data, inflation-adjusted average wages for nonsupervisory workers grew by around one-third over this period. ... After factoring in social insurance benefits (from Social Security and unemployment insurance, for example), government safety-net benefits (such as food stamps), and federal taxes, the CBO finds that median household income increased by 55% from 1990 to 2019, which is significantly faster than wage growth and certainly not stagnate. The bottom 20% of households enjoyed even greater gains, with market income growth of 51% and after-tax-and-transfer income growth of 74%."

(3) Holman W. Jenkins, Jr., a leading financial columnist, wrote that economist Thomas Piketty's has characterized CEO pay as "insider theft." Jenkins counters that outside recruits for top corporate jobs don't have the jobs yet, thus corporate boards "couldn't have been in the pockets of executives they had yet to hire." It's a valid point. What if executive pay were cut to provide more for low-end employees profits, while keeping payouts to shareholders and owners the same? Then prices don't need to rise. Who can prove this? Do higher-paid executives cleverly produce more profit for owners, or do more loyal, stable employees produce more profit for owners? On distribution of income, Jenkins states that Piketty's data missed "...the role of growing government transfers in the financial strategies of individuals and households." Thus "...all income groups have seen rising real income over the past 40 years with no shift toward the rich...," citing Auten and Splinter's report above. ("Capitalism Works, Says ChatGPT," by Holman W. Jenkins, Jr., Nov. 21, 2023, Wall Street Journal). In this Holman concludes that bargaining power does affect pay in offers made and accepted, between company boards of directors and the executives. Michael Lind concludes that bargaining power, or a lack of it, affects pay for the lower-end workforce (pp. 1-2, 148, Lind, 2023). So, we report agreement on something: bargaining power exists.

Among conclusions of worse or unfair results for U.S. employees are:

(1) The Economic Policy Institute reported "Since 1973, hourly compensation of the vast majority of American workers has not risen in line with economy-wide productivity. In fact, hourly compensation has almost stopped rising at all," This is cited by analyst Anand Giridharada. He writes, "The institute observes that the average American worker grew 72 percent more productive between 1973 and 2014, but the median worker's pay rose only about 9 percent in this time. In short, America doesn't have a problem of lagging productivity so much as a problem of the gains from productivity being captured by elites" (p. 40, Giridharada, 2018).

(2) In Congressional testimony, economist Ben Zipperer of The Economic Policy Institute (cited p. 152, p. 210, Lind 2023) reported that from 1938 to 2019, the U.S. national minimum wages rose in conjunction with profits from productivity gains, until 1968. [After that, we surmise, profits from productivity gains went to business profits and manager salaries, while most employees received no effective raises from those profits.] The federal minimum wage adjusted for inflation (2019 dollars) peaked at $10.15 an hour in 1968 (which was $1.60 in 1968). See "Gradually Raising the Minimum Wage to $15 Would Be Good for Workers, Good for Businesses, and Good for the Economy," testimony before the U.S. House of Representatives Committee on Education and Labor, Feb. 7, 2019. Lind writes "Had the minimum wage continued to rise with productivity growth, in 2024 it would be $22.19 an hour (in 2019 dollars)" (p. 152, Lind, 2023).

(3)"After Inflation, People Making U.S. Minimum Wage Are Earning Less Now Than 60 Years Ago," by Nicholas Vega, CNBC, July 2022 (cited on p. 210, Lind 2023). Citing Vega, Lind writes, "A minimum wage worker in 2022 made $5,000 less a year in inflation-adjusted dollars."

(4) Another source of income data is from the Social Security Administration. CNN published an opinion report from researchers Elise Gould and Josh Bivens of the Economic Policy Institute, Jan. 18, 2024. They write, "The latest SSA data demonstrates how vastly unequal earnings growth has been between 1979 and 2022. Over that period, inflation-adjusted annual earnings for the top 1% and top 0.1% skyrocketed by 171.7% and 344.4%, respectively, while earnings for the bottom 90% grew just 32.9%. This unequal growth has seen a rising share of total earnings in the US economy accumulate at the top of the wage ladder." The article is: "Why a new study gives a misleading view of inequality in America" (https://www.cnn.com/2024/01/17/opinions/inequality-earnings-economy-gould-bivens/index.html).

The Asset Tax, i.e., Wealth Tax: Profit and earned income for personal use is the proper thing to tax, if any tax revenue is needed, set by democratically-elected governments, which is fair.

One flaw of the asset tax is if it attempts to target "unfair" levels of profits, by adding a set cost, a set tax, to only part of the transaction. This may have flawed results, skewing transactions, or failing to remedy the unfair situation. Fines or tariffs on unfair commerce are more targeted.

Trying to bring fairness to profits, by identifying the "unfair" component of "unfair" profit by taxing each of these components or only the "unfair" component is a waste of time, when no laws have been broken, but rather the commerce consists of transactions between willing customers and willing sellers. Tax the profit taken for personal use, high, or low, huge, or minuscule, ongoing, or a one-time bonanza.

The futility of placing a moral tag on each dollar of a transaction can be shown in the example of a small business startup in a garage, or a dorm room, or a single store. People root for the little guy starting out whose few dollars of profit in the transaction are fair and morally unimpeachable, a good thing, without any doubt.

When those people working in the garage, dorm room, or one small town store are successful for decades, and now their dollars of profit are many, should they stop? If they become billionaires, legally, with products people want, are they now immoral? The same people from the garage, the dorm room, or the small town store. Which dollar earned was the line crossed to "immoral" commerce, "obscene" profits, and "unfair" assets? What about for your income level? When will your pay level become immoral? Which things that you own are unfair?

Is a large amount of money always immoral? Not when used for the good of society, certainly. Pooling money and production into large amounts can help many people. A small or mid-sized business can't summon the billions need for an off-shore wind farm. But a huge corporation can. So are large off-shore wind farms immoral? If you own a business, to remain morally good, how many willing customers will you turn away, who are seeking your legal, good product at a price they like? Tell customers no, to remain a little guy. Otherwise, the income is "unfair," to be taken, by tax, out of existence. How does Congress know when a sale of a product or service becomes immorally too much in profit for a small company, a mid-sized company, or a large company?

Should business people fail to make a profit, in order to keep good personal morals? Or succeed? By being profitable. The highly successful people are the same exact individuals, obeying the laws, but who went from being the little guy to root for, "fair" when in a garage, dorm room, or small store, to "unfair" only by a matter of math, of selling more of the same products, like books, computer services, or household goods.

Those little guys were the founders of Amazon (selling books from a garage), Google (providing computer services from a dorm room), and Walmart (selling household goods in one small town store).

Assets of any type, intellectual, land, or equipment, vary widely over time and circumstances, and any of them can become crucial, or become worthless, which is another reason why the asset tax is flawed.

The logical ambiguity and economic murkiness that arises in asset taxes come about when there is no income to be made from the asset in a given year. If there is no income derived from something, is a tax fair? Like cash savings, or durable goods held for personal use. Without income from renting or selling these assets, then the tax must be paid from savings, or debt from borrowing, or from a forced sale of the asset. Now, are any of those things fair, when it's your property, your stuff? That you've already paid for, after paying your income tax, sales tax, use tax, or transaction tax? An asset tax is triple taxation of the same income, at the least, after

(1) income tax and
(2) standard sales or transaction tax to purchase the asset, then would come
(3) an asset tax,

All from the original personal income, like your paycheck, for example.

A clear illustration of a pure asset tax would be a tax on a savings account balance (after you paid income tax, again) but not on any interest earned as new income.

In summary: Economies have only 3 types of status:
(a) growth status,
(b) neutral, even status, or
(c) contraction status.

Everyone is busy debating how to effect each status, (a), (b), or (c). But each year, an economy will be in either status (a), status (b) or status (c), so the final decision in (a), (b), or (c), each year, is how to split up the profits that are present, taken for personal use. How to split up the profit is distribution. Distribution, remains a primary question. See more in note 119.

(118) p. 19, "Data Visualization in Capital in the 21st Century," by Noah Wright, University of Texas Inequality Project Working Paper No. 70   p. 47, (https://utip.gov.utexas.edu/papers/utip_70.pdf). Also cited on p. 120, Galbraith, 2016.

(119) Distribution

Economist Robert Lucas, Jr. has recommended that growth would be the optimal, fastest way to bring more income to the masses. His paper on this topic to the Federal Reserve makes the case that without such vast growth for the past 200 years, the population would have had less sustenance from any distribution. Thus, stunted growth is a most dangerous thing. In concern for the masses, the poor, and for the equal value of each person, to Lucas, growth is the best method to show such help.

Here is a quote from "The Industrial Revolution: Past and Future," the 2003 Annual Report Essay, delivered to the Minneapolis Federal Reserve, May 1, 2004. (https://www.minneapolisfed.org/article/2004/the-industrial-revolution-past-and-future)

"Of the tendencies that are harmful to sound economics, the most seductive, and in my opinion the most poisonous, is to focus on questions of distribution. In this very minute, a child is being born to an American family and another child, equally valued by God, is being born to a family in India. The resources of all kinds that will be at the disposal of this new American will be on the order of 15 times the resources available to his Indian brother. This seems to us a terrible wrong, justifying direct corrective action, and perhaps some actions of this kind can and should be taken. But of the vast increase in the well-being of hundreds of millions of people that has occurred in the 200-year course of the industrial revolution to date, virtually none of it can be attributed to the direct redistribution of resources from **(a)** rich to **(b)** poor. The potential for improving the lives of poor people by finding different ways of distributing current production is nothing compared to the apparently limitless potential of increasing production."

We added the labels (a) and (b) above to guide the reader. We note:

(1) The potential for production increases aren't limitless, not for a given year, nor for each decade, nor for the coming century. Growth was limited in each year of the past 200 years as profitable production was limited by the number of customers with income to pay for items produced. At some point, when people have already spent their income, and can't borrow more, for the month, for the year, for a century, sales stop, profits stop, so does production. Potential is not "apparently limitless" as stated above.

(2) In each year of past stages of production, there were different amounts in levels allocated to:
  (a) the rich; and
  (b) the poor (employees at the bottom of the pay scale)
     which could have been adjusted by distribution in the first place by higher wages,
     leaving the rich owners with less (but enough?) and the poor employees with more. That's not redistribution, but different distribution ratios in the first place.

(3) The differences in the past, and now, between the citizens of the U.S. and the citizens of India are still differences in distribution in the first place of production and profits of the combined economies of the world. And the ratios of distribution present in each nation also are factors. Each citizen is affected in all these ratios. Economist James K. Galbraith points out that such ratios are hard to track, since so little data is collected.

We have seen Lucas' "most poisonous" quote isolated by some economists. It is perhaps a poor choice of words on Lucas' part for Lucas' intent. He stated that it's poisonous, thus irresponsible, to bring up changing the current distribution (the wages) to the workforce, but more responsible to seek growth to help the workforce. In other words, if the people lack enough income, let us find growth, to pay them more. A first reaction to the remark, could be that Lucas seems flippant about the condition of the world's workforce, when those words, "most poisonous," are quoted about the debate on distribution. This choice of words, most poisonous, can seem like a comment that if the people have no bread, let them eat cake.

And that seems far from Robert Lucas' intent, if you read his whole speech to the Minneapolis Federal Reserve. He comes across as very concerned about the world's people in his intention to stress free market growth as being a prudent goal, to help the world's masses. Especially, rather than trying ill-conceived interventions for workers that end up reducing production with which to pay people. That happens in central planning, like in the old Soviet Union, when factory managers purposely lowered output and neglected equipment maintenance, so the central planners would send them more supplies and new equipment. So the poor suffered. As the old Soviet Union joke went, we pretend to work and they pretend to pay us. So, yes, growth is a reasonable goal.

Let's next examine Lucas' logic about the increase of sustenance to people over the last 200 years. That would include in each given year. Lucas states that " ...virtually <u>none of it can be attributed to the direct redistribution of resources from rich to poor.</u>"

Look again, if you might, at the item we underlined above. None of the extra pay to workers was from redistribution. Yes, that's accurate. But is that all there is to it?

[Or this is accurate for most of the pay, as some people will point to income supports such as Social Security and regular Medicare as redistribution. Such social supports date back to Bismarck in Germany. Even including those items, Lucas' main point is still accurate, that primarily the workforce income increase came from overall growth, not redistribution.]

Some two hundred years ago there was no minimum required for anything, as reported by economist Adam Smith in 1776 (pp. 71, 83, 148, Smith). Distribution was allowed that included undernourishment to the point of death, or starvation, to use another term, or what the market will bear, to use another term, so take your pick of labels. That was during the existing growth, in those years, at the beginnings of modern economic methods. So, yes, work conditions and living quarters are much better for many workers, compared to previous years. So yes, today with no redistribution, growth has provided significant workforce gains.

Speaking about an annual income, distribution occurs in the year to both parties:

(a) the rich and

(b) the workforce,

of a share of income each year.

Because of the annual distribution to both parties of paychecks and profits, of course " ... none of ..." this can be attributed to " ... redistribution .... " from (a) the rich to (b) the poor. On that one level, yes, it logically holds water. As far as that one facet goes. Yes, as Lucas states, no redistribution occurred. In 200 years. Things are better with no redistribution. Case closed. Is that correct? Has every relevant ratio been covered, properly, in the discussion? Perhaps not.

If you back up a bit in the chain of events, there is a missing facet. The distribution in the first place could have been *much different* in the ongoing, simultaneous pay outs to each party, payday by payday, deposit by deposit, out of the economy, each year, for the 200 some years.

In 1776,

There was the annual distribution to

(a) the rich, with some evidence of the levels, shown by the luxury mansions of the time.

And there was the annual distribution to

(b) the workforce, which provided sustenance as shown by reports of living conditions, including want in many nations.

This continued each year, each century. What were the exact ratios of income paid out to each category, of the world's GDP? What were the effects, of variations, like in various nations? It would be enlightening to calculate that out, but we didn't have the time for this book. Let's let the past 200 years of exact ratios remain not calculated. We can still examine the logic of this distribution ratio between (a) and (b), using general categories.

Certainly, examples exist of differences in various nation states and regions, which show the effects that this initial distribution can have.

One example is between Haiti and the Dominican Republic. The nations are next to each other, in the Caribbean region. They are different in size, (Haiti is smaller) but the per capita wealth (amount of wealth per person) measurement is still valid as a comparison.

In Haiti, the ruling classes distributed as little as possible to the conditions of the masses of workers.

In the Dominican Republic next door, the ruling classes, prodded by religious leaders of the nation, concluded that they had a responsibility to distribute more to workers to improve their conditions.

This was distribution, not redistribution. The effects are clear. After 200 years of higher distribution to the workers, with inter-generational compounding effects, the Dominican Republic has better living and social conditions and higher per-capita wealth than Haiti, which had 200 years of lower distribution to the working poor.

Out of the whole world's GDP, had distribution to (a) the rich been a lot less, then, distribution to (b) the employees would have been a lot more. Instead of investors and owners taking more out of the equation, for example, had they paid employees more, that also would have been logically and statistically accurate that "none of it," the extra sustenance, cash, and goods for the masses, would be "attributed to the direct redistribution of resources from the rich to the poor," the key logical point from Lucas.

No redistribution at all would have been needed for the poor to receive a lot more, because they got it distributed to them in the first place, so redistribution need not have raised its miserable head. But that wasn't the decision made by owners and investors, usually, was it?

They did not change the ratio. It was what it was, from then to now, what the market will bear and what society will allow.

This part of Lucas' logic in his Fed paper is a case of changing the topic. Was this intentional? We don't know. Again, it seems to us that in this discussion, Lucas personally was highly concerned about people.

In that case, a changing of the topic would be an oversight, perhaps. We don't know.
In either case the topic was changed from:
Topic #1; higher distribution to employees in the first place, to
Topic #2, redistribution
Or another method is fully avoiding topic #1. This method is stated as such: "During the coming year there's no need to discuss how the production and profits will be split up, not when we need to discuss growth first and foremost. Let's stay on growth. What's going on with growth?" Then, if not "enough" growth occurs, or activity stays even, or activity drops, again, any discussion of how to split up the proceeds of what was produced is put aside amidst calls to "Fix the growth." But the split occurs. And if the growth was good, then what? Who gets what, in the split of more proceeds?

Again, Lucas's use of the words " ... most poisonous ... " raised some hackles, and is what gets cited as a bad example by some.

But what's worse?

- the choice of two words, or
- avoiding a highly relevant topic altogether? Which is topic #1 above, the split of the proceeds.

Take *most poisonous* out, and there still remains the topic of initial distribution to the workforce, as a highly relevant topic, leaving the topic of redistribution as a moot point.

Economists who bring up topic #1, higher distribution to the employees (or in other words, why the employees do not get more to live on in the first place) are told to quit pushing that dreaded redistribution down everyone's throat. Well, the topic is distribution, in the first place. Might you first explain your logic on that? Confiscation is another term used to change the topic away from fair distribution in the first place.

Proper distribution eliminates redistribution and prevents urges from the masses towards confiscation of the capital of others.

> (As an aside, this discussion is mainly about conditions in democratic republics. Systems with dictatorial power and criminal conduct will have redistribution and confiscation, because that is the very goal of the narcissist leaders, and their followers, who set up dictatorial, criminal systems.)

This debate-team rhetorical method of topic-changing is used full bore by many commentators on any examination of *distribution*, to immediately jump to the topic of the dreaded and unholy *redistribution*. The term redistribution has become a U.S. equivalent to a cuss word, describing a damnable abomination as unpatriotic as outlawing Girl Scout cookies or banning apple pie.

The method of topic-changing to the dastardly redistribution, however, misses responsibly answering the question, out of GDP, out of full profits, what is the *initial ratio* of the distribution in the first place.

So, again, distribution is the initial ratio to examine. Initially means; in the first place, That's income received in the first place, monthly, or by the end of the fiscal year. The topic at hand is to achieve fair distribution, so redistribution wouldn't even be a second thought. At what point will enough production and profit have been made in this world of ours? So, perhaps, one day, with proper, good-intentioned, patriotic distribution in the first place, there never, ever again, need be an occasion to use the terrible, divisive, despotic economic method of redistribution.

(120) p. 133, Galbraith, 2016.

(121) Robert Rubin, wrote this about income inequality, "I now believe income inequality is counterproductive to our society even if it is accompanied by broad growth," p. xxi, *The Yellow Pad: Making Better Decisions in an Uncertain World*, by Robert E. Rubin, 2023, Penguin Press, New York. Economist and banking official Christine Lagarde agrees. She told the IMF and the World Bank " ... that recent IMF research tells us that less inequality is associated with greater macroeconomic stability and more sustainable growth" (Atkinson, p. 12). If that's true, then advocates for growth can have both, fair distribution and growth, or growth and fair distribution, whichever emphasis one prefers. Bread *and* cake, perhaps.

(122) pp. xxiv-xxv, Ahmari, 2023. Ahmari titled his book *Tyranny, Inc.: How Private Power Crushed American Liberty - and What to Do About it*. Amari writes of " ... private tyranny ... " of "... class domination ..." of "... the power of the asset-rich few ..." which leaves "... younger Americans inheriting a much less prosperous and equitable economy ..." (pp. xxiv-xxv).

(123) p. 15, Piketty, 2022.

Index

A

affordability agreement contracts
    terms and conditions 95–99
    to get a good deal, you give a good deal to the next person 96
Amann, Dr. Wolfgang, European housing expert, provided Austrian housing statistics 152
Amari, Sohrab, economist, advocates for working families 124 135 142 152 161
appraisals 61–62
Arizona, citizens living in cars in Sedona 36
Arlington, Va., has some starter housing 72
asset accumulation, see also distribution
    accumulation by the middle class and upper class increases home prices 26
    an asset tax is problematic 157
    world wide asset accumulation is debated 124
Atlanta, Ga., is comparable to Vienna, Austria 81
The Atlantic magazine, has housing review by Madeline Carlisle 52
Austria in Europe
    Austria has wide availability of housing for all income levels 1 52 75
    explanation of Austria's housing and comparisons to U.S. housing 71–80
    has options which remove landlordism 52
    life-long leases at fair prices 86
Auten, Gerald, economist, Office of Tax Analysis, U.S. Treasury Department reports that income has risen for the workers and middle class, and that income share for the wealthy has dropped 135
avoiding mistakes 59

B

Baltimore, Md., example of safety concerns in Sandtown-Winchester neighborhood 63
banks
    banks and landlordism 127–128
    banks have adequate profit 106
Berkshire Hathaway, example of capital availability 84
Beverly Hills, Calif., can remain a rich area 50
Birdsall, Nancy, economist, concludes that extra money to investors spurs overall economic growth 124
Boise, Idaho, housing affected by Portland, Ore. and Seattle 26
bonds, see also financing
    housing bonds 74
    long-term rollover of U.S. and U.K. bonds 147
The Brookings Institution, has housing research 67
Brooklyn, New York City, N.Y. see New York City, N.Y.
Brooks, David, policy and social analyst, observes that economic unease prompts distrust in a system 25
Buffett, Warren, investor
    example of capital availability 84
building permits, limited effect on housing inventory, compared to profit margins 126
businesses
    employee-owned companies give workers control of production and profits 133
    payroll costs affected by housing 50 106 123 125 151
    productivity, affected by high payroll costs, due to high housing costs for workforce 50
    S & P 500 index, employs only 17% of U.S. workforce 125
    U.S. housing customers, ready to buy & rent starter homes 82
    with adjacent housing 77

C

California
    Beverly Hills will remain a rich area 50
    citizens living in cars in Silicon Valley 36
    Los Angeles, has starter home commitment 9
    Orange County homeowners renting half their houses 36
    Prop. 13 2% property tax cap 47
    Salinas, example of an area concerned with safety 62
    Some blocks of Compton and Fresno declined in price after the 1950s 98
    South Central Los Angeles, example of an area concerned with safety 62
Canada
    Canadian Network of Community Land Trusts 100
    examples of housing developments at lower prices 100
    Greater Vancouver Housing Corporation 100
capital
    capital lost? not if you can't ever buy, or save any money 97
    capital paid to labor 133
    capital paid to landlordism 77 128
    capital threatened by social instability 131
    labor is capital's only customer 133

capital cont.
    lack of access to loans for capital 148
    lack of capital, when half the population owns nothing 124
    levels of available capital 84
    privatized profit with socialized costs 124
    taxation of saved capital, i.e., an asset tax, is problematic 157
capitalism
    capitalism is dependent upon labor 133
    classical 97
    democratic capitalism 143
    free market doctrine 51 76
    no market limits 50
    risk and reward doctrine 76
    workers control and own production and profits 133
Chicago, Ill.
    has examples of neighborhoods with safety concerns 62
    Lincoln Park neighborhood, example of working-class neighborhood that became a wealthy neighborhood 97
China, declining population lowers housing demand 55
City Point Development, New York City, N.Y., example of successful lower-priced units added in 9 102
the commons, use of the commons 27–28 33–34
communist-style exclusion 51 76 143
Compton, Calif., example of price drops after 1950s 98
conservatives, who actively support social housing apartments in their area 72
constitution, as example of change 119
Cooper, Ryan, economist, housing analyst
    proposes financing at U.S. Treasury rate plus a basis point 87
    supports public component of housing funding 76
Cooper Square development, Manhattan, New York City, N.Y., example of lower-priced home ownership, now and in the future 72 95
corporations
    a corporation can be any business, just one with shares for sale 133
    corporate payroll to the workforce doesn't change housing inventory 123
crime, see neighborhood safety

D

democracy
    does not cap income 29
    people have freedom of choice in spending, and protection of private property 25
Democratic Party, U.S.; Democratic voters say they're concerned about getting by economically 143
democratic republics
    are set up to guarantee freedoms, not more wealth 76
    as an example of change 119
development
    housing developers are free to limit production 27
    housing developers avoid open competition 76
    U.S. customers would buy and rent starter units 82
development patterns, see Bruegmann 135
discrimination, see unfair discrimination
distribution 159
    differing conclusions on distribution 123
    proper distribution eliminates redistribution 123
    when half the population owns nothing 124
down payment assistance 104
Drozda, Zarek, policy analyst, has research on property tax caps 1

E

Ecclesiastes, example of unfair economic inequality debate, from 3,000 years ago 30
economic emancipation
    example of personal story 108
    landlordism is removed 52
    steps to take 108
economic inequality, see unfair economic inequality
    definition 142
economics
    altering economic curves 37
    distribution 124
    economic inequality, see unfair economic inequality
    economic markets, with a social designation, like electricity 27–28 32–33
    economic stability: household level 26 34–37 108
    inter-generational economic disparity 88
    economic stability: national level 23 106
    economies have only 3 modes 124 158
    growth 124 158
    guaranteed income 123 155
    household economic instability 35 92 108 124 131
    inequality, see unfair economic inequality
    Laffer curve 124
    minimums and maximums 29

economics cont.
   monopoly 18 26 122
   privatized profit with socialized costs 124
   r > g equation 124
   recession 158
   redistribution 123
   regulated markets 27
   steady growth 158
   to avoid anarchy 124
   unfair economic inequality, see unfair economic inequality
   unfettered markets, what the market will bear 27
economics is about distribution 124 159
economic subjugation
   creates social problems 108
   in modern economics, who is responsible? 124
economic unease
   creates distrust 25
   housing costs contribute mightily to economic unease 131
Economist Steffen Wetzstein 147
Ellickson, Robert C., legal analyst and zoning expert
   cites residents devotion to their children in housing decisions 145
   uses term "cartelization" of housing inventory by restrictive supply 18
eminent domain can be used fairly for public good 76
employee-owned companies distribute all profits to workers 123
employees
   net income boosted when housing costs are lower 123
   when employees decide profit distribution 123
empowerment means having assets 133
Europe, see also Austria in Europe
   articles and websites about Austria's housing system 146
   avoids pockets of poverty 69–70
   example of income tax rates 80
   examples of major changes that occurred to benefit workers 118
   has a lower ratio of social dysfunction than the U.S. 63 146
   has a properly educated workforce 59
   has a social designation for housing 71
   has widespread starter homes in Austria 1 9 71–73 96
   Housing Europe website 147
   housing finance in Europe 147
   in Europe, average employees vote regularly, so they get results 119
   investors choose starter homes 18
   preserves low prices for future generations 95
   the wealthy in Europe want for nothing 119

F

federal housing budget 173
federal taxpayer welfare 127
Feldstein, Martin, economist
   opposes minimum wage increases, with wages supplemented by welfare 155
   promotes education for upward mobility 124
   refutes Thomas Piketty's income totals for 1980-1986 124
financing
   examination of factors and examples 83–88
   financing, long term 83 148
   lack of access to capital 148
   market supported financing 74
   private capital 84 148
first-time home buyers assistance 104–105
401(k)
   as an example of property rights to assets 77
   citizens can save more in 401(k)s, if their housing prices are lower 77 95
   full 401(k)s provide independence from government and private exploitation 51
   reduced by high housing costs and high property taxes 54
free enterprise
   free market failure in housing 126
   includes open bidding for government contracts, including for starter homes 89
   in housing, without exclusion of starter homes 76
   lets businesses raise prices, or quit selling 27
   should embrace risk and reward 76
   subverted by socialized costs to subsidize private profit 124
   unfettered markets, what the market will bear 27
   with some markets, like electricity, with a social designation 27–28 32–33
free market failure in housing 126

G

Galbraith, James K., economist 124 136 155, 159
Gary, Ind.
   Gary is the home town of two winners of The Nobel Prize in Economics 152
Gates, Jr., Henry Louis, examines economics of human trafficking 150
gentrification
   caused by growing middle class and growing upper class 26

gentrification cont.
    effects 53–54 123
    in rural areas 26 122
    rent trap 68
gentrification curve 14–15 15–16
Georgia, a U.S. state is equal in size and population to Austria in Europe 81
Germany, example of hyperinflation from government overspending 124
Giridharadas, Anand, policy analyst
    sees need for higher political participation of populace 136
global economy
    as a factor in labor rates 123
    debate on overall taxation and distribution 156
government budget needs; a property tax cap for seniors and working families is fair 44
government housing spending is 1% of GDP in U.S. & Austria 78–79
government is for graver purposes 119
Gowan, Saoirse, economist, housing analyst
    proposes financing at U.S. Treasury rate plus a basis point 87
    supports public component of housing funding 76
gross domestic product (U.S. GDP) as compared to taxpayer housing spending 78–80
guaranteed income; will not offset housing price increases 123
Guzman, Benjamin, policy analyst, has research on property tax caps 1

H

The Hamptons, N.Y., will remain a rich area 50
Hong Kong, China, small units for lowest-paid employees 35
household income
    drained by housing cost 35
housing
    appraisals 61–62
    compared to other essential products 27–29 33
    housing discrimination in appraisals, leasing, and loans (see also unfair discrimination 61
    inventory commitments 37 73
    inventory pricing ratios 18 71
    inventory ratios to population income groups 50 73
    is biggest cost to most households 123
    list of U.S. housing programs 125
housing new construction
    can be at lower prices with no government involvement 16–17
    construction firms will bid on starter-unit contracts 91–92
    open competition in housing construction is needed 76
    opportunity cost 31
    housing with private investment 74
    raises business payroll costs 50 106 125
    and retirement 45 48
    in rural areas 26 54 71 72 122
    housing and safety 62
    "should ever be held sacred," after "many years of toil," per classical economist David Ricardo 137
    status as essential 27–29
    and U.S. customers 82
workforce housing
    help the lowest-earning employees own a home 104–105
workforce housing, opponents of 77
housing activists ask for more money, which goes into higher prices 88
Housing and Urban Development (U.S.) agency, has housing financing 88
housing bonds 74
housing discrimination, see also unfair discrimination
    documentation of unfair discrimination in housing, see Taylor 138
    housing discrimination in appraisals, leasing, and loans 61–62
    incremental successes to complete daunting tasks can overcome opposition to change, see Rothstein 137
    vigilance and enforcement against unfair discrimination should prevail, see Trounstine 139
H.U.D. (U.S. Department of Housing and Urban Development has financing availability 88
Husock, Howard, economist, housing analyst, identified problems in public housing 59 136

I

Idaho, housing affected by Portland, Ore. & Seattle 26
immigration, level of immigration affects national wage scales 123
incentives for lower prices fail 89
income
    discretionary spending 29
    income supports 67
    inequality, see unfair economic inequality
    no income caps in democracies 29
income distribution, see also distribution
    variety of essays on income distribution, see Boushey 135

India
    example of dense new urban units, see Berger 135
inequality, see unfair economic inequality
investors
    can effect unfair economic inequality through starter homes 87
    can investors always create never-ending profit, if they just need not pay any tax for a government? 124
    in Austria, many investors did invest in starter homes 74

J

Japan
    declining population lowers housing demand 55
    Tokyo has demand for urban development 104
Journal of European Real Estate Research 152

K

Kansas City, Mo., along with St. Louis, Mo., and the state of Missouri are comparable to Austria in Europe in size and population 81
Korea, in Seoul prices have risen for starter homes 35

L

labor
    capital accumulation through home ownership or low rent prices 77
    immigration labor levels 123
    labor is capital's only customer 133
    landless status of laborers 127
labor market
    affected by many factors 123
    participation rates 123
landlordism
    landlordism is removed 52
    landlords have been raising prices on workers and business payrolls for centuries, when pay goes up. 123
    reversing landlordism, transfers assets to average households 129
land trusts
    are successfully used, but not extensive 125
    examples of successful land trusts 100
legislation, sample housing statute 7
let's reduce the use of tax money 91
Lind, Michael, economist, promotes worker bargaining power for higher pay, for national stability 124 136
listing of successful developments at lower prices 100
Lloyd, Toby, housing developer
    cites development costs can be paid by users of the housing 147
    promotes land trusts, supported by voters 137
London, England, U.K., high home costs have pushed one million people into poverty conditions 35
long term bonds 147
Los Angeles, Calif., has starter home commitment 9
Low Income Housing Tax Credit 87 125
Lucas, Jr., Robert E., economist, to help employees, focus on growth 124 159

M

Macfarlane, Laurie, economist
    notes that development costs can be paid by users of the housing 147
    promotes land trusts, with social/governmental mitigation, supported by voters 137
Manhattan Institute 59
Manhattan, New York City, N.Y., see New York City, N.Y.
Mari, Francesca 52
market, real estate; demands average people's largest single monthly payment 131
Medicaid is a vast cash asset to the U.S. working class 124
Medicare
    is an example of a huge change from when 75% of seniors had no health insurance 12
    is a vast cash asset to the U.S. working class 124
    Medicare costs can go down if more people have higher retirement savings with lower housing costs 92
Memphis, Tenn.
    example of an area concerned with safety 62
Miami, Fla.
    example of area with safety concerns 63
    example of some employees who rent entryways of homes to sleep in, using cots 36
Michigan, Upper Peninsula, example of social housing run and supported by conservative Republicans 72
middle class
    middle-class home prices can remain stable 96
    middle class stagnation 118
    when the middle class can't buy a home or condo 73

minimum wage
    business owners only raise wages when they have to 123
Missouri, a U.S. state is comparable in population and size to Austria in Europe 81
monopoly economics
    gentrification creates a monopoly effect in housing 122
Mortgage Credit Certificate (MCC) 125
mortgage interest deduction; is one of the U.S.'s biggest housing welfare programs 125
Mundt, Alexis, European housing expert, examined European housing systems 152

N

National Assistance Corporation of America (NACA) has starter home mortgages 108
national interest; starter homes benefit the national interest 12
Navi Mumbai development, India; example of successful urban development 135
neighborhood safety
    both the middle class and working class are protective of neighborhood safety 57
    housing inventory and buying decisions are affected by neighborhood safety 62–64
    research sources about improving neighborhood safety 62
New York City, N.Y.
    Brooklyn has successful rental units at lower prices 9 102–103
    has examples of neighborhoods with safety concerns 63
    Manhattan has successful starter homes with private ownership, with affordability agreements 72
New York state, see also New York City, N.Y.
nimby (not in my back yard); nimby conclusions block free-market housing 77

O

open competition, should be available in housing 76
opportunity cost; definition; as relates to housing development 31–32
Oregon, housing prices in Portland, Ore. affect surround regions 26

P

Paul Douglas Institute, has research on property tax policy 1

payroll costs for business
    83% of U.S. business payrolls are mid-size and small businesses 125
    can be lower with employees in stable housing 106
    essential employees on payroll need housing 50 124
The People's Policy Project, research advocates housing for working families 76
personal stories of housing effects 107
Piketty, Thomas, economist 124 132
    Piketty's conclusions are refuted by Holman, W. Jenkins, Jr. 156
political power
    and economics 118
    change in political power 117–119
    examples of change, made for the national interest 12
    definition of power 117
    lack of power of non-voters 118–119
    power reveals intent and motive 149
population declines
    can end the need for affordability agreements 99
    lower birth rates are offset by increased immigration 55
    may lower housing prices 55
    will have varying effects on land use and prices 104
Portland, Ore., rising housing prices affect nearby regions 26
power, see political power
prejudice, see unfair discrimination
pricing equilibrium, lack of equilibrium in housing pricing 19
private property, should flourish for average households 76
property rights, exclusion of working families from property rights 76
property tax
    examination of property tax factors 43–48
    gentrified property tax 35
    property tax cap 43–48
        California Prop. 13, 2% cap 47
public housing, see social housing

Q

questions for students 176

R

racial segregation, see discrimination
raise the wages 123
real estate market
    2008 housing bubble 105
    declining areas 104
    growing middle class and upper class affects housing market 96

real estate market cont.
    has similar risks to other business markets 98
    real estate profits take from business payrolls & household earnings 123
    selected by investors 88
    speculators, decried as "gamblers" not "soberminded proprietors" in 1817 by classical economist David Ricardo 137
    standard market pricing can support starter homes and rentals 16
redistribution, can be avoided by proper distribution 123
referendums, can be used to provide starter housing requirements 32 39
rent trap
    example of household loss of assets 68
    U.S. taxpayer spending goes to landlords 126
Republican Party, U.S.
    against white supremacy and slavery 150
    Republican-run social housing 72
    Republican voters say they're concerned about getting by economically 143
retirement
    people can't remain in the same area in retirement when housing costs rise 48
    proper retirement comes from proper income distribution 124
    threatened by housing costs and high property taxes 45
reversing landlordism
    for better world stability 129
    is a worldwide revolution worth trillions 127
Rolls Royce automobiles, as an example of high prices 49
Rubin, Robert, U.S. Secretary of the Treasury, Wall Street executive, concludes that higher inequality is counterproductive 124
Ryan-Collins, Josh, economist
    notes that development costs can be paid by users of the housing 147
    promotes land trusts, supported by voters 137

S

safety, see neighborhood safety
Schuetz, Jenny, economist, housing analyst
    concludes government accountability is needed for housing progress 138
    finds that exclusionary policy deserves sturdy penalties 138 141
    provides review of all U.S. housing options 52
Seattle, Wash.
    city council voted for some starter units 9
    example of housing inventory 9–10
    housing prices affect nearby regions 26
Section 8
    reaches 2% of U.S. 125
    transfers taxpayer money into landlord profits and price increases 151
Sedona, Ariz., citizens living in cars 36
Seoul, Korea, housing prices rising 35
Singapore
    has one variation of starter housing units 82
    used social compact to boost development and provide reasonable housing prices, see Mallach 136
single-family homes
    can be included as starter homes 102
    can be lower priced 71 104
    lower payments possible over time 95
    single-family home prices rising along with gentrification effects 26
    single-family zoning can include starter homes 126
60-Year High-Payment Plan 35
social housing
    mistakes in social housing 59
    social housing supported by conservative Republicans 72
    200 units in City Point, Brooklyn, New York City, New York 102
social improvement
    can lower taxpayer spending an lower tax rates 94
    funds are available 87–88
    results from less strain, when housing costs are lower 94
social instability
    causes unneeded pain and sorrow 94
    costs taxpayers a lot of money 92
socialism
    corporations use socialism, when privatized profit is supported by socialized costs (welfare) 124
    current examples of all profits paid to workers 123 133
    social designations for certain economic markets, such as electricity 27–28 32–33
    the workers can control production and profits, within capitalism 133
Social Security
    as an asset worth billions to U.S. citizens 124
    example of change for the national interest, to keep the elderly from destitution 12

Social Security cont.
    seniors on Social Security caught in rent trap 126
    taxpayer spending on Social Security can remain level or be reduced with lower housing costs 92
    won't cover housing costs for seniors, forcing them back to work 54
S&P 500 index, employs only 17% of U.S. workforce 125
Splinter, David, economist, Joint Committee on Taxation, U.S. Congress
    reports that income has risen for the workers and middle class, and that income share for the wealthy has dropped 135
sprawl, may abate with population decline, but sprawl is popular 103
St. George, Utah, affected by Portland, Ore. and Seattle 26
Stiglitz, Joseph, economist, advocates for working families 124 138 152
St. Louis, Mo., and state of Missouri are similar in population and size to Austria in Europe 81
suburbs
    author Jane Jacobs was dismissive of suburbs 136
    suburbs are popular with many citizens 104
    suburbs attract U.S. middle class (see Ehrenhalt) 135
    suburbs have ample space for starter homes 103–104
    worldwide suburbanization (see Berger) 135
summaries of housing proposals and methods 1 5–17 52–53 82 125

T

tax money
    asset tax can problematic 157
    avoiding use of tax money 90–92
    housing tax credit 123
    ineffective uses of tax money for housing 126
    required to avoid anarchy 124
    tax money savings 92
tax rates
    a warning about unfair property taxes from classical economist David Ricardo 137
    lowering tax rates 93
    U.S. to Europe comparison 79–81
The 60-Year High-Payment Plan 34
Tokyo, Japan, example of density with lower prices, with willing buyers and renters 104
2008 housing bubble, included risky loans to be avoided in the future 105

U

unfair discrimination, see also unfair economic inequality

unfair discrimination cont.
    documentation of unfair discrimination in housing, see Taylor 138
    in appraisals, leases, and loans 61–62
    incremental successes to complete daunting tasks can overcome opposition to change, see Rothstein 137
    in housing appraisals, leases, and loans 61–62
    reducing economic disparity with housing helps people that have been unfairly discriminated against in the past 88
    vigilance and enforcement against unfair discrimination should prevail, see Trounstine 139
unfair economic inequality, see also unfair discrimination
    definitions of related terms and concepts 142
    income and spending caps are unworkable, under freedom to work for more 29
    minimum standards are essential 29–30
    more studies? or more housing that people can actually afford to buy or rent? 87
    targeting most households' largest single expense 38
    unfair discrimination in housing appraisals, leasing, and loans 61–62
    when half the people own nothing 124
unions, union members lose their pay increases to housing price hikes 123
United Kingdom
    Community Land Trust Network, examples of development at lower prices 100
    London, England, high home costs have pushed one million people into poverty conditions 35
    London, England, St. Clements Community Land Trust 100
Upper Peninsula of Michigan, has Republican publicly-run Housing Commissions 72
urbanism, can mix into suburban settings 104
U.S. Census
    Analyzing U.S. Census Data: Methods, Maps and Models in R, by Kyle Walker 152
    tidycensus, analysis of census data 152
U.S. customers, will support homes at reasonable prices 82
U.S. Federal budget and housing, comparison to Europe 78

U.S. Housing and Urban Development (HUD) agency, has available funding for starter homes 88
U.S. population, doubled since 1950 26
Utah, prices affected by Portland, Ore. and Seattle 26

V

Venezuela, example of hyperinflation from government overspending 124
Vermont, has starter homes and lower rental prices available in some developments 1 72
Vienna, Austria, see also Austria in Europe
   Alt-Erlaa housing complex 75
   has reasonable prices with nice units 71
Virginia, example of starter units in Arlington 72
voting
   non-voters, lack of power 118–119
   the homevoter hypothesis, see Fischel 136
   voting by U.S. household income level 121
   voting, effects of 119
   who selects the U.S. Congress 120

W

wages
   housing prices overtake wage increases 123
Walmart employees
   could afford housing, if the prices are reasonable 71
   Walmart full-timers are responsible citizens who deserve homes at reasonable prices 106
Washington state, see Seattle, Wash.
wealth and lack of wealth
   reversing landlordism over time would transfers trillions to working households 128
   summary of economic debate 124
wealthier neighborhoods
   can remain wealthy 19 29 50
welfare
   privatized profit, supported by socialized costs (welfare) 124
   U.S. welfare rut 86
   welfare to upper income households 125 173
Wetzstein, Steffen, economist, supports long-term financing because access to adequate housing is perhaps the social problem of our generation 147
Will, George F., political and social analyst, identifies graver purposes of government 119
Wolff, Edward N., economist, found that assets minus liabilities at 0.2% for the bottom 40% of households 124 155

working class
   half the people own virtually nothing 124
   instances when workers receive all profits from production 123
   when workers lack political power 118
working families
   asset accumulation for working families
   low rental rates allow asset accumulation for working families 77
   lack of political power 118
   net income 123
world economy
   affects wage levels 123
   discussion of overall economics, with a summary 156
world wide housing market
   examples of successful developers and developments of moderately-priced housing 100
   is 80% of real estate value, about $250 trillion 128
Wright, Noah, economist, notes that r < g from 1920 to 2000 124

Z

zoning, any type of residential zoning can include starter units 126

Additional Information

Appendix

2018 - in millions of dollars
SPENDING ON HOUSING OF U.S. FEDERAL TAX DOLLARS:
52% for middle-and upper-income households and
48% for moderate and lower-income households

TOTAL IS JUST UNDER 1% OF U.S. REAL GDP (0.724%)
COMPARED TO AUSTRIA IN EUROPE, ALSO UNDER 1% (0.9%) OF GDP

From: Budget of the U.S. Government, Fiscal Year 2020, Analytical Perspectives, ISBN 978-0-16-090573-5, U.S. Government Publishing Office, Washington, 2019, from the White House, Office of Budget and Management: https://www.whitehouse.gov/wp-content/uploads/2019/03/spec-fy2020.pdf - in millions of dollars

2018 figures are used, since Table 17-2 has actual outlays for 2018, not estimates. Table 16-1 indicates estimates, but was published in 2019, so the 2018 figures should match actual outlays closely. The authors have placed the amounts into middle- and upper-income spending (wealthier and middle-class households) and low-income spending (low-income households) with estimates, as discussed on the next page. Page numbers refer to the pages of the item in Analytical Perspectives Fiscal Year 2020.

Table 16-1 - Line Items - Estimates of Total Income Tax Expenditures - Total from corporations and individuals (in millions of dollars - i.e. add 6 zeros)	Page & Item in Analytical Perspectives	Middle- and Upper-Income Spending	Lower-Income Spending
Exclusion of interest on owner-occupied mortgage subsidy bonds (note 2 next page)	p. 176, item 58		$890
Exclusion of interest on rental housing bonds (note 2, next page)	p. 176, item 59		$910
Deductibility of mortgage interest on owner-occupied homes (Itemized on Form 1040)	p. 176, item 60	$37,160	
Deductibility of State and local property tax on owner-occupied homes (Itemized on Form 1040) (*2019 estimate used, as the recent change was a significant decrease for this deduction which will reoccur.)	p. 176, item 61	$6,250*	
Deferral of income from installment sales	p. 176, item 62	$1,700	
Capital gains exclusion on home sales (note 3, next page ($43,760 split)	p. 176, item 63	$22,974	$20,786
Exception from passive loss rules for $25,000 of rental loss	p. 176, item 65	$5,720	
Credit for low-income housing investments (Low Income Housing Tax Credit - LIHTC) (note 2, next page)	p. 176, item 66		$9,140
Accelerated depreciation on rental housing (normal tax method)	p. 176, item 67	$2,460	
Exclusion of interest on veterans housing bonds (note 2, next page)	p. 179, item 168		$40
Deductibility of nonbusiness State and local taxes other than on owner-occupied homes (*2019 estimate used, as the recent change was a significant decrease for this deduction, which will reoccur) (note 1. next page)	p. 179, item 171		
Table 17-2 - Line Items - Federal Grants to State and Local Governments			
Department of Housing and Urban Development - Discretionary			
Public and Indian Housing Programs			
Public Housing Operating Fund	p. 244		$4,382
Revitalization of Severely Distressed Public Housing (HOPE VI)	p. 244		$18
Native Hawaiian Housing Block Grant	p. 244		$2
Tenant Based Rental Assistance (Section 8)	p. 244		$21,384
Public Housing Capital Fund	p. 244		$2,708
Native American Housing Block Grant	p. 244		$755
Housing Certificate Fund	p. 244		-$4
Choice Neighborhoods Initiative	p. 244		$58
Family Self Sufficiency	p. 244		$71
Rental Assistance Demonstration	p. 244		....
Community Planning and Development			
Homeless Assistance Grants	p. 244		$1,340
Home Investment Partnership Program	p. 244		$1,362
Housing Opportunities for Persons with AIDS	p. 244		$352
Rural Housing and Economic Development	p. 245		$1
HUD Shop Program (see note 7, next page)			$10
Permanent Supportive Housing	p. 245		....
Housing Programs			
Project-based Rental Assistance	p. 245		$285
Department of Housing and Urban Development - Mandatory			
Public and Indian Housing Programs			
Native Hawaiian Housing Block Grant (all lines above in millions, add 6 zeros)	p. 245		$2
The Bottom Line: Total 2018 of all standard U.S. Government Tax Spending for housing (in millions, add 6 zeros)		$70,014	$64,492
Percent of two categories listed.		52%	48%
Total U.S. Housing Tax Spending with all zeros included		$134,506,000,000	

173

2018 SPENDING ON HOUSING OF U.S. FEDERAL TAX DOLLARS CONTINUED

	Page & Item in Analytical Perspectives, or as noted		U.S. Real Gross Domestic Product (GDP) Chained 2018
Table 2-1 (See note 4)	p. 10	(A)	$18,575,000,000,000
Total U.S. Housing Tax Spending on Housing 2018	previous page bottom line	(B)	$134,506,000,000
Percent of U.S. Real GDP of Federal Tax Spending on Housing 2018)	(B) ÷ (A) from above right		0.724% Or, 3/4 of 1% Or, almost 1%
(The above U.S. percentage is near to the percentage of total federal tax spending in Austria of about 1% (0.9%) on housing. Thus, both nations spend about the same on housing.) (See note 5.)			
Total U.S. Housing Tax Spending on Low-Income households	previous page 3rd line from bottom	(C)	$64,492,000,000
Percent of U.S. Real GDP spent on Low-Income households	(C) ÷ (A)		0.347%
Table 11-1 - Totals for the U.S. Budget and the U.S. Federal Government	p. 108		
2018 Total Actual Outlays Unified ($4.1 trillion)	p. 108		$4,109,000,000,000
Total U.S. Housing Tax Spending ($134.5 billion; from above)			$134,506,000,000
Percent of U.S. Federal Budget (not GDP) Spent on All Housing			3.3%
Percent of U.S. Federal Budget Spent on Upper-Income and Middle-Class Housing			1.7%
Percent of U.S. Federal Budget Spent on Low-Income Housing			1.6%
Notations:			
Table 16-1 - Line Items Excluded			
Addendum: Aid to State and local governments; These items are duplicates from other Table 16-1 Line Items already listed above.	p. 180		$0
Exclusion of net imputed rental income (This is listed by federal budget staff and Congress, but is widely ignored as a potential realistic tax item. Such a tax would be on homeowners based on rent they theoretically [imputed] would pay to themselves to use their own homes.)	p. 176, item 64		$116,590,000,000
Discharge of mortgage indebtedness (This special item from the 2006 housing bubble ended in 2018, so it is excluded as it won't be a standard reoccurring cost.)	p. 176, 68		$210,000,000

1) From p. 180, endnote 17; Items 61 and 171 have "interactions" with each other and thus have a combined larger total each year. The singular figures are used for ease of following the tables, since the differences are not overly dramatic; 37% for 2018 and 8% for 2019.
2) Government bonds for housing (Table 16-1 - Items 58, 59, 66, 168) are placed in Low-Income Spending, since the proceeds of such bonds are not used for primarily upscale housing, but for moderate and low-income housing, although some housing might be considered solid middle-class (for households in the median-income and just above range). Such bonds do also provide a tax reduction for purchasers (which are the actual Line Items dollar amounts), many of whom are wealthy, but bond purchasers may also include pension funds for workers. Thus, these Item costs could also be split on a 50/50 or 40/60 basis between higher- and low-income households. If the split on bonds was 30/70, the difference would be $4 billion and the total spending split would be 55/45, not a huge difference from the 52/48 split we report in our Bottom Line. But we have chosen to bypass the direct tax benefits to wealthier bondholders and count that tax cost instead as benefits to housing users of the bond proceeds. In part this is to not be accused of trying to skew the numbers to increase federal tax spending that benefits wealthier households. In total of federal housing tax spending, low-income households do not receive more than middle-class and wealthy households, unlike the popular perception.
3) For Table 16-1 - Item 63; 47.5% of homeowners earned $49,000 or less in 2015, which is 13.3% below the median income in 2015 of $56,516, according to the Brookings Institution (https://www.brookings.edu/blog/the-avenue/2017/10/09/who-is-the-new-face-of-american-homeownership/). So finding that 47.5% of homeowners are at that level gives a rough estimate for a starting point and below of lower income homeowner, the authors split the Item 63 total of $43,760 billion into $20,786 billion (47.5%) for Low-Income Spending and $22,974 (52.5%) for Regular Spending. We will use this for 2019 as well. This is not an exacting calculation of the tax savings to the lower-income homeowners to the wealthy, as the profit per home sale per capita is likely higher on upscale homes. We used this estimate, so as not to be accused of attempting to skew the numbers to overestimate benefits for the wealthy on this exemption. Tax savings to those with higher income may be higher as a percentage, as the capital gains on more expensive homes would yield higher gross tax savings.
4) Regarding gross domestic product (GDP), from Table 2-1; the Real GDP (chained) figure was used because the U.S. Bureau of Economic Analysis (BEA), which produces the GDP statistic, most often cites the Real GDP (chained) in its reports.
5) Austria's total state support for housing is 0.9% or about 1% of GDP, at 2.7 billion euros, from page 254 of "Housing subsidies and taxation in six EU countries," by Robert Weiser and Alexis Mundt, Journal of European Real Estate Research, Vol. 7, No. 3, 2014, pp. 248-269, © Emerald Group Publishing Limited, as provided by Alexis Mundt to Troy and Lydia Deckert, Oct. 2019. See also: "The following observations on the overall housing situation in Austria can be made: The total expenditure on housing subsidies is 1% of GDP." from Sect. 5 Conclusion; first 2 sentences, from a report "The Austrian System of Social Housing Finance, by Dr. Wolfgang Amann and Alexis Mundt, 2013. Dr. Amman is Director of IIBW - Insitut fur Immobilien, Bauen and Wohnen GmbH, the Institute for Real Estate, Construction and Housing, Ltd, Vienna, Austria and Alexis Mundt is an independent housing researcher based in Vienna, Austria.
6) See: http://cms.siel.si/documents/170/docs/socialhousing-finance-amman-mundt.pdf. These totals match up in categories of funds spent, as Weiser and Mundt include the following: the mortgage interest tax exemption, the reduced capital gains tax in primary home sales (held for 2 years), direct tax spending on housing, and tax exemptions on housing bonds. These categories are in the U.S. totals compiled by Troy Deckert and Lydia Deckert. The other main tax category, that of tax exemption on imputed rent, also matches, as it is not included in either the Austria or U.S. totals. This is because apparently only one country in the world, The Netherlands, taxes people for imputed rental income for living in their own home, and that is at a very low level. (p. 257, Weiser, Mundt, above). The U.S. and Austria do not tax imputed rent, thus this supposed tax break isn't included as a tax break. Thus, the housing tax spending totals for the U.S (0.724%). and for Austria (0.9%) as a percentage of GDP are statistically similar.
7) A $10 million cost of the HUD SHOP program under Rural Housing came from the HUD website totals for 2018, which we don't see included in Table 17-2, so it is added here. (https://www.hudexchange.info/programs/shop/).
8) We didn't include the effects of FHA loans, VA loans, or of federal involvement in Fannie, Freddie and Ginnie, because those programs don't change affordability of pricing drastically and often those programs operate at a profit for the budget rather than at a loss to taxpayers.

Appendix

2019 - in millions of dollars
SPENDING ON HOUSING OF U.S. FEDERAL TAX DOLLARS:

From: Budget of the U.S. Government, Fiscal Year 2021, Analytical Perspectives, ISBN 978-0-16-095404-7, U.S. Government Publishing Office, Washington, 2020, from the White House, Office of Budget and Management: https://www.whitehouse.gov/wp-content/uploads/2020/02/spec_fy21.pdf

The authors have placed the amounts into middle- and upper-income spending (wealthier and middle-class households) and low-income spending (low-income households) with estimates, as explained in note 2 previous page. Page numbers refer to the page of the budget item in Analytical Perspectives Fiscal Year 2021.

Table 16-1 - Line Items - Estimates of Total Income Tax Expenditures - Total from corporations and individuals (in millions of dollars - i.e. add 6 zeros)	Page & Item in Analytical Perspectives	Middle- and Upper- Income Spending	Lower- Income Spending
Exclusion of interest on owner-occupied mortgage subsidy bonds (note 2, previous page)	p. 151, item 54		$790
Exclusion of interest on rental housing bonds (note 2, previous page)	p. 151 item 55		$1,030
Deductibility of mortgage interest on owner-occupied homes (Itemized on Form 1040)	p. 151, item 60	$25,130	
Deductibility of State and local property tax on owner-occupied homes (Itemized on Form 1040)	p. 151, item 57	$6,010	
Deferral of income from installment sales	p. 151, item 58	$1,460	
Capital gains exclusion on home sales (note 3, previous page) ($43,610 split)	p. 176, item 63	$22,895	$20,786
Exception from passive loss rules for $25,000 of rental loss	p. 176, item 65	$6,070	
Credit for low-income housing investments (Low Income Housing Tax Credit - LIHTC) (note 2, previous page)	p. 176, item 66		$9,140
Accelerated depreciation on rental housing (normal tax method)	p. 176, item 67	$2,460	
Exclusion of interest on veterans housing bonds (note 2, previous page)	p. 179, item 168		$50
Deductibility of nonbusiness State and local taxes other than on owner-occupied homes (*2019 estimate used, as the recent change was a significant decrease for this deduction, which will reoccur) (note 1, previous page)	p. 154, item 164	$4,430	
Table 17-2 - Line Items - Federal Grants to State and Local Governments			
Department of Housing and Urban Development - Discretionary			
Public and Indian Housing Programs			
Public Housing Operating Fund	p. 214		$4,458
Revitalization of Severely Distressed Public Housing (HOPE VI)	p. 214		$13
Native Hawaiian Housing Block Grant	p. 214		$1
Tenant Based Rental Assistance (Section 8)	p. 214		$22,208
Public Housing Capital Fund	p. 214		$2,150
Native American Housing Block Grant	p. 214		$657
Housing Certificate Fund	p. 214		....
Choice Neighborhoods Initiative	p. 214		$109
Family Self Sufficiency	p. 214		$71
Rental Assistance Demonstration	p. 214		....
Community Planning and Development			
Homeless Assistance Grants	p. 214		$1,149
Home Investment Partnership Program	p. 214		$939
Housing Opportunities for Persons with AIDS	p. 214		$358
Rural Housing and Economic Development	p. 214		$1
HUD Shop Program (see note 7 previous page)			$10
Permanent Supportive Housing	p. 245		....
Housing Programs			
Project-based Rental Assistance	p. 245		$285
Department of Housing and Urban Development - Mandatory			
Public and Indian Housing Programs			
Native Hawaiian Housing Block Grant (all lines above in millions, add 6 zeros)	p. 245		$2
Fair Housing Activities	p. 215		$65
The Bottom Line: Total 2018 of all standard U.S. Government Tax Spending for housing (in millions, add 6 zeros)		$73,995	$63,821
Percent of two categories listed.		54%	46%
Total U.S. Housing Tax Spending with all zeros included			$137,816,000,000

Questions for Students

1. Is any additional supply of starter priced housing needed for your immediate region? If not, or if so, supply statistics to back up your assessment and conclusion.
2. If and when it is needed to do so for the public good, what are the best methods to alter residential real estate development practices and inventory? Are any such methods properly justified?
3. Prepare a short home buyer's guide of a few pages. Explain the following lending options and factors: conventional, non-conforming, private notes, self-directed IRAs, owner will carry, rate buy down, closing cost credit or assistance, down-payment credit or assistance, and private mortgage insurance. Explain amortization and provide examples with full interest paid per amortization schedules in different numbers of years. For U.S. students, explain the U.S. home loan programs from the FHA, USDA, VA, and NACA.
4. How much would a homeowner save with a 15 year mortgage instead of a 30 year mortgage? Is it worth the extra money per month? Or not? Is owning better than renting? Or not? In what situations?
5. Compare the ideas of constitutional freedoms regarding:
    - freedom to control one's own person decisions;
        - travel, association, assembly, speech, petitioning
    - freedom of rights to private property;
        - deciding how to spend one's own money
        - protections of private property (your money)
            - preventing fraud and theft of your money by other private parties; what are proper methods for redress and penalties for theft and fraud of your money?
            - preventing unfair confiscation or taxation of your money, or of items you bought, by a government; what are proper methods for redress?
6. For extra credit: This requires research on material not covered in this book. Explain the history of private property laws.

    How does commonly owned property (sometimes referred to as the commons) play a role?

    What abuses of the commons have occurred, and can occur, compared to good uses of the commons.

    Which community-owned, cooperatively-owned, and socially-owned (government-owned) enterprises have succeeded; and why? Which have failed; and why? Examples could be infrastructure, business operations, housing and living developments, and agriculture operations.

Made in the USA
Coppell, TX
06 December 2024